Dostoevsky, 1876.

THE UNPUBLISHED DOSTOEVSKY

DIARIES AND NOTEBOOKS (1860-81)

IN THREE VOLUMES

GENERAL EDITOR
CARL R. PROFFER

VOLUME II

translated by

ARLINE BOYER AND CARL PROFFER

ARDIS   **ANN ARBOR**

CONTENTS

ILLUSTRATIONS

THE UNPUBLISHED DOSTOEVSKY

DIARIES AND NOTEBOOKS 1872-1876

ГРАЖДАНИНЪ

ГАЗЕТА-ЖУРНАЛЪ ПОЛИТИЧЕСКІЙ И ЛИТЕРАТУРНЫЙ.

Журналъ „Гражданинъ" выходитъ по понедѣльникамъ, исключая 4-хъ лѣт-нихъ мѣсяцевъ—Мая, Іюня, Іюля и Августа, когда ежемѣсячно изданіе дѣлается выпускомъ большой книги (5—10 л.). Въ случаѣ чрезвычайныхъ полити-ческихъ событій будетъ выходить, кромѣ означенной книги, также и главное изданіе.

Объявленія принимаются до 10 коп. за строчку петита въ Гражданинъ, въ главной конторѣ при книжномъ магазинѣ А. Ѳ. Базунова и въ Office de publicité гаве. Михайловская улица № 2.

Редакція (Николаевская ул. № 9, кв. 1) открыта для личныхъ объясненій отъ 12 до 2 ч. два ежедневно, кромѣ дней праздничныхъ.

Рукописи доставляются исключительно въ редакцію; непринятыя статьи воз-вращаются только по личному требованію и сохраняются три мѣсяца, принятыя, въ случаѣ необходимости, подлежатъ сокращенію.

Подписка принимается въ С.-Петербургѣ, въ главной конторѣ „Гражда-нина" при книжномъ магазинѣ А. Ѳ. Базунова; въ Москвѣ, въ книжномъ мага-зинѣ И. Г. Соловьева; въ Кіевѣ, въ книжномъ магазинѣ Гинтера и Малецкаго. Иногородные адресуются въ Редакцію „Гражданина", въ С.-Петербургъ.

Подписная цѣна:

За годъ, безъ доставки . . . 7 р.   съ доставкой и пересылкой . 8 р.
— треть года . . . . . . 3 „

На другіе сроки подписка не принимается. Служащіе пользуются разсрочкою чрезъ гг. казначеевъ.

Подписчики, желающіе получить полное собраніе сочиненій А. Н. Майкова, прилагаютъ два рубля.

Отдѣльные №№ продаются по 20 коп.

№ 34	1872	25 Декабря.

ОТКРЫТА ПОДПИСКА

НА

ЖУРНАЛЪ „ГРАЖДАНИНЪ"

НА 1873 ГОДЪ

Изданіе будетъ выходить разъ въ недѣлю, по понедѣльникамъ, въ размѣрахъ отъ 1½ до 2-хъ боль-шихъ листовъ, въ теченіе всего года, безъ перерывовъ.

Введены будутъ значительныя улучшенія; но направленіе остается неизмѣннымъ.

Цѣна годовому изданію журнала „ГРАЖДАНИНЪ":

безъ пересылки и доставки . . . 7 руб.
съ пересылкою и доставкою . . 8 „

За полгода: безъ пересылки и доставки . . 4 р.
съ пересылкою и доставкою . 5 „
За треть года: безъ пересылки и доставки . 3 „
съ пересылкою и доставкою . 4 „

Для лицъ служащихъ допускается разсрочка платежа подписныхъ денегъ чрезъ казначеевъ.

Подписка принимается въ С. Петербургѣ, въ редакціи журнала „ГРАЖДАНИНЪ"—Николаевская улица, № 9, и въ книжномъ магазинѣ А. Ѳ. Базунова. Въ Москвѣ: въ книжномъ магазинѣ И. Г. Соловьева. Въ Кіевѣ: въ книжномъ магазинѣ Гинтера и Малецкаго.

Иногородные адресуются въ редакцію „Гражданина", въ С.-Петербургѣ.

Первые пятьсотъ новыхъ подписчиковъ годовыхъ, на 1873 годъ, получатъ безплатно, въ видѣ пре-міи, полное недѣльное изданіе за 1872 годъ, или лѣтнюю книгу въ 37 печатныхъ листовъ.

При редакціи предполагается, въ теченіе 1873 года, выпустить особымъ изданіемъ слѣдующія книги:

а) Романъ „Одинъ изъ нашихъ Базаровыхъ", съ иллюстраціями.

б) Романъ Б. М. Маркевича „Забытый вопросъ".

в) Англійскій романъ въ переводѣ: „Тома Брауна школьные дни".

Всѣ годовые подписчики на 1873 годъ будутъ пользоваться правомъ пріобрѣсти каждое изъ этихъ изданій на 1 р. дешевле противъ продажной цѣны.

Сверхъ того, всѣ годовые подписчики на 1873 годъ будутъ имѣть право, предположенный къ изда-нію „Альманахъ", въ составъ коего войдутъ лучшія беллетристическія произведенія,—пріобрѣсти за поло-вину противъ продажной.

Въ теченіе 1873 года, редакція надѣется помѣстить въ журналѣ „Гражданинъ" новое произведеніе Ѳ. М. Достоевскаго.

На обмѣнъ изданій съ редакціями, предложившими и имѣющими предложить таковой,—редакція согласна.

First page of *The Citizen*, December 25, 1872.

NOTEBOOK VI

(1872-1875)[1]

23 December 72.[2] //
Current phrases.
Belinsk/y/: he just kept longing.[3] Why not now, why not so fast. Of course, he had vanity, but there was nothing show-offy about him. He foresaw a higher goal.

The general public, you know, turned and ran; they betrayed you, they grabbed their money and ran off to Europe.
And in Eur/ope/ they could feel their prosperity with pleasure.[4] //

About who is healthy and who is insane. An answer to the critics.[5]
Decide beforehand. Such a Russian idealist is Kirillov.[6] His instinct is true (like Belinsky: first we must decide about God, and only then will we have dinner).
A laughable prince.
NB. Article about the diversity of modern society, people have lost their forms; they were immediately obliterated, and new ones are still in hiding. The gentry, the hereditary serf-owners, gave the government service in exchange, and the shaping of a tradition; gentry literature, concepts, suddenly chaos, people without forms—there are no convictions, no science, no points of special emphasis, they preach some secrets of socialism. —People, like Kirillov, using his own intellect, suffering. The main thing is that they do not understand each other. This entire jellied mass was seized by cynicism—the youth, lacking guidance, welcomes it with open arms. How could it be that Nechaev could have been successful.[7] Meanwhile a few preconceived ideas, the feeling of honor—a false concept of humaneness. The pettiest vanity. Look at literature, with what restraint it expresses its goals, its rage, its abuse, its haste.
Kirillov. He is beautiful; you could never pound into his skull that he is more harmful than useful.
Sometime or other we will express this haste of theirs.
The Citizen must present the picture.
Nechaev—surely someone must say that this is actually vile.
They picked at it!
There is absolutely no one to respect (that's the present-day plague), how the enlightenment of the past is not taken seriously today among us Russians. Faces without forms.

On the other side of the coin, the Stundists. //
But you must have noticed that [everything] even the grandest deeds in

the world have begun with horribly simpleminded and naive exam/ples/.

So often a man adheres to a given /sort/ of convictions not at all because he shares them personally, but because it is glamorous to adhere to them, he is given a uniform, a place in good society, often even an income.

They left without even admitting their guilt [before], and it could not have been otherwise. They themselves did not understand what they had done. Just as there is already a rejection—of the French, of the German—etc., included in the word "European," it's the other way around with us, the word has come to be a rejection of the Russian—an abstract term has been provided for our upper class.

All reforms have been done by people of the past, bypassing the help of our youth—they only gave cat-calls.

Decembrists a gentry uprising (Westernizers).

Of these amused landowners.

(absolute truth/?/) //

After that. We accepted all of Europe's gifts and took them with such fury that we could not take its core, i.e., the direct living life of Europe. And while over there even the most general philosophical and social teachings take on a national shading, here in Russia N. M/ikhailovsky/ keeps talking about how the *national* is harmful to the people.[8]

—all the strong and capable young men have condemned themselves to the blindness and deafness of socialism, they have no opinions about anything, lies and contradictions, no one dares to express an opinion about Nechaev (or even about Tatyana).

A duel between suicides. Grekov. Jungdorf—a diligent mother. //

The worth of the appearances /?/ of Nechaev is exactly equal to the worth of his being passed over in silence; i.e., in the sense that they have the same absolute value: both point out all the shakiness of our liberalism, all its cowardly weakness, its slavish fear of what people will say and so forth. //

Near the Assumption on Mogiltsiye, Pribytkova's house.[9]

N. M/ikhailovsky/ Febr/uary/.

This is why: not one single monastic society, not in one monastery was it good, even from the very beginning of Christianity, while there were always individual monks, individual holy men, and still are now.

Nationalism is unnecessary.

And from that it follows that if the people do not obey you, then you will immediately get angry at the people and walk away from them. And what little despots you are! Now that's just what you want because it is reasonable. But they will tell you directly that this is not reasonable because you are predetermining their nature.

I am so glad that I have the opportunity to speak with a good-natured and warm, so pleasantly warm, person.

I wish that this would be disproved, like the correspondence about the governor who was hunting—he suddenly came out of it completely innocent.

The middle, though, the newest liberals, live God knows how and make do with I don't know what.

That you will change the face of this world very little with your theories (of reason).

N. M/ikhailovsky/ In vain they say "frivolous."

Mr. Pypin.[11] Pypin is not frivolous, Mr. Pypin is a blockhead, a sullen blockhead. What he has read—it's only a haywagon—and the cart is falling apart. Old Believers who consider themselves young and original. In this sense, of course, Slavophi/lism/ is an innovation and a new idea.

Socialism—this is also Christianity, but it proposes that it can succeed through reason.

Fortunately, they judge you to be a man of about 30, i.e., in your early youth. //

Remark/able/.

A little worm
Even though it would be impossible without him, besides his drinking, he also had good qualities.

No I want an ideal, that is I want everything at once.

Probably he did not have it, *ponny* and a weakness for caprices. He is outrageous, but this outrageousness is the same as, not even more horrible than, breaking mirrors and plates.

It's a pity, but indignation, revulsion.

Newspapers and the public were what was needed—

O why have you never seen anything more intelligent.

They say the public is impudent, why then did they agree to come?

No, there was no real live feeling here, there was a certain book in mind (if she is a well-educated lady).

Self-will and the modern idea that everything belongs to me, and I do not owe anything to anyone.

To shoot yourself to music.

Where did this society come from? O, you, historians of ours, celebrating the two-hundredth jubilee,[12] tell me, whose work this is, what ever caused or contributed to the uprooting from the soil.

Our society is riper for nihilism than any other society. Thank God not the people though. The people were transformed into a taxable unit by the monstrous will of our other ancient hereditary rulers. Their faith was the same: it's all the same to me, just so the double *obrok* gets paid. But we are breaking it off, this song won't be sung now. We know that this song is much too old now.

What elements led to the formation of this society.

Mindless misfits[13]

What if he should finally go as far as to regard a priest as only a government functionary.

What if this movement actually does have the idea of self-salvation from corruption, then it is possible for it to envelop all of Russia. The mindless misfit type may die and fade away, but another one like it may appear at any time.

To Saltyk/ov/. This is a secret, but just a simple one. —So simple that I will even let it out: I suspect that Gambetta... No, I've changed my mind, I won't tell it. //

Avvakum:[14] The task of woman is not always attractive.
Another poem.
Work on form.

Art gives form[15] to lived feeling, or gives a prophesy if a feeling has not yet been experienced, and is only beginning to catch fire among the people.

But still this deep human question, and so not all esthetic questions are questions of idle curiosity.

In this sense what a great thing is art?

Burenin's very subtle comments,[16] but he admits the possibility of admiring the line about Altay's peak.

Many things happened through Peter's great designs; Peter, who practically turned priests into government functionaries.

Karl Friedrich Wilhelm *dans le ventre.*[17]
Esthetics is the discovery of beautiful moments in the soul of man, but by the man himself to achieve self-perfection.

I am not astonished that the most burning questions look like Spanish affairs.
About Russia as if about Spain.

And the people of N. M/ikhailovsky/ who discovered them (with the best intentions, however [and with a praiseworthy aim] and with the most praiseworthy aims, incidentally). //

6

In essence, republics are aristocratic governments (see 35 No., *The Citiz/en/.* France) and also a product of classical education.

Communists, the destruction of private property, want general prosperity and through the confiscation of private property they wish to limit the misguided will of the people, but it is precisely this *misguided will of mine* that I need, and *all means to them* to *be able* to reject them.

Our society, which was broken of the habit of any activity by Peter the Great.

The idea of the article: *Absolute freedom.*

Suppressing the sense of duty in yourself and not recognizing any obligations, and at the same time, demanding all your rights—is simply piggishness, but after all, it is so alluring.

A man lives by good example

A two-bit dump.

Materialists recognize the beginning (movement, heat). They therefore recognize a *before the beginning.* Their conclusion—there is *nothing* that has always been in existence.

A fair maiden is a rose. A little worm. She needed the public and newspapers.

But temperate understanding will come through in the end. *Wednesday. Suffering.*

Countess Heidelberg. For there, you know, the Anti-Christ speaks a language which is difficult to withstand.

But we have *The Voice.*

Nationalism is nothing more than a people's identity. A people, having become a nation, has left its childhood behind. //

There are now R/ussian/ writers who, despite their unquestionable talent, have built houses for themselves through literature.

For any German beaten up by a Russian undoubtedly considers that his entire nation is being insulted through him personally. A Russian beaten up by a German will think nothing about his nation, but will be consoled by the fact that at least his slap in the face was from a civilized person.
Such is the noble passion for civilization.

For all Westernizers are only the left-over generation of landowners. This is all their ideas, their trend, and their occupation. Abstractness and so forth.

And besides that, having private capital.

Both of them shame-faced, vile men. Ashamed of their own vileness, but still intending to carry the vileness through to the end. What is better: to be naive and vile, or shame-faced and vile—which is preferable. A direct answer: to be simply vile.

These are some of the "shame-faced vile men," who were separated from the commonfolk through the system of serfdom.

NB. You have brought the situation to the point where they no longer like their own ideas. We stood on the execution block with belief...and left with hope. But your adopted children shoot themselves without any hope whatsoever, or even any kind of ideas, what is worse, they consider it foolish to have ideas. Life is boring to them!

O, you monsters, poisoned generation.

Not you, N. M/ikhailovsky/, the roots are deeper!

What could he wish for? What does he have to live for? A cook lost 5 rub/les/.

What a shabby and stupid trick.

A suicidal person wants to kill himself, he is looking for vengeance.

A dying mother on the stand argued with her daughter to try to get her daughter to support her.[18] The judge decided against support.

The daughter tore her mother apart.

This passionate thirst for science! It leads to such brilliant results!

The mother, asking to be provided for, this sober glance at life—where will it lead us!

NB. What you give to the commune goes in equal measure to yourself.

Life and experience will decide.

Old people got old.

But old things get old with horrifying speed.

NB. Where are the writers? Where are the poets?

Poor old things, they couldn't even answer anything. The most ridculous are old things that try to join up with the young.

Atheism is an aristocratic disease,[19] a disease of higher education and development, and therefore, it must be repugnant to the commonfolk. (The Jesuits finally want to take advantage of this idea.[20] See No. 153 (20 June) *Mosc/ow/ News*. The news from the Roman correspondent of the *Times* dealing with Queen Isabella's visit to the Pope.) (NB. What I already foretold in *The Devils* and always.)

Can independence of thought, even the least little bit, really be such a burden?

About verse. Easier to think. L. P/apko/va.

Classical languages—Europeanism, liberalism.
(The fruitless and pointless liberalism of Mr. Pypin—dead liberalism.)
At one time there was the idea of *mésalliance*. But constant exceptions to the general rule have already demonstrated its [one] unsoundness.
A woman [if she is morally worthy of it] is born an aristocrat and, if she is morally worthy of it, is the equal of everyone, the equal of kings.//
That is exactly why a part of my self-will is demanded from me, and I do not feel like giving it up.
Therefore, in essence, socialism evokes the protest of individuality and will never be realized...
Your reasoning is totally unreasonable; for it does not indicate what to do with the protest of individuality, other than a despotic relationship toward it.
But it is reeducated to reason and so there will be no individualities.
But how will you prove to me that individuality is unreasonable.
All of your arguments boil down to that new share of the average profit which your reason gives me. But neither you nor your science will prove that this exhausts all of man's individuality.
What are you going to do about protest?
What kind of protest?
Any kind. Bad or good protest of the individuality against the herd instinct in general, no matter what—to simply take it for granted that this protest is misguided and to chastise it. This is like China.
(NB. What's so disgraceful about it? What stupidity, just build your stupid society, otherwise not even *2* "oh!-oh"'s will have any disturbing effect at all.)
Protest of the individuality. It will always be, but you skipped over it.
If you want, I will take it off your shoulders, I will now formulate your whole problem for you. I kept listening to you and letting this rot go on through lack of anything better to do, but to finish and be done with you,

9

I'll give it to you in a couple of words: and so: there is and still remains something that exasperates you (a little piece of baggage) and despite all your arguments about the non-existence of man's moral side—it exists. And that is just where all the power is.

Program for 10 No. of *The Ci/tizen/.*[21]
From "one person's" letter.

The person furnished this strange article. This person, the same person who

What kind of person? (Description and biography.)

What is a thought about graves.

40 letters to the editor. A disturbed man. He can't stand the tone—the tone of the feuilletons.

Attacks on me made his blood boil. He suggested I write. I declined.

But here he is, furnishing it himself, he just would not give up. A strange letter: the force of the style is equalled only by the naivete of the thoughts.

You can't do too much about it, so let him go ahead and have his say. But he intends to do too much about it, and writes a severe admonition.

The first half of the article is my defense. Again, and sharply this time, I informed him that I am able to defend myself, but I do not even want to try—and therefore I am not putting in the first half of the letter.

And besides, this isn't the right time.

The attacks have ceased lately.

N. M/ikhailovsky/ and *Z.*—This T. Z.

The insinuation of a Jesuit. But this is something I definitely intend to answer, i.e., not directly, for it does not pay for me to speak about my own novel myself, but in connection with this, for I write everything, but only "in connection with this." But I did not allow myself to answer. The verbal abuse has stopped: at least 3 weeks *after* it should have, so why disturb the anthill. But then, the letter has a second part. The second part, although wild, still deserves attention. It teaches the rules, so to speak, of morality. There they are not called

I don't deny the fact that it is written for Petersburg and Moscow, but it may serve as a rule for feuilletonists of all times and all nations.

I add that the force of the style is equalled only by the naivete of the thoughts. In order to avoid annoying the man and to get rid of the 41 letters, I am putting in this second half of his letter, removing from it, by the editor's right, a few barbs, since *The Cit/izen/* states that it, in the case of necessity, revises articles.

Take the style as in the *familiar,* but without addressing anyone personally.

The *familiar* form was even used in odes to the Empress.

But, I admit, I retained from the first part of the letter just a few pig-elucidating words.

Thus: "One Person's Letter"

...and does the word pig really have such an attractive meaning?//

Let us be decent people, my friends. Have a sense of shame and at least a little restraint over your wrath. And then I will respect you not only for your intelligence, but also for your honesty. The sacrificed generation.

Showing your private parts.

So what if I put up a notice that on Saturdays or Sunday afternoons I will show one naked spot.

I believe that enthusiasts of this sort of thing will be there, and come in hordes, but [now] will they respect you. Ask yourself this: do they come in order to show their resp/ect/ for you—they will come to spit on you and ridicule you, for such spectacles are getting more and more common. But is that what you wanted! On the contrary, you wanted to be fascinating, as far as I can tell, and even you are/blaming/yourself for it now. Now tell me again what I am to think about your intelligence.

For you see, you keep showing a naked spot every Sunday.

You're fighting.

It's you who's fist fighting.

I'm an admiral.

You're ly-y-ying.

You dared me.

You're ly-y-ying!

But now if Avseenko[22]—I'll forgive him, what can the poor man do, anyway.

Let the novel writer who is annoyed by the editor's rejections try being a critic.

Scandal—Nechaev—Kostomarov.[23]

You have no thoughts.

Help.

A turkey.

So who does not know what a subscription is, and you're going after yourself—at your master's command.

Spring Rites.

Help!

You're obliged to your editor because of your family and home, and you attack anyone he sets you on.

But don't you agree, disgrace is revolting.

But don't you agree, that it is even more revolting for you to attack someone not because he has insulted you, but just because you are egged on by the editor, for the sake of his own pocket.

In respectable society there are sometimes sharp wits.

Well if you meet each other in society.

Photographic illustrations.

Your expression changes and you sit down in the corner—a brawl takes place and they lead you away.

Do not have respect for society. Sometimes a character is good, sometimes bad, everyone has the same ideas.

They don't know what is liberal and what is not.

Shaggy.

But who doesn't know that you curse the rival newspaper because you are afraid they will take your subscribers away.//

The times that children fight with each other are precisely when they have not yet learned to express their thoughts.

Who shouts out abuse using all the words at the same time.

An impossible, naive method, found only among primitive peoples.

A new newspaper, but it expressed itself like [some kind of] some Petersburg bustling idiot.

I do not ask deep insight from you. The face of society is rapidly changing, and no one believes you. So why do *you* believe.

Why are you so naive and frivolous, that is what I find unforgivable.

You enter into a literary friendship with him, you keep your intentions secret, you praise him, you lie in waiting for him, and suddenly you spring on him. You held out, you say, for a long time, but, you're sorry, you just could not wait any longer, and so then you catch him. It was disgraceful and vile; but there is, of course, something sneakier and shrewder than what you did, something you just cannot wait around for.

Your internal rage flares up and you are constantly blurting out something.

You have no idea at all.

I cannot forgive you for thinking that you do have.

Write: Affirm, vow, and swear that you have ideas—I must forgive you, for this is your game. But you do not believe yourself. If you do believe that you can have ideas also, what am I to think about your mind. And I will be reconciled with you for you will thereby demonstrate that you have a mind. I cannot respect you but I will be reconciled with you because of your mind.

But then how can you count on my respect after that?

But what a beating you have taken and what a beating you are still going to get.

Subscribers. Pigs. (Odessa.) The proposal was so absurd that even the other Petersburg newspapers decided not to take advantage of it—which apparently means that absurdity has its limits even for them—a comforting thought in any case.

Now you do not believe that they believe you, or do you? Stupid. So write that way because you are itchy, so to speak, art for art's sake.

This is exaggerated.//

One person's n/otes/.

The force of his style is equalled only by the naivete of his thoughts, for he [is deeply astonished that] revealed as if for the first time something that people have known for a long time, and what he finds astonishing is something that people no longer find the least bit astonishing.

They write necrologies of each other.

I fancy that you, like the drunkard and the admiral, are lying in the mud, insulted by each other and all beaten up, each under the window of his own editor's office. And your voice resounds afar through the squalid streets of Petersburg—but no policeman comes to pull you out of the mud, and you continue to lie in it, getting smeared up and choking on it.

For you are not at all as vile as you portray each other to be.

And it would be good if you stood up for your own sake, or else at least for the entrepeneur who hired you.

For you know, nobody will believe you, since you can never make a villain out of an honest man.

Is the word pig really so magical and alluring in meaning that you could never take it for yourself, why should it be?//

A heavy candleholder of bronze, of which the master of the house is proud.

The editor admits this picture to be a little exaggerated, despite the further proofs by the author.

And your partner claims the crown.

13

An occurrence which may even be quite impossible.

The nature of the relationship, so to speak, disturbs and agitates him.

A candleholder, you aim it at his forehead.

Your partner, a young woman, who was expecting so much cleverness from you when she sat down to play with you, goes off with an exclamation to find refuge under the wing of her husband, a distinguished lieutenant colonel of the engineers, who [looking] gazing at your behavior, along with the rest of the guests, says to her: "You yourself can see now, my dear, what you can expect from [him] these 'leaders of society'." Tossed out. You missed the enjoyment of society, the pleasant though innocent moments with the lad/ies/ of Peters/burg/—and dinner. But you hurry to reward yourself. Every one of you [at one time] rushes straight to your writing desk and by morning has scribbled down an in/sult/, an extremely venomous article with a very detailed description of the whole incident (for this is what you will probably do because of your stupidity), mentioning his father and mother, his wife, and even his innocent children. Then it hap/pens/ that the editor will nag you—

For even you are a familiar figure in respectable society. To judge from your feuilletons, you speak casually with generals, with financiers, with tavern waiters, with foreign travelers, and you even deliver admonitions to ministers... We became acquainted with general such-and-such, I was at Prince so-and-so's, at Palkin's I met such-and-such, spoke with so-and-so, he told me something and I stated something else.

According to what you say, your wide circulation in high society is truly amazing and is perhaps equalled only by the indispensability of your presence in society, for according to the sense of your feuilletons, no activity can be done without you and your witty words, but even here you are clumsy.

For all this abundance of many things, you have none at all.//

You cram into your feuilletons so many generals and financiers who have need of you and your witty words, that willy-nilly one concludes that you have none at all, that you spoke with no one and no one asked you for your opinion, but that you simply have a little herring and onion snack somewhere near Palkin's.

You are going to show yourself stark naked or, even better, show one of your secret spots exposed.

A proven shaggy-haired bum in the feuilleton squabbles as well.

This brilliant cry to Antropka[24] and the anguish—it can be repeated not only among little country boys, but also among grown-ups in the final stages

14

of graying, members of our reform-torn and unsettled, society. For between these two publishing entrepeneurs of two present-day newspapers surely you can discern Antropka! They know that their attacks on each other, the abuse, and even their reasoning will be utterly in vain, for no one listens to them and no one in this progress-minded society really cares anything about them, and still every day they repeat them with anguish and spite—isn't this the same Antropka?

Everyone knows that you curse because /of/ the subscribers, that there is no way that they can take subscr/iptions/ from each oth/er/, maintaining these two capital-city Antropkas.

Your pen pulls you down to a position of degradation because, judging by your literary impatience and your lack of self-control, I am justified in concluding that you also are impatient in private gatherings.

A host who feels himself so much at fault would ask his gathering to forget what happened as though it had never taken place.

Stark naked, i.e., without even a stitch of clothing, so that every [pay] visitor who pays his money can examine you down to your most intimate [disgusting] details.

The main thing here is the anguish: for he know that Antropka would no longer respond to him and no practical result would come out of his exclamations, but he continued to shout for so many years, overcome with impotent anger: Antropka.//

I agree that there is much in this approach that is immoral, and even more immoral than anything else you have written. But you must agree it's more intelligent. Please, stupid, sit down.//

Each of you is dashing along in a cab, prodding the coachman on the back to get you home fast. You keep rushing along in the coach, the coachman keeps prodding his poor innocent nag, but the horse is dodging away from his driver and does not understand your haste and, alas, does not know what literature is.

In passing you envy his innocence and are aware of your duty to him as that of the rich class toward the commonfolk.

But the idyllic feelings /are/ replaced by furies.//

An organ for people with independent convictions.[25]
403 for ticket 105 *minimum.*

My editing.[26]

Diary of a Writer. Current Life. St. Peters/burg/ Review.[27]
Politic/al/ Rev/iew/. Curr/ent/ Life.

Diary of a Writer. Curr/ent/ Life.
Internal Rev/iew/. Curr/ent/ Life.

Have articles by Yurkevich?[28]
                Pogodin?[29]
                Kelsiev?[30]
Something   Putsykovich.
                Novels.[31]
                Comedy.[32]
                and ladies' novel.[33]
Expected:
                Something from Filippov.[34]
                Definitely from Meshchersky.
                Something Sokolov.
Regular cooperation of Strakhov.[35]
Keep *Poretsky* in mind.
Secretary Soloviev.[36]

Keep Bogdanov in mind[37]
and someone is to send—

Each issue will more or less regularly appear with the following names

                Meshchersky
                Strakhov
                Putsykovich
                Myself
                Kelsiev *et. al.*
                Current Life
                Novel.
Have manuscripts:

On monks[38]   —Fadeev's[40]
On *zemstvo*   —A Stranger's[41]
NB. On opening of school   —Parfeny's Wanderings[42]
  Letter of a Lady[39]   —Apostolic Rules
  Kelsiev   —With Filippov
  Belov   —Take *Saints' Lives* and Polevoy's[44]
  Strakhov   —My penal servit/ude/ notebook[45]
  Story (Meshchersky's   —Part of *War and Peace*
  M/oscow/ Notes   —*N* of Citizen Stanley[46]
                    —Syllabus[47]

Inform Meshchersky whether Gorbunov[48] has a story.
Answer Shitov//

31 December. A lady came:[49] on the threshing floor and about the *clergy among* aliens. Probably give her an answer on Wednesday.

Legend about Bulgakov—missing.

Bogoyavlensky seminarian, about the education part of seminaries— left the article to some indefinite time. It will come in February (by 3-month deadline for articles). //

A count of important articles now being edited
Novel of a Moscow lady.

X   On Pugachev by Salias[50]
X   Apartments
X   On Slavs
?   Nikolaevsky's *Vienna*[51]
?   Danchenko's article
?   Gensler's[52]
?   Meshchersky's "Bismarck"
?   On London life[53]
?   Nikolaevsky's analysis. Pan-Slavism and the Greeks.[54]
?   Bibliography by Strakhov—
?   Mine[55]

Look over:[56]

      Grain-sack
      Exercise and education[57]
      Home industries[58]
      Female question

Memento
March 73

1st /of/ March. Two articles received: Bogdanov's about the exhibition and *one lady's* on the female question. //

Memento
(Society of all useful initiative.)

Society of mutual insurance for success in life— reading of Kokhovsky in the town of Solyany[59] *Labor-Rest.* A public reading by Pertsov, Rogov, Shalfeev, Genike and Tarapygin.

Correspondence about orphanage children in *The Voice.*
Pr/iest/ Ioann Nikolsky in *Petersburg Leaflet. The Voice,* 9 March, No. 68.

Letter from Prezhevsky from Vologda, asks about Toshma. Asks to inform him whether he can count on work with *The Citizen.*

13 /March/. Mrs. Grunilion, story, "because of old age," send answer to town of Rogachev, Mogilevskaya guberniya.

16 /March./ *Butagov's* legend about Bulgakov—on Friday. Satur/day/.

/Manuscript?/—given back.

Later, on Monday (on the threshing floor.).

On the life style of the Chubashsky clergy.
Given back to Bogdanov.[60]
The seen and the unseen sides of mastery /?/, two stories taken.
Glinka, story.
Mosc/ow/ theater, given back. //

Moscow, 4 April. What use is it for the sun
                    To pour its hot rays on the gravestone?[61]

Into the article.
The Protestant church is a negative one. If Rome falls, the *raison d'être* of Lutheranism disappears.
Moscow News. April IV—11. //

Essential material. 1st June 73.

Literary works.   Drama
                         "Lot/tery/ Ticket" (story)
                         Maybe another drama (?)
                         Large novel
                         Story by Kazantsev (answer him)

Other articles —   Filippov's
                         Kelsiev's
                         Vienna Exhibition
                         Diary of a Writer
                         Poretsky's
                         Putsykovich's
                         New contributor's
And then—Strakhov's

                         Meshchersky will send
                         Yurkevich?
                         Current Life

NB. Expected articles.—
Moscow Notes //

Next No. (24)
"Khiva" X[62]
Mosc/ow/ Notes   X[63]
Diary of a Writer
Filippov's X[64]
Vienna Exhibition X[65]

Kelsiev's[66]
2nd act of drama X[67]
Verses[68]
Putsykovich's X
Current Life X

Putsykovich's Khiva[69]	−500
Mosc/ow/ Notes	−350
Verses	−100
Filippov	−400
2nd act of drama[70]	−750
Vienna Exhibition	−800
Current Life[71]	−600

No. 25

"Khiva"[72]
Filippov's
Ob/last/ Review
Drama
Diary of a Writer
Verses

Plan 26 No.

	Khiva	300 now
X	M/oscow/ Notes	400
X	V/ienna/ Exhibition	800
	Belov	500
X	Strakhov	450
X	Meshchersk/y/	600
	Verse[73]	

Monk Kelsiev or open/ing/ of
school, lady. //

Diary on the Journal

21 June. Wednesday. Returned from Staraya Russa. Nothing in the journal suffered because of my absence. Putsyk/ovi/ch does nothing, he cannot even compile anything somewhat interesting on Khiva from the other newspapers. Asked him to turn in a receipt for distributed money and he did not, I have to remind him again. Remind him too to have all the letters received by the editor shown to me. I've already told him a hundred times.

Saw Strakhov. Saw Filippov, talked about publication of issues of *The Citizen,* where his article is in many 1000s of copies. He said that the prince will be in Usov, around 20.

22 June. Thursday. Strakhov said about the article: German books. It would be good to put in a "European Review," even if only once a month. But Strakhov can only take the literary part.

Belov's article is sensible but too modest and, it seems, he is not much of a literary man; but a useful person. //

Important articles in connection with the journal.

Mosc/ow/ N/ews/, No. 153. 20 June. On the Prussian army from Zinoviev and news from the Rom/an/ correspond/ent/ of the *Times* about Catholicism's readiness to bypass the tsars and go straight to the people.[74]

St. P/etersburg/ News, No. 169 (22 June). On *Bobrovsky's* book *Cadet Academies*[75] and news about the Tambov remount officers. From France and Prussia. And about the arrest of 300 idlers in one day in Odessa.

Mosc/ow/ News, No. 154, June 21.
Lead article on the return of the Krasnovodsk detachment.
Extract from *The Invalid* on the same.
Bambury on the Khiva march.[76]
The Shah in Manchester.[77]
Judge's sentence on wife-selling in a Wars/aw/ trial.[78]//

Plans for articles in *The Citizen.*
Articles: Newspaper *The Voice,* being prepared all summer (before subscription). //

32 No. of *The Citizen.* Current Life.
On popular books. //

Memento   *Memento*

The very last page

A female nihilist proud and glib:
            Since the time she first had dreams
            About the female rights question

2 August, Thursday, feuilleton in *The Voice.* W— praise for secular burials.
Thursday, 9 August. Wimpfen, *The Voice,* about the reading in the "History of Russ/ian/ Antiquity" society (on Katkov).[79] //

About how to teach God's law to children in primary school
(NB. Samarin and Meshchersky, No.'s 34 and 35 of *The Citizen* and 33.)

Fires. A number of court sent/ences/ in Penzenskaya Province (modern times).

Mother and daughter
Monk *(Russian News).*[80] Resettlement.

They weakened.
Wife-killing. Mme Bovari (last year cooked on the stove). //

Expenditures[81]

For No. 23	To Strakhov ten rub. 50 k.	−10 50 k.
	To Putsykovich	13 20 k.
		23 70 k.
For No. 24	To Papkova	2 40 k.
	To Strakhov	27 20 k.
		48 36 k.
	To Putsykovich	18 76 k.
For No. 25	To Putsykovich	4 80 k.
	To Poretsky	21 60 k.
	To Kishensky for whole drama 142, but deduct the 8 he sign/ed/ for	134 169 60 k.
	Costs for distributing and changing money	1 20 k.
	To Gladkov *Kishensky's signature* 8	
For No. 26	To Putsykovich	10 40 k.
	To Strakhov	48 32 k.
	To Belov	23 90 k.
	To Danchenko for everything[82]	24 90 k.
	15-16 No. to Lichkov /?/	4 36 k.
	For sending money	98 k.
	To Nekrasov	24 25 k.
NB. For my work[83]		
For No. 27	Offic/e/ expenditures	22 k.
	To Poretsky	19 50 k.
137 r. 11 k.	To Putsykovich	11 28 k. 30 78
NB	To Putsykovich, salary 5 June 50	+ 50
		————
	[To Papkova]	80 78
		+ 22
		81

21

For No. 28	To Belov	30 25 k.
	To Putsyk/ovi/ch	7 20 k.
	To Poretsky	15 60 k.
	To Nekrasov[84] with an additional 2 k. each for 26 No.	38 58 k.
	To Strakhov for 27 and 28 No.	34 44 k.
	To Kulakov for "Lot/tery/ Ticket"	23 25 k. 149 32 k.
For No. 29	To Belov	18 70 k.
	To Pa/pko/va	3
	To Poretsky	25 30 k.
	"Khiva"	22 16 k.
	Shtorkh	8 80 k.
	Strakhov[85]	21
	? "Lot/tery/ Ticket"	
	Petty expenditures	54 k.
	? Mine	
	Total	113 50
For No. 30	To Putsykovich	12
	Storkh	14 20 k.
	"Lot/tery/ Ticket" for No. 29 and 30	43 50 k.
	To Belov[86]	25 45 k.
	To Porets/ky	11 25 k.
	Total	106 40 k.

169, 60		9 July
48, 36		376, 63 k.
23, 70		81
———		149, 32 k.
241, 66		———
134, 97	Total	606, 95
———	16 July	113, 50 k.
376, 63		———
	Total	720, 45 k.
	23 June	106, 40
		———
		826, 85

For No. 31 Oblas/t/ Rev/iew/		21 90 k.
Storkh		19 64 k.
Monast/aries/		24 44 k.
To Prishvitsyn		8
To Belov		22 80 k.
		96 78 k.
NB. To Strakhov in advance		25
		121 78
	Total 23 July	826, 85
	Total 30 July	121, 78
		948, 03
For my work from 23 No. on		106, 71
	Total	1055, 34 k.

(Nem/irovich/ Danchenko)
To Putsyk/ovich/ to 1st of Aug/ust/

	salary	50
	Total, to 1st	1055, 34,
For No. 32	[To Peleshevsky]	17
	To Shtorkh	20 80 k.
	To Bunaev	10 20 k.
	To Poretsky	9
	To Putsyk/ovi/ch	17 50
	Total	57 50 k.

For No. 33	To Porets/ky/	14 10 k.
	To Shtorkh	24
	To Puts/ykovi/ch	10 58
	To Kazantsev	7
	To Danchenko	32 70
	To Belov	42
	To Strakhov	17
	To same, former debt	2 70 k.
	To Danchenko, former debt	14 40 k.
	Changing and sending money	90
		165 36 k.
	To Shtorkh	44, 50
	To Porets/ky/	23, 10
	To Puts/ykovich/	28 6
	To Bun/aev/	10, 20
	To Kazants/ev/ 1	7
	To Danchen/ko/	47 10

To Str/akhov/		19 70
To Belov		42
P/etty/ Exp/enditures/		90 k.

		222,86
Total, to 13 August	in all	1055 34 k
for No. 32		57 50
for No. 33		165 36
[and former] debt		

	Total	1328 20 k.

To 20 August

for No. 34 To Poretsky		8 40 k.
To Putsykovich		11 55
To Kishensky (with remittance)		59 25
[Puts/ykovi/ch has 70 k.]	Total	79 20 k.

NB. From No. 32 on I did not count my own articles.

To 27 August

for No. 35 To Poretsky		22 50 k.
my article		33, 39 k.
	Total	55, 89

In all to 1st September spent:

From 23 No. through 33 No. inclusive	1328 20 k.
for No. 34	79 20 k.
for No. 35	55 89 k.
Also for my work in No. 32 and in No. 34	28 70 k.

Total, through 1 September	1491 99
To Strakhov, in advance	15
	1506 99
	or 1507

298 of debt
1491
  298
―――――
1789

My articles 266 pp., 32 No.

144	34 No.	266
477	35 No.	144
		410

1220 r. salary to Puts/ykovich/

24

1105, 34

114, 66	1270
162, 5	1105
276	185
	165
	133
	298

Total, to 19 August debt was	−165
Overspent to 1 Sept/ember/	−133
Total, debt to 1 Sept/ember/	−298

28, 77	
5, 32	
5, 39	
33, 39	

57 50	
165 36	700
79 20	570
55 88	520

received 1790
sp/ent/ 1491
Total August cost   357, 95

520	357, 95	386, 65	520
357, 95	28 70	250	386 65
162, 5	386, 65	136, 65	133, 65

For No. 36	To Putsykovich	31 35 k.
	To Nekrasov	34 44 k.
	To Strakhov additional	2 8 k.
	To Poretsky	12
	Total	79 87

On top of that, old debt to Peleshensky	14
Salary to Putsykovich to 1st Sept/ember/	50
	143 87

10 September for No. 37 To Poretsky	24 10 k.
To Strakhov	5 80
To Putsykovich	13 44

25

To Germany	To Boldakov	32 80	
	To Mrs. Loboda	34 15	
	To Naumov	9 60 k.	

	Total, for No. 37	119 89 k.
NB. To Shkliarevsky in advance		20
	Total	139 89 k.

Total: through 1st September expenditures stood at 1507
Then to 3rd September (for 36 No.) with

	salar/y/	143 87
To 10 Sept/ember/ for No. 37		119 89 k.
And *in advance* to Shkliarevsky		20

Total, *total*	1790 76

13 September. For Mrs. Kokhnova's article published in March, at her sudden

demand for 1550 lines at 4 kop. per line	−62	
17 /September/ for No. 38 To Shtorkh	−22 20 k.	
To Danchenko	−20 90 k.	
To Putsykovich	− 8 19 k.	
To Poretsk/y/	− 7 40	
To Naumov	− 3	
	61 69	

Total, to 17 September of all expenditures	1790 76

NB. My article in 38 No. of 495 lines is not counted.

To Kokhnova	62		
for No. 38	61 69 k.		
My article in 38 No. [at 5 k.]	34		490
at 7 kop	[30] 9 k [490]		7
			3430

2360		193
2313 31		1948 75

346 49 k. remaining	June	−520	
	July	−570	
	Aug/ust/	−700	
	Sep/tember/	−570	
		2360	

24 Septemb/er/	To Putsykovich	7 50 k.
	To Poretsky	14 85 k.
To same for /The/ V/ery/ Last P/age/ in 38 No.		2 10 k.

To Peleshevsky		12 90
To Strakh/ov/		14 50 k.
My work for 2 articles		22 33 k.
	Total	74 18 k.
Total, to 24 Sept/ember/ in all		1939, 20
		74, 11
		2013, 31

Received 2360		
2036 86	Total	2024 85
323 14	Mine in 40 No.	14
		2036 86

To 1st October all together for me *321 15 k. //*

Tolstoy says: If in teaching children history, you try to appeal to patriotic feeling, then you will come out with 1612 and 1812 and nothing else. Deeply untrue and terribly crude: every fact of our life, if interpreted in a Russian spirit, will be precious to children, not at all because in such-and-such a place at such-and-such a time we repulsed the attackers, pounded, beat down, and killed the enemy, but because in all places and at all times, for 1000 years, in our triumphs and in our downfalls, in our glory and in our humiliation we were and we always remained Russians, unique, in our own right. The Russian spirit will be precious.

The Westernizers are not antagonized by the Slavophile thought that Russia is predestined to a great role in the future in relation to Western civilization, but by the idea, the one dream, that Russian too can raise herself, be something good and fine-looking, it's Russia that they hate—that is what it is more than anything else.//

NB. Renan is a Slavophile.[87] The peasants watch their master's luxurious wedding and are joyful, Mikhailovsky and Tolstoy[88] are indignant with the peasants on the basis that the luxury of their master's wedding in no way increases the peasant's well-being. And Tolstoy and Mikhailovsky even consider it their sacred duty to bring the peasant to his senses right away and to explain to him that he is stupid if he is happy at the happiness of his master, and that his master's happiness does not increase his well-being. This way, both Tolstoy and Mikhailovsky are forgetting that *this* peasant *is happy anyway, you see,* and, by making him listen to reason, they are taking happiness away from him. Why? Are they his enemies or something? No, it's because they are brought down by the false idea that happiness is limited to material well-being, instead of the abundance of good feelings characteristic of a human being.

7 August 75

The technicians of ancient times always stand out in front and give us sci-

27

ence's thought and impulse, while our own earlier educated technicians and special-ists (professors) always were just the pitiful mediocrity, blind implementors and *yes-men.*

A man, so to speak, who is perpetually snot-nosed.

Marvelous region, across Altay...[89] etc.

in these lines of verse, in which there is something that seems to dance, the greatness of Russia is portrayed.

He was of the Orthodox-Lutheran religion, like all Russians of our times who still continue to believe in God.

—Givetoallday.[90] I propose this be accepted as a new verb. You cannot ima-gine anything funnier than the city of Valday giving a gift of little bells. Besides, this verb is well known to all of Russia, to three generations, for everyone knows the *dashing troika,* it caught on not only among cultured people, but it has even reached the elemental strata of Russia, speaking in Rostislav Fadeev's style.[91] But everyone, in all strata, sang gift of Valday not as gift of Valday but as givetoallday, i.e., as a verb expressing swaying and ringing—you can say that every swaying and ringing or knocking thing is givetoalldaying. You can even make the noun the give-toallday and apply it to all those who keep making up "To Be Or Not To Be" bro-chures. What are we, what will we be. It is strange that in the past ten/se/: Giveto-alldaid, especially in the feminine gender: she sat and sat with me and she givetoall-daid and givetoalldaid. But why is it so strange? You know the commonfolk say: She sat and sat with me, or she knocked and knocked and went away. I have in-vented, or, rather, introduced only one *word* into the Russian *language,* and it has been accepted, everybody uses it: *the verb "to fade away into the shadows"* (in Go-lyadkin)... (in Belinsky, to be in *raptures over), all-too-well-known literary men*[92] my most important underground man type (I hope that this boastfulness will be forgiven in view of my own recognition of the artistic failure of this character type).

She sat and sat, kept givetoalldaying such foolishness! (Now that's not bad, really.)

You can even make a surname Givetoallday, to use in a novel or a light come-dy to portray a superficial young man who makes a pretense of being a conserva-tive or a liberal, it's all the same.

To make somthing fade away to nothing but a shadow is somthing else. So I let the slang word out, don't know if anything will happen. I, you givetoallday; he, she, it givetoalldays; we, you, they givetoallday.//

He who loves mankind in general too much is, to a great extent, unable to love any man in particular.

He who very much pities an evil-doer (a thief, a murderer) and so forth, is quite often unable to pity his victim.—I am not in a position to believe that the evil-doer *could not* avoid killing, as a result of the oppression of his surroundings and I am only willing to grant the smallest [slightest] number of exceptions in this case, while it has been accepted as the rule among us.

"The worse it is, the better it is" is also a general rule.

Fizz. Every one of our journals is a nest of envious fizz, isolated in order to... etc.

Our feuilletonists all sign themselves exclusively with pseudonyms. Are their names really so precious to them that they need to be so carefully protected from shame by pseudonyms? Could it be that everything they write is so disgraceful that they absolutely have to conceal themselves, and are their names really that precious to them?
Rostislav Fadeev and Fourier. No, for Fourier I...I [one t] even endured punishment partly for Fourier...and I rejected Fourier a long time ago, but still I will stand up for him. I regret that our general the philosopher treats the poor socialists so condescendingly. I.e., all these scholars and youths, all these former believers in Fourier are all such fools that all they'd have to do is come to Rostislav Fadeev to smarten up immediately. There must surely be something else to it, either Fourier and his successors were not such complete fools, or the soldier-philosopher is just too smart. Probably the first.

Mlle. Ishchenko and Count Tolstoy.
They say the northern and southern factions[93] have finally agreed to appeal to Yasnaya Polyana, and whatever Count Tolstoy decides, that will be it. It's about time.//

1) Complete freedom of the press is essential, being without it so far has given rotten little people (crummy little minds) the right not to spell things out and to drop a word with the hint: "We will suffer, you might say." This way they've got the reputation not only of "sufferers," "driven by despotism's arbitrariness," but also of wise people. It is supposed by the good reader that just in what they did not spell out their pearls are hidden. And full freedom of the press would be a most unpleasant surprise for them. Suddenly they would see that they must not lie, that everyone might start laughing at them. They would be frightened—and this fright would be stronger than the censor for them, /stronger/ than all the 1st, 2nd, and even 3rd preliminary security inspections, which now only encourage them and put them up on a pedestal (they would be forced to bring all their foolishness right out into the open).
/.../

None of the intelligentsia of Russia, from Peter the Great on, participated in the direct and current interests of Russia, but was always dragging around abstract European frippery (Alex/ander/ I, the Mordvinovs,[94] the Speranskys,[95] the Decembrists. The Herzens, Belinskys , and Chernyshevskys and all the contemporary trash.

Dramatic scene: Doctor N. N. (with a stupid but impudent smile) or with an incongruous look of personal dignity—and entered looking like a lackey in gentleman's dress. With unwashed hands and a cigarette.

If a man isn't just starting out to get *Tolstoy-cized,* like Strakhov is, he has already gotten *Tolstoy-cized.*[96]

2) People who know how to filter in and latch on.

3) They write verbosely (in *N/otes/ of the Fath/erland/*) and this is really a bad vice. It implies some degree of harmful self-satisfaction.
/.../ / /
All reforms of the present tsarist reign are the direct antithesis (in essence) of the reforms of Peter the Great and the nullification of them in all respects. The liberation of the commonfolk is, f/or/ exam/ple/, the direct antithesis of Peter's view (he bound the commonfolk) of the Russian commonfolk as tribute-paying—with money and services—material and nothing more. Self-government is the direct antithesis of Peter's (narrow) view of Russia as a land-owning economy based on serfdom, where the commonfolk "be not alive" and where everything is governed by a few governors from among the landowners, i.e., by bureaucrats with the landowner Peter at the head, collecting income for his war with the Swede.
Classical education, finally, is the direct antithesis of Peter's views on education, which never went beyond technology and urgent utility, demanding midshipmen, foundrymen, blacksmiths, metalsmiths, and so forth, and never posing the question of what an educated man is. —The present tsarist reign can definitely be considered the beginning of the end of the Petersburg period (such a long one) of Russian history. (The suffocation of Russia in Peter's narrow frame.)

NB. Wherever education began with technology[97] (Peter's reform here), Aristotles have never appeared. On the contrary, an unusual narrowing and impoverishment of thought could be noticed. But wherever it began with Aristotle *(renaissance,* 15th century), the event was immediately accompanied by great technological discoveries (book printing, gunpowder) [astro] and the broadening of human thought (the discovery of America, the Reformation, astronomical discoveries and so forth). / /

Horrible news and changes will befall the world in the very near future. Even if only from the point of view of population (NB. France and Russia, the population in both in about 40 years). /.../ The rise of [central] Asian kingdoms suddenly (Tamerlane) due /to/ a factor which has existed there from ancient times.

Lermontov, mirror, sloop, *the individuality being crushed under its own weight (The Voice.* Feuilleton 18 September 75), the play *Masquerade* the beginning, Lermontov's duel the end.[98]

It is not so much Peter the Great who is guilty as his adulators who follow

Peter's view of the Russian commonfolk as money-paying material and nothing more. / /

4) Our European glory and our Europeanism in general may perhaps be pointed out to us as an example of how our own Russian thought has broadened since the Petrine reform. But our European glory was produced not by the Petrine reform at all, [for it is difficult to imagine that] (if it had been, the entire reform would then have boiled down to a technological exchange, which the Moscow tsardom could also have done)—but actually by the ancient popular Russian view of power (as an unlimited sovereign)—a power which Peter did not encroach upon, in view of the only too obvious advantages to himself, and which dismayed Europe and the world with its strength and solidarity (the last manifestation of this strength was the freeing of the peasants at a single word from the tsar); but our military glory and our strength brought no benefit to us, precisely because of the narrowness of our thought, which could not develop into a popular ideology and was torn away from the commonfolk. Examples: the war with Napoleon ended to Europe's advantage, Alexander freed the Poles, which no former Moscow politicians or any government after Peter would ever have dreamed of doing, and our society even went as far as considering the greatest possible honor and goal for itself would be to become Europeans, to Europeanize once and for all; while, on the contrary, if there had been a broadening of Russian thought resulting from Peter's reform, Russian would not have made such political blunders as occurred in the 19th century (i.e., having both success and strength, but not knowing how to direct them to our own advantage), —and Russia would have considered it neither a goal nor any particular honor to be Europeans, but, on the contrary, the idea that would have been accepted would be that a Russian first and foremost is not a European, that he first and foremost must not be one for any reason, but that he is something unique and nothing else. / / And when foreigners had to announce (many times) out loud and in various forms that we are not Europeans and that they, as Europeans, did not in any way acknowledge us as their own, we began to get angry (because of our narrowmindedness) and did not understand (and even to this day cannot understand) that the Europeans, by their very failure to acknowledge us as their own, afforded us a great honor and acknowledged in us independence and supremacy in the great Slavic family of peoples and as the leaders of the Slavs to independent goals, and although they rebuked us, they nevertheless feared us. We did not understand this and were angry at the narrowing of Russian thought that began with Peter the Great.

5) Russians who do not know French, but speak the language with all their might just to be in style and rack their brains trying somehow or other to express their thoughts in a foreign language. While those Russians who speak French with facility (upper classes) most often have facile thoughts, in other words: they have no thoughts at all.

(Before the classical reform.) God only knows what was taught in our universities, all in fits and starts and unsystematically, some kind of scientific scraps; it is possible to be a specialist (with the problem compounded, for an uneducated person rarely turns out to be a good, first-class specialist), but still a thoroughly uneducated person. I remember the most talented people who had come out of the universities (Maykov, Krestovsk/y/). These people still do not know anything or know how to do anything, they are defenseless against all the temptation and the intellectual seduction of science, and if they learned anything, it was only later, on their own. /.../

They point to literature, but Pushkin (an admirer of Peter)[99] was essentially a negater of Peter through his love for the old Russian popular spirit (*Captain's Daughter,* Belkin, and so forth).[100]

He was the beginning and the first leader of the Slavophil/es/. And Gogol was the direct negater of the consequences of Peter,[101] and as for the writers who followed him, none of them, for example, produced a single new art form (they said nothing new and were content with the European ones. //

6) General principles exist only in heads, while in life there are only particular events.

7) Morality, social foundations, tranquility and maturity of the land, and order in the government (industry and complete economic well-being also) depend upon the degree and the successfulness of land ownership. If land ownership and agricultural management are weak, erratic, and disorderly, then there is neither government nor citizenship nor morality nor love of God. To the extent that land ownership and management are strengthened, all the other things can be established (NB. The change of all our [other] former laws of land ownership has brought chaos to Russia). And wherever land ownership has already been strengthened—when popular settlement is attracted and people without land and the proletariat start to appear, there industry develops (and with it such things as, for example, education are strengthened, and with education everything else is strengthened). But if the population of the earth increases very greatly, then revolutions appear. But this only proves that all must have the right to some land and that when this right is even slightly abridged, there is a shake-up and a disintegration of society. Our Russian Decembrist Yakushkin—a most sincere person—understood this.[102]

Industry and capital have a corrupting influence; torn away from the land, and therefore, from his native place and from his own people, every working man must have land. *Ergo:* is not the whole thing a matter of land.

They strongly desire that the landowners be Russian /.../ Energetic land ownership is an achievement of all Russia, one of many great /?/ achievements, sciences of all /?/ I warn the young peop/le/ in advance.

8) An ideal, its presence in the soul, a thirst, a need for something to believe in, something to worship, and the complete absence of belief. From this, two feelings are born in a superior modern person: unlimited pride and unlimited self-con-

tempt. Look at his hellish torments, observe them in his desires to assure himself that he too is a believer...

But the conflict with reality, where he turns out to be so ridiculous, so ridiculous and petty...and insignificant. He surmises that he needs to work on himself, humble himself and that this goal is worth unlimited labor. And so he commits himself to the duty of self perfection and he is happy, in raptures... he chooses some ridiculous penance chains to wear. Feelings of tormenting disbelief and skepticism afflict him now and then, but he stands firm and is seemingly achieving his goal... And so in the conflict with reality he falls down horribly, terribly, feebly. Why? Torn away from the soil, child of the age...

You are angry that such people exist. To take a close look at them, to discover them requires love for people. Then you will have eyes and you will see there are a multitude of them.

The underground man is the principle person in the Russian world. More than all other writers it was I who spoke of him, although others did speak of him for they could not fail to notice

We are amongst those who cannot keep calm in a void /.../

Fadeev's brochure,[103] the complete annihilation of the gentry and the gentry spirit through the squeezing out of their rights or the loss of land by small owners, the very people in whom the old noble families and the spirit of the gentry found refuge, fat-bellied merchants who hoard petty estates will drift in and replace the gentry. At that very moment education will cease. Every merchant will say: so, the 100 year per/iod/ of the gentry spirit turned out to be just a poof, nothing at all. Came and bowed to capital, that's what. When I have my own capital, whatever I want to do I can do, education is very important, while admitting that money is *above everything else* (NB. chapter IV. The right of a merchant to demand to become a gentleman.)

And so, even while fighting for both the unity and the unification (centralization) of Russian spiritual strength through the gentry, he himself turns out to be the first enemy of the gentry. That is how developed our gentry is. But then, perhaps General Fadeev is only a general and nothing more (soldier-philosopher)...

—But then, besides that (nevertheless, the most substantial and significant mistake), the thoughts of Fadeev are true and worthy of complete sympathy, i.e., the two main ones: the unification of spiritual forces and the role of the gentry (only not in detail, not of the leading gentry nor of the merchants). Without that unification, everything goes poof, all honest men are at a loss over what to do, everything is shameful, everything is just a triumph of the shitheads.

Inexhaustible cynicism from above (i.e., from the courtiers who surround the Tsar). //

The gentry and its preservation are essential, for its very establishment expressed a kind of *vital bond* between the tsar (signific) and the commonfolk, and the gentry class had within itself all the possibilities for the further social development of the land. It preserved the spirit of this bond, the *spirit* which was to be understood as *civil obligations.* There is no one to replace them. It is impossible without the best people (the Decembrists and other mistakes which occurred because of the crude reforms of Peter, based on contempt for the independence of historical Russia).

Moscow News, No. 229. —Interesting article about Old Catholics.

The Voice, No. 251, about how rats chewed off a child's hand in Penza.

Markov's two-faced article: Spoilers of Modern Society.[104]

Fadeev 174 pp. Without a devoted class (the gentry), supreme power that rests only upon indifferent predators and lazy bureaucrats who have no political ideas, with the commonfolk and upon those whose feelings have been corrupted by seminarians—will not last very long or go very far. The autocracy, in destroying the gentry, struck a blow against itself.

I will expose the enemy of Russia—it is the seminarian.

These rotund pipe-smoking generals, who have finished everything. (At all times we have always had generals who finished everything themselves.)
Fadeev, p. 120. The power which has cheated everything in Russia. Fadeev forgot what Orthodoxy stipulates. If one power betrays Orthodoxy then the commonfolk will choose another power. Orthodoxy, i.e., a form of religious belief in Christ, is the beginning of our morality and our conscience and therefore the beginning of social strength, of science, of everything. On the other hand, in Europe sciences and development have always made society atheistic. This, though, is really only because of Catholicism. But due to the fact that since the time of Peter's reform (formative period) those brought up during the period learned only to disdain Russia and crap on her, they too got atheism in accordance with their degree of education. Now let the rotund pipe-smoking general imagine that education in the European sense forced its way to the commonfolk: Orthodoxy will fall down before it (education)—so then why does it (Orthodoxy) have supreme power?
To look then at the Decembrists and nihilists as petty events is stupid.
Not all who wished for Siberia and the gallows filled out the numbers: many also remained behind. Russian Europeans are inevitably atheists while they are torn away from the commonfolk. This is the most substantial and significant result of Peter's reform.
They expect the world

I /:/ if your success is also worth nil, thoughts of novels [I am falling, but with glory, but you have] Wife-murderer. Children ran away from him. "Kids, kids, who told you?"//

To Kozlov.

The Dresden Madonna,[105] Lizav/eta/ Kuzminishna. I. (A bedraggled dog sticks around.) Strakhov. Match-making. I could not resist before dinner. I ate. I have no explanation. I will marry you. Laughs loudly, etc. //

9 March 75

Strange Tales (of a madman).

1) Exchange of heads.
2) Miracles in Russia.
3) Miracles in Paris (long arm).
4) Ungern-Sternberg.
5) Arrow and nose of Napoleon III.
6) *Le grand Orient.*
7) Crucifixion in our times, 4 martyrs.
8) ...Feodor—
9) Duel witn Kr-y, bullet in the rump.

Composer. Great musician. Sentenced by the judge to give an opera. Gave a *pastoral.* Lady, you loved me. Ruined the effect.

Forty Days' Prayer.[106]

Book of Wanderings

Sufferings 1 (2,3,4,5,6 and so forth.)

(Satan: You were all deceived.)

Y/oung/ Man. What irritates me more than anything else is that you keep hanging on to me. I am disorganized... What an empty, stupid trick, how stupid you are.

Yes, but you know, you also regarded God as something *poured out* (spilled).

1 August 1875.—Pushkin.

—Children. Torture of children (why is it you did not help?)
—On the stairs (I forgot).
—The closer you are, the farther away you seem.
—David.
—Avisog /?/
—Steamship on the Atlantic Ocean.
—*Butte aux Caèlles*
—Future world, the commune, golden calf, slavery, crowdedness and more crowdedness (woe to those who bear fruit).
—The suicide's protest.
—The court and a wish.
—Good spirit, turning into evil.
—Bedbug's breeding ground (Russian intellectual's filth).
—Pictures of the world. The pope. Contact between things, the millionth drop on the scales of the world.

History of Peter the Great: the mistake of the historian Soloviev[107] that in all of Peter's history there are no mistakes. This is not a history, but a panegyric.

Essential books
1) *The History of Emperor Alexander I* by Bogdanovich.
2) *Great Book of Daily Devotions* of Makary (in Moscow) at S. T. Bolshakov's on Maly Okhotny Riad (five parts).
Part 1—5
2—3
4—3
3rd—print. cop.
5th—3
3) The Gentry Class in Russia—Romanovich-Slavatinsky. *Son of the Fatherland,* No. 35 (Sunday 31 August). 75.

Editorial office Nevsky Prospekt, at the corner of Karavannaya Street, Mednikova House, apt. No. 4.
"What Is Needed More?"
Yury Samarin's answer to Rostislav Fadeev's book *What Should We Be?*

Moscow News, No. 242, Tuesday, 23 September /1875/, remarkable leading article about resettlers.[108]
Nil Popov's book *Russia and Siberia.*[109]

Fits

After interval of 5½ mon/ths/ /in/

1873	1874	1875
20 April	28 January	4 January
4 June	16 April	19 January
1st August	13 May	8 April
3rd and 19th November	27 June	4 July
27 December	8 October	
28 January 1874	18 October	
	28 December	

On Thursday also
2 shirt/s/
3 handkerchief/s/
3 cl/ean/ sh/irts/, received 1
2 n/ight/ sh/irts/
3 undersh/orts/
5 handkerchiefs

A. N. Pleshcheev, Troitsky Lane at Five Corners, House No. 27, Apart. 30.

In Grebetskaya (Yamskaya) Street Tulyakov House apt. No. 47. Rudin.

Konst/antin/ Iv/anovich/ Ivanov, Povarskaya Street (or Povarsky Lane) near Vladimirskaya Street, House No. 13.

Emilia Fedorovna. Peterburgskaya, Siezhenskaya Street, Danilov House (nearer the park, nest to Borodulin's candle-works).//

5 April 1875.
From Suma. Telegram No. 92 (answer of 20 words from Suma to Bologoe Nik/olaevsky/ r.r. paid)
Ilinskaya Street Leontiev House Dostoevsky.
Fedor Mihailovich, give me the chance to *get to see* Nyuta in Petersburg, *where I will be on Tuesday the 8th in the morning.* If it is impossible, then have cashable check sent off by registered letter right away to Elizaveta Snitkina, send answer to Bologoe station, general delivery, answer paid for.

Ivan Snitkin[110]
Verno Pivovarov//

4 February
To 1st of April—To Zamyskov/sky/	−1000	
To Pechatkin[111]	−2300	
To Vargunin	− 600	
To Goyzhevsk/y/		
and the house	− 600	
	———	
	4500	

19 September by promissory note to Pechatk/in/−266, 2nd note
To Pechat/kin/	− 954	(without interest)
To Alonkin	− 425	
Things	− 86	
For furniture	− 140	
To Vargunin, To Prats		− 156
To Trish/ins/		− 104
To Iv/an/ Gr/igorievich/		−2240
19 Septemb/er/ in cash		
balance	− 137	
plus	−1000	
plus	− 85	
	———	
	−1222	
Advertisement	−100	
To Polyakov	− 25	

37

Fur Coat	— 15
To Landlord	— 50
Live on	—300
	490

I will have [can receive]

From journal	— 700
House	— 400
Isakov's	122
From Moscow	— 245
Kozhanchik/ov's/ promissory note	— 350[112]
Nadein's	— 245
Can sell more for	— 300
Total	2162

If business goes well		—2500
To 1 April		
To Zamysl/ovsky/	—500	
To Polyakov	—125	

My personal expenditures since *6th of June*

6 June to landlord	— 50
To Alexandra for my expenditures	— 3
Dinner and petty expenditures	— 2
7 June. Promissory note to Pechatkin	—100
Overdue promissory note	— 1 80 k.
To Iv/an/ Grigor/ievich/	— 50
To Ana	—100
Trishins	— 10
Cab and pett/y/ expenditures	—150

Income since *10 August*

From Anna Nikolaevna given to her for safekeeping	—500
of her own	—150
from Wolf for 25 cop.	— 61 25
Total	711 25
from Klein 12th	—75

38

Expenditure

To Kolya	— 10
To Katya	— 3
V.	— 5
Expenditures	— 5
Petty items	— 3
	26
To Pasha	— 8
Given to Misha earlier	— 10
No. 165	— 36
79	— 20
Given to K/olya/	— 10
To Katya	— 3
To Ver/?/	— 5
To Pasha	— 8
	270 56
	286
	270
	516

134. It was 137

To Iv/an/ G/rigorievich/		— 5
Wasted		— 3
	Total	— 129
	plus	— 200
	Total	329
45		
30		
18		329
		150
40		
20		179

Novel

450 pages at 2 signatures per week

Total 329

Expenditures

Transport	17
To yardkeeper	5
For apartment	— 7
To new landlord	— 25
Transport	— 25
For cottage	— 60
For trip out of town	15
	154

installment — 25

240 cop/ies/   — 8   17½ k.
2400   — 80   1 75 k.

In all   — 45

155   17 50 = 100
          175 = 1000

420
175

245   245
          15

1225
245

3675

240	—	8	4800	—	160	400	380
2400	—	80	Print/?/			240	70
Printing	—	40	and all		80	160	420
Total		150			240		150
							240

3000 at 25 each at 2 signatures give   3250
                                           650

3900

48	— 8	650	700
480	— 80	300	700
			560
6		950	1960
			750
2880	— 480		2210

Printing 200
Stitch/ing/ of pub/lication/ 60

40

```
320                740                  4000 cop. = 950           2800
 64            740  or  750                                       1800
____                                                            = 5400
384                                                             = 5000


480 cop/ies/          − 80                  700
  5                      5                  700
_____            ____                 ____
2400 cop.             400                  280
                                          _____
Remain/ing/          250                  1680

                    _____
                     650
```

        Year. At 3 signatures per No.   3 signatures

        15 May   160   −   8
        15 July   1600   −   80
        15 Sept/ember/   Printing and everything   −   50
                                                      _____
                                                          130

        15 November
        15 January   Publication   −   30
        15 March   _____
                                                          160

```
              1600        160
                30
            _____              Pap/er for cop/ies/
             320,00
                                       320    −   160


        60 copies                   Printing
        600      −   8          Publicat/ion/        50
          5                     and everything       40
   _____                                 ____
   3000          5                                   250

   Printing   −   150
   Publ/i
   cation/    −    50
```

Wide distri-
bution   —   600   1500   2700

Every 3 months

```
        80   −  8
       800   − 80                400 for 4 thousand   8050   850
      3200      4
             _____
               320              350      270      820
                               _____   _____   _____
                                 6        6        4
                               _____   _____   _____
Type-setting  −  110           2100     1620     3280
Public/ation/ −   40           1300

            _____
              470                 4
                               _____
               80              5200

            _____
              550
```

600
150 printing
  50 pub/lication/
_____
800 editing
  60 cop.   −   8
600   80
  4   4
_____
2400   320
Printing   − 150
Paper cov/er/ for pub/lication/   −   50   75   500
_____
                             500
                 520
Var/ious/ ed/itions/   =   550
                 700   1200
                 400   520
                 280   _____
                1680   680

$$\begin{array}{r} \underline{\quad\quad\quad} \\ 550 \\ \underline{\quad\quad\quad} \\ 1130 \end{array}$$

3000 v.

600	80
5	5

3000	400
Printing —	150
—	50
	600

160	— 8	65	30
6	6	55	125
		10	
960	48 = 50		205
		125	

200 profit

Pap/er		1600	— 80	1600	270	27
All the rest			80	100	162	6
	Total		160	185	432	162

	270	3550	220
	270	710	220
	540	4260	440
	185		

8 February. Expenditures in Petersburg since 5th (not detailed)

Was to have come	30
Plus from Nek/rasov/	200
	230

Expenditures 8th of February

In hotel for everything	17 (from 5th to 8)
To Simonov	17 50
Also to Kornilov ent/er	45
	79 50

Should have left   — 150.
but I have in my pocket — 139

That means, 11 r. spent in Petersburg on cabs up to the 8th
— tobacco
— cigars
— dinner at Wolf's
— tips to servants
— for bath
— for buying petty items   — stamps
                                pomade
                                candy
                                etc.

       Had left — 139 r.

9 February gave to *Polyakov*   — 50
                                               10
     Dinner, cab and petty expense   5
                                          _____
            Total   65

       Remaining   —   74
       To Kolya   —   10
       To Katya   —   20
                                        _____
                                          44
                                          14
                                        _____
                                          30

13— Promissory note to Kozhanchikov/?/   202

                To Misha   3
     At post office for/?/   4,20
     [To Alonkin 100] To laundress   1
     For tobacco and petty items   4
14— To Vargunin   159
     To Trishin   30
     To Bunting   3
     Purchases   46
                                             35
14 February. General total of expenses

     To Simonov   17,50
     To Kornilov   45

To Kornilov	45
To Polyakov	50
To Nyanya	50
To Kolya	10
To Katya	10
Vo/?/	202
To Misha	3
At post office	4, 20
To laundress	1
Cigars and tobacco	9
To Vargun/in/	159
Purchases	46
Toys	35
In hot/el/ for 3 days	17, 40
Dinner and petty items	14
Cab	12
	688, 20
	900
	293
	1881, 20
To Misha	3
To Bunt/ing/ /?/	3
To Ko/lya?/	1

45

NOTEBOOK VII

(1874-1875)[1]

Feuilleton in the *St Peters/burg/ N/ews/*, 20 Octo/ber/, about the Russian character.

266 43 k. to Vyach. Pechatkin.

28 Jan/uary/ fit (rather severe).[2]
Fits. After a break of 5 1/2 months in 1873 (the year of the editorship):
—20 April
—4 June
—1 August
—3rd November
—19th November   NB. Total, for the year 8 fits.
—27 December
—28 January /1874/
—16 April (one of the severe ones, headache and sore legs).
(NB. *Saturday, 20 April,* it had barely started clearing up in my head and soul; it was very gloomy; apparently I was hurt; 3 twenty-four-hour periods 19th was the most painful of all. Now, 20 April, at 10 o'clock in the morning, although still painful, but as if *beginning* to go away).
13 May (one of the rather severe).
27 June (rather severe).
9 July (Saturday, 29 June. Very painful in the head and in the soul, and legs still very sore).
15/27 July (rather weak). Full moon. Sharply changing weather, about 5 days, sun, wind, rain, calm—all continues to be in the day.
8 October (at night, severe. At 5 in the morning).
Dry and clear days.
18 October fit at five o'clock in the morning, rather severe, but weaker than the preceding one.
Clear days.
28 December, in the morning, at 8 o'clock, in bed, one of the very most severe fits. My head suffered most of all. The blood pressed into my forehead intensely and the pain is reflected at the back of my head. Groggy, mournful, pangs and fantastic. Got very irritable. Clear day. 1.5 degrees of frost.
Total, in 1874 from 28 January in the year 8 fits.
From 28 December two more fits, one the 4th of January /1875/ and the other—11 January.
8th of April /1875/ Fit [morning] at 1/2 [two] past twelve in the day. I had a strong premonition from evening on and even during the day yesterday.

All I did was make cigarettes and wanted to sit down in order to write at least two pages of the novel, when *I remember* I flew, walking in the middle of the room. I lay for 40 minutes. I came to myself sitting by the cigarettes, but wasn't making them. I don't recall how the pen came to be in my hand, but I was tearing apart my cigarette case with the pen. Could have cut myself. Dampness all week, only today (tonight) full moon and, it seems, a mild frost. *8 April* full moon.

NB. Thirst the hour after the fit. I drank three glasses of water at once. But my head doesn't ache all that much. Now it's almost an hour after the fit. I am writing this and still getting words mixed up. My fear of death is already beginning to pass, but still it is there and extreme, so I don't dare lie down. My sides and legs hurt. I went to wake up Anya 40 minutes ago and was surprised to hear from Lukeria that the mistress had left. I questioned Lukeria in detail, when and how she left. An hour and a half before the fit I took *opii banzoedi:* 40 drops with water.

The whole time of my complete lack of awareness, i.e., when I had already gotten up from the floor, I sat and filled cigarettes, and by count filled 4 of them, but not neatly, and during the last two cigarettes I had a severe headache, but for a long time couldn't understand what was wrong with me, until I went to Lukeria.

Slight hemmorrhoids, constipated, the beginning of hemmorrhoidal lumps.

*Printing*3		900—7	160
5 k. @		3600—28	N = 120 pro/fit/
4000—160		4000 —32 with printing	if 4000 cop/ies/,
4		and total 40 r.	240 per month
	640		
cost	160		
	480 per month		

And if only 2000 cop/ies/, then 240 r. per month.

If 800 cop/ies/, then each No. costs — 75
Per year — 1800
At the 1/st/ subscription rate, per year — 7200

Roughly	2000	cost
	5200	

If 12 thousand. . . ., then each No. costs [103] — 110

Subscription	— 10, 800
Per year cost	— 2, 500 (roughly)
profit	— 8, 300

240–6
2400–60
4800–120
Pap/er/, printing, bind/ing/
and all   – 200
Publica/tion/ 50
                  _____
                  250
10,000–400 for a cop.

year of publ.–5000
Total–   9000
Clear   –4000

If at 10 k. –5000 cop. – 400
            Cl/ear/ profit – 150
If subscription   – 1
        3000–2700
If at 15 k.
this means, with 1000–120

with 4000–480
            250
            _____
profit   230
with 5000   600
            250
            _____
Cl/ear/   350

Figuring

If 4 times per year, at 6 signatures per month.
Printing, bind/ing/ etc.   –100
Paper: 80 cop/ies/   –6 signatures
    800   60
                          _____
    4000   300
Total, all   400
With publica/tion/ etc.   500

Price   –50 k.
Discount   –37½ k.
1000 cop/ies/ will give   –375
                                  4
                              _____
                               1500
                               500   cost
                              _____
          will give   1000 income

Figuring 1½ signatures per month, format of *The Citizen,* but not more than
                                                        3000 lines

Printing & bind/ing/   –25   –30
Paper: 320 cop/ies/   – 6
    3200   –60
    4000   –75
                          _____
              Total   –105
              Advertisement –125

48

No.   −10 k.

1000 copies with discount to booksel/lers/   −75
                                      −300
                                      −125
                                      _____
                                      175

      Pap/er/ 8000 cop/ies/ −150.   8000 cop/ies/ No cost   −225
           7200
     Cost   2700
            _____
           4500

If price No. 15 k.   −12k. cl/ear/, 1000 co/pies/   −120
                             3000   −360

      If price of subscription 150 k.
      with post /age/   175   −1−   35 k.
                                 1000 co/pies/   −1350
                                    4000   −5400
                                               _____

with 4000 subscri/bers/ cost per year 1500, clear profit to 4000

Price of subscr/iption/   145
with post/age/   2
If one signature per month
Typography, binding,
           advertis/ements/ −75
Paper   −60
                       _____
                     135

    4500 cop/ies/
         If 10 k.   −80
                            4
                           _____
                          320

      roughly [200] profit
        If 15 k.   120
                            4
                           _____
                          480
                          135
                           _____
                          345

If 6000 cop/ies/, cost 175

    900−12   480
       5   175
   _____   _____
   4500−60   305

1½ signatures per month
paper for 4000 c/opies/   −75
Printing & bind/ing/   60 −75

                Total −150
      Advertise/ments/ − 50
             All −200

300 cop/ies/ subscrip/tion/   5, 250

Separate sales   1800

               7050
               2400

Profit   4650   − with 4000 cop/ies/
For the novel   3000

      Total   7650   cl/ear/ income with the novel

Novel 20 signatures long   −in 2 parts−[4]
    24   −6
   240   −60   If 6000 co/pies/ ed.   −300
  2400   −600   −1450

                              Gros/s/   10, 500
  3600   −9000   3, 600

4000 c/opies/   −10,000   Clear prof/it/ to 7000

Print, correspondence, adverti/sements/   −500
    Total, novel − 1500 (*maximum*)
       at 2 r.
    Cl/ear/ pro/fit   − 50
    Gross   −6000
    cl/ear/ prof/it/   −4500   //

Not every (man) can offend one. //

Diary of treatments in Ems, 1874.

Thursday, 25 *June*. At 7 o'clock in the morning, during a hard rain went
to the spring for the first time—Kesselbrünen; two /?/ glasses. Although it cleared
up, it was rather windy towards evening and cool. It seems I managed to take cold,
I coughed at night and congestion in my chest. At night afterwards dreams
(Golitsyn, my brother, Anya).

    For four days now quite severe hemmorrhoids (bleeding). Stomach's all right.

Friday, 26. Rainy & changeable day. More dry coughing. Towards evening my chest even got bad (upper chest *gocka).*

I fall asleep trembling. Slept without bad dreams. My stomach's tight, but my tongue feels clearer than ever before. (NB., both days, despite the bad weather, I've been walking a lot.)

Severe congestion when I breathe.

27, 28, 29 /June/. All rainy days, only occasionally did the sun peep through. Probably because of the dampness I'm worse, the cough more intense, primarily toward night and sometimes it's even dry. Changeable stomach, mostly a tendency to constipation. Went to the doctor the 29th and told him how my stomach feels. Prescribed drinking Krenchen instead of Kesselbrunen, *three* glasses a time. (NB. as I've noticed there are far fewer people drinking Krenchen than sick people drinking Kesselbrunen.)

30 /June/. Went to drink Krenchen for the first time; in spite of the barometer moving toward clear weather since yesterday,—cloudy and even a light rain, though it's warm and gentle. The night of 29th to 30th congestion in my chest with a loud noise, like at the worst time last winter. I am coughing, however, much less than last winter. But nevertheless too much compared to the eased days of the sickness even in Petersburg.

No shakes tonight. //

Wednesday, 1st July. Splendid and hot weather. Yesterday I walked a great deal, went up into the mountains, got tired and my legs hurt. The congestion in my chest continues. Constipation. Tongue very good. Went to the bath. Again in the evening I walked too much and got tired.

Thursday, 2nd July. Even more severe congestion in my throat. Even though I don't feel especially like coughing I do cough, just to clear it out, the build-up of matter is such I notice it's harder for me to breathe than before. Fine weather, but at seven o'clock in the morning a solid cloud of fog lay over the city and it was burned off by the rising sun.

At 7 o'clock it was only 14 deg/rees/ in the shade Réau/mur/. (NB. maybe from the bath, or maybe from the great amount of walking through the mountains and tiredness the congestion in my chest has intensified?) The constipation continues. An hour before noon it was 24 degr/ees/ Réaumur in the shade. Towards evening the desire to cough intensified, and extremely severe irritation in the throat, and towards morning the next day even more difficult to breathe apparently.

Friday, 3rd July. After the Krenchen it seemed to be better and the build-up of matter in my chest broke up; but still coughs in bursts. Tendency to biliousness, my tongue, extremely clear until now, turned somewhat yellow. I want and *insistently* asked the doctor to increase the dosages of Krenchen, and mainly, with milk. A splendid day today and hot, the barometer on *beau temps,* but as if with a threat to turn a bit back, to changeable.

NB. All during the last three days a certain weariness and even pain in the legs. I definitely attribute it to my extreme amount of walking during these three-four days and, mainly, in the mountains—maybe the intense exercise is harmful to my chest too. //

Saturday, 4 July. I asked the doctor if I could drink Krenchen twice a day, in the morning 3 glasses, and the evening 2, 6 ounc/es/ of Krenchen to 2 ounc/es/ of milk.

Saturday, 11 July. Generally seem better, but the fit I had Wednesday intensified the build-up of matter in my chest. Since yesterday, i.e., since Friday (10th) the weather's gone bad, there was a storm, and today, Sunday morning, rain. Dampness and build-up of mucous with intensified coughing—this is inevitable. Will the next week of Krenchen do something? And will there be any permanent good from it finally?

Sunday, 19 July. At the start of the week fever for 2 days, and I sweated for about three days. Beginning Friday the sweating decreased and even stopped. The doctor, Thursday, decided to add another glass of Krenchen, in the morning. Thus, in the morning 4 glasses, and the evening two. He examined my chest very thoroughly: everything's healed everywhere, except two places: down low in front and in back at the back. Indeed, when coughing I even feel pain there.

However, all week my breathing has *apparently* been easier; it's incomparably less congested in the chest, and it's three days now that the cough has definitely let up. No cough even when getting up in the morning. (NB. it's remarkable that this began simultaneously with the 4th glass of Krenchen). Even cigarettes, cause almost no scratchiness in my throat. The doctor added another week to the former time-period. Thus, according to the current schedule, I've to remain here until approximately the 30th of July Ne/w/ Style. In this case the doctor guarantees the treatment's success.—But the patients say that given such a long catarrh as mine, although one can get great relief, nevertheless there is no way one can be cured *radically* by a single round. On the contrary one has to come next year for a second round of waters, and then one can hope for *radical cure.* (All functions superb. Appetite // marvelous, I sleep beautifully. I have physical strength. Irritability even less. In a word, everything *is going well for now.)*

Wednesday, 22 July. Yesterday exactly three weeks had passed since I started drinking *Krenchen* (total of 3 weeks, but Koshlakov ordered it drunk for six weeks). The cough and tickling in my throat have noticeably decreased and are decreasing more and more with *every day.* Physical functions are superb. Sweat/ing/ at night has sharply decreased, but not passed: I change shirts once regularly each night. However I am not losing any strength. Yesterday was a day with rains, today it's windy and rather damp, although the sun is shining; in spite of this the cough and congestion are evidently less. It wouldn't be bad somehow to stretch out the Krenchen to 5 weeks. The main change, that the tickling in my throat is evidently decreasing; even cigarettes no longer irritate.

Saturday, 25 July. Yesterday and today (and also partly the day before yesterday) it was damp, sun with scattered showers, and fogs in the mornings as yesterday and especially today. The dampness was reflected in my chest: more congestion, from which it is clear that the sore parts have far from healed yet. True, less tickling (although some, for ex/ample/, yesterday)—and my breathing is nevertheless freer than before. All evacuations very good and I even feel far stronger than when I came here. //

If I stay until August 2 (Sunday) I'll have to pay the landlady a total

	—35 thalers	
Food 12 days	—12 thalers	
Wine	— 3 t/halers/ 20 grosz	
Tobacco at	— 7 t/halers/ 5 thaler/s/	
Linen	— 6 t/halers/ 5 thal/ers/	
Doctor	— 6 t/halers/	
Misc.	3 t/halers/	//

72 or economizing 70 t/halers

The fairytale Fedya told me September 4, 74 in Staraya Russa, in the morning at tea.[5]

"There was a house, to the ceiling, like a birch tree. Suddenly a wolf and arap assaulted the inhabitants. They went into the house and ate everyone up."

Fedya was *three* years old and a *month and a half.*

NB. He himself made up this fairytale, on the basis of fairytales he had heard of course. But nevertheless he made it up. Here the remarkable words are: *inhabitants* and *assaulted.* That means he already knows quite well what inhabitants are. But even more curious that he knows the word "assaulted" and had assimilated its meaning so completely. //

Moscow News, No. 225, 74. September 9 (Sunday page). In their article, "Commonfolk Education" they praisingly cite the Novgorod zemstvo's most base ultrawesternizing reaction—that in teaching seminars the sooner the student is torn away from the commonfolk the better, and that the greater the separation and alienation from the commonfolk "in the name of the civilizing influence of science"—the more consoling it is.[6]

13 Sept/ember/ 74.[?] Drama. In Tobolsk, about twenty years ago, like the Il/in/sky story. Two brothers, an old father, one has a fiancee with whom the second brother is secretly and enviously in love. But she loves the elder one. But the elder one, a young lieutenant, debauches and acts foolish, quarrels with his father. The father disappears. For several days not hide nor hair. The brothers talk about their inheritance. And suddenly the authorities: they dig up the body in the basement. Clues against the elder (the younger one doesn't live together). The elder one is tried and sentenced to imprisonment. (NB. He quarreled with his father, brags about the inheritance from his deceased mother and other rubbish. When he entered the room and even his fiancee was repelled by him; drunk, he said: can it be that even you believe it. The clues were falsified splendidly by the younger one.) The public doesn't know for sure who the murderer is.

Scene in prison. They want to kill *him.*

The Commandant. He doesn't give them away. The prisoners swear brotherhood with him. The commandant rebukes him for killing his father.

After 12 years the brother comes to see him. The scene, where *silently* they understand each other.

Since then 7 more years, the younger brother has a rank, a position, but he is tormented, hypochondriacal, he declares to his wife that he is the murderer. "Why did you tell me?" He goes to his brother. The wife runs to him too.

On her knees the wife begs the prisoner to keep silent, to save her husband. The prisoner replied: "I'm used to it." They're reconciled. "You've been punished even without this," says the elder one.

The younger one's birthday. Guests gathered. He comes out: I am the murderer. They think it's a stroke.

The end: the other returns. The former on the transport. They exile him. [Slanderer ask] The younger asks the elder to be the father of his children.

"I've set out upon the right path!"

NOTEBOOK VIII

(1874-1875)[1]

Memento. S. Petersburg News, (list of noteworthy things) April Tuesday 30 on Atkinson's English book about Russian art.[2]

May 1st, Wdnesday, No. 118, about the district scribe of *Pinsk* province *Borisovsky county* who whipped a peasant woman (birches!).[3] (NB. They don't dare touch the base district courts (even to curb drunken caprice). True freedom but not nominal! To the devil with republics if they means despotism!) (the girl's murder of her child), of the illegitimate daughter, whose mother married the peasant from Novgradvolynsky County, the village of Serbovskaya Slobodka. Because of jealousy (took her away to the mill, choked her and bit her with her teeth). In the *Russian Messenger* 74, No. 4 April in Peter Petrov's article about France the most interesting details about Ledru-Rollain. A kind of trickster trading in liberalism.[4]

Memento from 1 May 74.

NB. In the May Prussian (German) laws (73).[5] All posts in the clerical offices are subject to government control. Disciplinary power (jurisdiction) of the bishops over the lower clergy is subject to government control. Future Catho/lic/ priests are obliged to pass a series of courses in public schools. The courts *for church matters* (the King's Court) henceforth is formed of members appointed by the government, and the cases under the May laws and *all church cases in general* come under the purview of this court. (NB. The case of the insane people.)

Prison examiner Makarov.

Warden of the juvenile delinquents Gasabov.[6]

1874
24 March cash on hand

Anna Grigorievna has	— 27
I have	— 15
Misha should bring	— 20
I have	—200
Note	— 70
Bazunov's	— 61
For editorial office sales[7] to	— 40
Total	433

26 March. *Cash.*

Anna Grigorievna has	550
and	17
I have —	71
Total	638

55

28 March there *was*   −71
    Gave the tail/or/   −25
    For shirts   −14
    Pool   − 3
    Misc., cab/by/, tobacco
    and bathhouse   − 3 50 k.   71

                                           45
            Total−45. 50 k

         Total in the purse   −   25 50

29 [March]. To Pasha   − 10   Total, 29 March −13 in my pocket
Purchases and misc.   − 2

                    12
30 and 31 March. Purchases, tobac/co/, cabby   −4
              Nanny and Liza/veta/   −3
              For vodka   −1

                               8
         In my pocket − 5
         Took from Anna Grigorievna −10 //

About 4th April Ann/a/ Grig/orievna/ had −407 (except 14).
In all 26 March there was − 63
4 Ap/ril/ (received by post−18).

From 4th to 9th April   Stolen from me   −8
                        Took from Anna
                            Grigorievna   −10
                        and also took   −10
Bought from them tea, tobacco, purse, hotel, wine, misc.−
9 April I had in my pocket 9

10 April received 61 r. 25 k. from Bazunov.
Given to Anna Grigorievna − 50.
Kept 11 r. 25 k.
Bought toys, tobacco, hotel, snacks, cabbies, theater, 3 r. taken to the doctor.
About 14 April *I had 11 r. 75 k.*

19 April took from Anna Grigorievna −15
Bathhouse, tobacco, tea, hotel, purchases etc.
On 21st I had in *my* pocket−with all the money taken,
left over−14 and some kopeks

To 23 [April]. Parfumerie, gloves −4

Tobacco etc.   −2

Total, in pocket on 23rd
5 rub. to Kalugin, taken from Anna Grigorievna −8 //

23 April I received from book/s/[8]   −125
And my own   7

Total, *I have*   132

Remaining in Anna Grigorievna's hands after deduction of all expenses
−210
And in Iv/an/ Gr/igorievich's/ hands   −100

Total   319
132

In all   447

Anna Grigorievna's own money, from stock subscription, *not counted.*
Received from Misha −10   447
10

457

From 23 [April] to 3 May Anna
Grigorievna spent   −90
and gave me   −25

Total spent   −115
Total, in Anna Grigorievna's hands 3 May   −114
Given away by Iv/an/ Gr/igorievich/   − 25

Total   139
Iv/an/ Gr/igorievich/ has left   −75

Total   214   Anna Grigorievna

Total, left over with me 3 May − 175
But I had   −132
and taken from An/na/
Gr/igorievna/   − 25

Total   157

Trip to Moscow, purchase of a shirt, and expense here since arrival −82 //

In total at home *cash* money 3 *May* with Ann/a/ Gr/igorievna/
with Iv/an/ Gr/igorievich/   −214
and me   − 75
Total   289

57

```
Received from Nekras/ov/⁹          −2000
            was                    − 139 (without Iv/an/ Gr/igorievich/)
            and I had              −  75
                              _____
                                  2214
```

NB. Books in the Ems Library to read, if there is time.
G. Sand. Césarine Dietrich. Journal d'un voyageur pendant la guerre.
Erckmann-Chatrian. Histoire d'un homme du peuple.
Belot. L'article 47.
G. Sand. La confession d'une jeune fille.
Erckmann-Chatrian. Waterloo.
A. Dumas. Affaire Clemenceau.
Proudhon. Le révolution sociale démontrée par le coup d'Etat du 2 Décembre.
NB. *Musset Alfred.* La confession d'un enfant du siècle.
Flaubert. Madame Bovary.
Octave Feuillet. Le roman d'un jeune homme pauvre.
Belot. Le drame de la rue de la Paix.
                    Femme de feu.
A. Dumas-fils. L'homme-femme.
Belot. Madame Giraud, ma femme.
NB. | Paris en Amérique.
     | On Zola's novels.

```
Iv/an/ Gr/igorievich/    −75
An/na/ Gr/igorievna/
     has in cash      −139
     Given her        −1300
                   _____
          Total       −1439
Expense
     To Trishin       −240
     For Kashpireva    −100
     To Goyzhevsky     −195
     Note for inter/nal/
          loan        −122
     Note payment     − 58
     For apartment    − 25
     6 days food      − 18
     Misc. purchases  − 38
                  _____
                       796

                    1439
                     796
                 _____
                     643
```

58

Given for debts:

To Trishin debt	−220	
To Kashperev/s/	− 181	8 May Anna Grig/orievna/ has 644
To Goyzhevs/ky/	− 200	I have 675
Things	− 5	1319

To Pechatkin	−659
	−112
	771
	360 debt [?]
	75 Iv. Gr.
	44 Pri [?]
	512

1319
512
1831

80000	365	2191	24	3 in 2 minutes
730	2191	216	91	30 August
700		31		725 with An/na/ G/rigorievna/
365				100 with me
2920				
431				
325				
500				
365				
185				

6 Febru/ary/   −70   10 October and to Anna G/rigorievna/−6½ left
10½
6
86 ½

12 Febr/uary/ An/na/ G/rigorievna/ has − 36 //

Print—37 rub. Paper for 2000 cop/ies/ 4 1/3—35 for each thous/and/ at 3 each

If twice yearly at 12 signatures each,

40 cop/ies/	−6
400	−60
8	8
3200	−480
Print	−240
Dustjacket, cover	− 25

59

Adv/ertisement/   −75
_____

All   820 or 800
Price 75 k. with 1000 cop/ies/   600
                       3
                _____

                1800
Clear profit   −1000
If 4000 expen/se/   −1000
Receipts   −2400
Clear pro/fit/   −1400
with 1000   −   750
                 3
            _____

            2250
            800
            _____
            1450
            2
            _____

With 2 thousand total   2900
At 1st−750 clear pro/fit/
With 4000 cop/ies/   −750
                     4
                _____
                3000
                1000
                _____

                2000 clea/r/ pro/fit/   //

If 4000 cop.
To expense 550
Receipts gross.   1500
                500
            _____
            950 = 3800   //

Describing nothing but priests,
Is boring and not fashionable, I think;
You're writing in a decaying genre,
Don't make a mess of things, L/esko/v!

The pettiness and secondrateness of "Peter's views."
—The fleet (just for Sweden).
—Petersburg—a crude shift of centers.
—He forgot and *did not understand at all* the idea of faith and Orthodoxy.
—The commonfolk as subservient material.
—The schismatics (so long as they pay money).
—Ranks   (turned into the very same gentry, but just slightly [?] undermined.

As if they did not realize what they were doing.

    —Absolute lack of economic sense in the idea of landowners and all his servants with the destruction of personal farms and personality. An idea worthy of a Persian Shah.

    —Debauchee and Nihilism. Concept of honor and the sword.

    —A monster—a filicide.

Анатолію Ѳедоровичу
Кони

въ знакъ глубочайшаго уваженія
отъ автора

ДНЕВНИКЪ
ПИСАТЕЛЯ

ЗА

1876 Г.

Ѳ. М. Достоевскаго.

С.-ПЕТЕРБУРГЪ.
Типографія ин. В. В. Оболенскаго, Николаевская, № 8.
1877.

Diary of a Writer for 1876 (published in St. Petersburg, 1877), with Dostoevsky's gift inscription to A. F. Koni.

NOTEBOOK IX

(1875-1876)[1]

1875.
Fits.

22 September /1875/ one of the stronger (but not one of the strongest), at night, toward morning, at 6 A.M., after a three-month break. Full moon. Tightness. Light thr/oa/t hemorrhaging, a very powerful rush to the head. Irritability.

Octob/er/ 13 (Monday) morning, in the morning, while asleep, at 7 o'clock, not so strong.

January 26 /1876/. Monday, morning, while asleep, at 7 o'clock, one of the rather stronger, [full moon] (1st quarter of the moon). //

12 February money—576 r. /expense diary/. //

Buy books: Belyaev "The Peasants in Rus."[2] //

Starting 24 October 75. *Bibliograph/ical/ Information. The Voice,* No. 294—1875[3]—Essay on *Servition de liste u servition de division.* //

1875. Of November 5 *Mosc/ow/ News* [Che] On the Egyptian legacy (Chernyaev).[4]

Of November 6 *The Voice.* Feuilleton from Berlin, on nihilism stuff in Russian schools.[5]

Diary of a Writer

Of November 8. Friday. On Wednesday Chernyaev was at Prin/ce/ Meshchersky's.[6] "We have a total of 6,400,000 cartridges, and since the powder is in metallic cylinders it chemically decomposed *(sic)* and it's impossible to fire. We have only 70,000 of the new model, and it is *impossible* to fire from any of the others." I said that the alliance of the three nor/thern/ powers would have the effect of not dividing Turkey, but each would protect her, and each of them will remain hostile to the others (because of the Turkish matters). And England meanwhile [who] will occupy Egypt too, to protect it, and once she occupies it will not leave. Chernyaev observed abruptly: "And so what do we care if England occupies Egypt, let her!" *(sic).*

Chernyaev also argued that the re-arming of Russia was scheduled to end by 1889 *(sic).*

At least Khlestakov prattled and prattled,[7] but nevertheless while he was prattling was a tiny bit afraid that they'd up and throw him out. Contemporary Khlestakovs are not afraid and prattle with utter serenity.

Our conservative part of society is just as shitty as the others. How many scoundrels have joined it, Filonovs,[8] Krestovsky,[9] the poet // with his long poem. Count Salias[10] with his frivolousness, the wicked fool general. The filthy family Avseenkos[11] and Krestovskys—Fadeev[12] with his Tsar in his head. //

All are serene, all are egotistical, and it would seem that this alone is enough to disturb things with eternal turmoil. On the contrary, the contemporary egotist does not worry about himself, how he entered, how he stands, whether he said something well. Nowadays all are serene and everyone is certain that everything belongs to him alone. And if not, he'll shoot himself.

Papa, forgive me, 27 years old and I haven't shown anything yet. I'll shoot myself. That's still good, there's a certain pride in it. While another person simply shoots himself because he is not as rich as Ovsyannikov.[13] What is there to live for if not for pride?

If not religion, then at least that which replaces it in man for a moment. Remember Diderot, Voltaire, [Rousseau], their age and their faith... Oh, what a passionate faith that was. With us no one believes anything, with us it's *tabula rasa*. Well, if only in the Great Bear, you laugh—I wanted to say it at least in some great thought. //

The fantastic idea of an *Order of Honor* instead of nobility (in the form of a humorous corrective to Fadeev's idea about merchants).[14]

But the seminarian [herd] works in a body like a herd. The seminarian is always in a herd. This is a herd animal.

Nekrasov's story about Reshetnikov's[15] last days (revolutionaries, old Gavrila)[16] parallel with the elegant Avseenko—Yukhotsky wept,[17] the armband, the foyer and delicatesse.

Talentless mediocrity (they flock... etc.).
Count Tolstoy. Turgenev's letter. The November issue of the *Russian Messenger* (se/e/ *Russian World*, No. 216).[18]

NB. The society of argicultural colonies and craft retreats (apparently significant, get to know it). The Childr/en's/ colony on the other side of the powder factories. NB. Check it out.[19]

The Voice. Sunday, 9th [October] November 75.[20]

"Sick works." But your very health is a sickness. And what do you do when healthy? //

The Voice. Monday 10th of November. Feuilleton. On the madness of the

64

double. Golyadkin.

Love for Russia. —How to love her when she gave such family names as So-
sunov, Sosunkov, they have to be done over into Sasunov and Sasunkov, so that
they contain no suggestion of sucking,[21] but on the contrary would suggest honorability.

A man who is happy to crawl from Baden to Karlsruhe [22] on all fours (on his
hands and knees) just to do something unpleasant to his literary rival. A man who
sits in his room and uses his time to think up what insulting *mots* he will say when
meeting one person or another, how he will address them, how he will offend them.

Ce n'est pas l'homme, c'est une lyre (of Lamartine). [23]

NB. In Simbirsk, one of the bas-reliefs on the monument to Karamzin de-
picts Karamzin reading his *History* to Alexander I, both are wearing ancient costumes, i.e. they are naked, at least 9/10ths.[24]

From Gogol's letter from the other world about spiritualism [25] and devils,
reference to the Epistle to the Romans, Chapter II, Verse 9. [26]

NB. *The Russian World* itself acknowledged it was 5-rubles-worth worse than
other newspapers. But [this] he says that this is for propaganda, if so,[27] there is
hope that next year it will be offered for free, and that the year after that maybe
even with an appended 10 rubles from the editors, and maybe even fifteen rubles
per subscriber—if only they read the opinions and surmises of fighting General
Chernyaev. //

Turgenev's jubilee, [28] a telegram from Petersburg from writers, such-and-such
and such-and-such and D/ostoevsky/ last, but only in sympathy for your talent,
not your person.

The Russian World is like a man who gets mad in the dark, "why isn't there
any fire, why isn't there any fire?"

...But why did Mr. Turgenev take the journey on all fours to Karlsruhe upon
himself specifically? I have never made reference to what I say about him, and who
knows, maybe there were others willing to crawl too? As for Mr. T/urgenev's/ sub-
sequent explanations, I think it would be unseemly for me to reply to them, for
if a person has prescribed crawling on all fours for himself, he could not answer
this other than [with squealing] in that nervous condition which people are in when
they run around the room beating the walls with their fists, squealing loudly and
wailing in a voice that wakes up the neighbors. In this kind of condition a man can
write God knows what, and how can one answer him?

A bottle-baby abroad. A Russian is a bottle-baby abroad.[29]

—Levites, seminarians, they are— they are the toilets of society.

Instantaneous thing (in the sense of momentary). //

Mos/cow/ News, No. 291, 14 November, Friday, the article "Literary Kunst-kamera," on *A Raw Youth.* [30]

Mos/cow/ News, No. 292. *Politische Corresponden.* Refutation of the sensational telegram of *The Russian World* about the cut-off of supplies into Chernogoria by Austria.[31] *The Russian World* urgently wanted subscribers, they take the public to some sort of Tashkent and storm it in the most unpardonable manner.
   The basic idea should always be unattainably higher than the possibility for fulfilling it, f/or/ ex/ample/ Christianity.

The absurdity is quite often contained not in the book but in the mind of the reader.

And you fail to understand not because [I] the writer is not clear, but because your abilities are underdeveloped, dull. Dull and underdeveloped.

The Citizen, No. 46, 16 November: news about the priests (with little cigarettes and not wanting to learn to read).[32]

Moscow News, No. 296,[33] 20 November. News about our foreign wheat trade (Odessa report). And Jean Lemoin's essay *(Debats)* on English politics, Egypt and the Suez Canal.

Prince Svetozarov—that charitable dimwit.

People made of paper. Princess Mary. [34] A person with taste cannot read that without boredom.
   Poor, dear, little ones. //

The current generation—the fruits of nihilism junk of the 60's. They are terrible and disgusting fruits.
   But their turn will come. A generation of children who will start to hate their fathers is coming into being.

Moscow News, No. 297, [35] 21 November.
   1) Summary of reactions of all the important English newspapers to the purchase of stocks in the Suez Canal.
   2) On compulsory education (from Petersburg).

The Russian World cheapened the newspaper.

And Balda said reproachfully,
It's cheap things you should chase, Kuzma.

About the incredible style people write in now, especially in provincial newspapers. Cf. the excerpts of Poretsky from *The Kiev Telegraph* [36] *(The Citi/zen/,* No. 47, 23 Nov/ember/.)* Print up excerpts in this spirit and in every issue of the *Diary* cite them as curiosities of how people write nowadays, in order to root it out and ridicule it.

And what can he say this man skinny in spirit (but not in body), but not in spirit? Even if the man is fat in body?

The Russian World—sanctuary for all talentless people and offended egoists.

Fibster.

He had dinner with me, I fed him.

Deskturning. Revolt of the desks in the Ministry of Education.[37] //

About how the *Mos/cow/ News* is our leading political newspaper.

Moscow News, No. 301, Wednesday, 26 November. From the brochure *Pro nihilo* excerpts[38] and a lead article on this theme.

The Voice, 26 November, No. 327

                        The Ovsyannikov case[39]

The Voice, 27 November, No. 328

Our liberalism is even retrograde, one gets an Order of Stanislav for it, Slavophilism is another matter: what stern demands! How hateful it is to the run-of-the-mill people trying to accomplish great deeds in a frivolous or swindling way. Liberals are put in the ministries so that they'll be, so to speak, *à la hauteur.*

Seminary editorship: what kind of total satisfaction, what kind of total blissfulness.

Sleep, honest laborer, he was dancing with a glass in his hand, stomping his feet, and with soldiers' verses ridiculing that which was not worth the dirt on his soles.

(Note of a person who shot himself.) [40]
                One shirt for the three of them,
                The rest God'll save.
                What's possible besides "Ah" ah!

To shout here—except maybe "oh!"

The Voice. Saturday, 29 November, No. 330. The Ovsyannikov case.

Moscow News, No. 303, 28 November. Lead article on the Herzegovinian uprising.[41] //

Once someone squashed this physiognomy with his heel, and went away, after this something as it were squashed remained in this physiognomy for its whole life.

Un homme heureux qui n'a pas l'air content.

On the artificiality and unnaturalness of the society for humanity to animals (man-loving) or a society for humanity to livestock, 15 rub. from the cab driver, to exterminate dogs with chloroform.

The Voice, No. 331, 30 November. The Ovsyannikov case.

Specialization of doctors, so that you don't know which to call for what, a torn-out eye, Sokolov, unwashed hands, the cigarette.

The Voice, 1st of December. The Ovsyannikov case and the article in *Independance Belge* about the change in the map of Europe, admitted to be insanity. But never, perhaps, has Europe ever been so close to precisely such a switch and redoing of territory *as in our time* (advertize this).[42]

On teachers of Russian letters (up to classicism—prattle, whatever occurs to you)—they made their careers.

Our civil servant is the embodiment of donothingism. In Dresden for the same money and what service with respect. In Russia putting on airs before the public with no respect. Let him put on airs. Railroad mailmen.

The dispatch [com] by the ministry of Forei/gn/ Affairs of money to Herzegovinia 12 November, and it was we who made the proposal. *Jonung.* [43]

Reminiscences of Committee Meetings. //

The Voice, 5 December.[44] Friday. Essay on the building in London for the preservation of rare and valuable objects, with the air being pumped out of the main vaults. The same issue. The brutality of a doctor to a girl who had shot herself /.../ Sardanapulus. (See *The Voice,* LaRoche's feuilleton.) [45]
Dances. The married woman and dances. The minuet as a declaration of love. The quadrille.

What are dances? The spring courtship rites of animals, only in a morally reasoning creature.

Perhaps he does have a lot of internal intelligence, but he has none that is external.

He'll say something and all you can do is stare at him, or exchange glances with your neighbor.

And he'll sit down to write and amaze the whole world. And now this g/entleman/ with intelligence more internal than external...

In the *Stock Exchange* of 7 December,[46] Sunday, in Suvorin's feuilleton, the funny paradox of Ovsyannikov: that even if he were not guilty of arson, nevertheless, because of his previous unpublished sins he should be indicted for arson now. //

The first striving of a diplomat is, it goes without saying, to have as few *enemies* as possible and as many friends as possible. Diplomat, his friends are always enemies, and then friends. Thus—more important are the enemies, so that the transition to being friends is closer.

But, my God, I am guilty before him, and therefore I must avenge him.

The Voice, Monday, 2 December, No. 339.

The case of the fist-fight on the street between the female teachers, the Candidate of Mathematical Sciences and Limberg.[47]

The conviction of the girl M. for indecent exposure and disturbing the peace on the street, the girl V. —speech in court about the defenselessness of weak women when girl M. was sitting on top.

The Citizen, No. 49, 7 December. About Ovsyannikov.

Smoke, about *beauty,* Potugin, abuse of Russia, the beauty of Belinsky.[48]

Turgenev and Viardot, translated Gogol's "Viy",[49] wanted to crawl under the table.

Potugin is precisely a person with natural ability who gets angry with himself.[50] Potugin—is Mr. Turgenev himself. The mistake is in Potugin being a seminarian, a seminarian would talk less, and more precisely.

Beauty, remember the lackey liveries of marquises and marquis's, falling on their stockings (Casanova).[51]

He confused the youth, predatory animal, monogamy.[52] *But the orphan homes?* The youth would not even start to speak, let alone weep, Potugin was lying.

(Turgenev and Pisarev.) //

"The Impolite Koronat"
All the comicality of the boy commanding the uncle.[53] *Lies*. Sucking up to youth shame.
Byron. Cain. Lies—lies since the times of the French Revolution.

The peasants are coming and they are carrying axes, something terrible is gooing to happen (apparently this is beauty in your opinion?).
And if the landowners suffocated us for a long time?[54]

On Mrs. Stechkina [55] —resurrection of the law of literary ownership (as about an advertisement).

In Turgenev—Churila's suit, but your flaps covering your rear area, and the glass in your eye, and the lackey-marquises, Churila's walk and your walk, thighs.

People have been terribly wrong about the beautiful. Bas-relief Karamzin and Alexander Pavlovich.

You sold off your estate and hightailed it abroad as soon as you imagined that something terrible was going to happen. [56] *A Sportsman's Sketches* and serfdom, but the villa in Baden-Baden, built on whose money if not on the serfs' money?

The girl Stechkina, feeling of measure destroyed, indelicately showing off to oneself that way, the end of your story and some kind of contemporary question.
Let me fall in battle, as not in measure, A frenzy of repulsive self-adoration with the most repulsive indelicacy and with the most repulsive showing off.

An article. 1) Potugin, Turgenev— (beauty).
　　　　Civilization.
　　　2) Civilization, by rejecting religion, has by that very fact admitted its own death, *for* it must introduce slavery then—if only in the form of the *proletariat* and the deification of the rights of personal property.
　　　3) Religion resolves all of that
(NB. How? The personal worth of the proletariat and freedom of spirit! without the carnivorousness of a proprietor).
(NB. It is difficult to say how this was resolved by Christ. Reciprocal grief for one another would soften capital and raise up the proletariat.)
It is Roman and Protestant Catholicism which is to blame. Katkov[57] (do we have the same faith as the Romans, the same Christ, Christ who needed the Jesuits). And finally the triumph of eight million proletarians and arsonists.

Lies since the beginning of the century. Lies in the journal, lies even in Cain

70

and the lies have been praised.

Cain—the reason: Byron lame.
Lermontov's tendency—the reason: an ugly person, he broke the poker.

NB.NB.NB.NB.NB. A political article. On [con] France and the illusory solidity of Germany.
Soon several representatives of Europe will die. We are on the eve. And the main thing is that one shouldn't forget the 8 million proletarians. Half of France will join the destruction.

The Germans could not have destroyed France. Destroy Paris, shoot the proletarians. Buy up the holders of land and keep it with Germans. Bismarck is not strong enought for that. //

"Impolite Koronat." The carnivorousness of youth. And after all you yourself wanted that. So there would be no spirit, you wiped out God. —But even without God one has to be humane, love humanity. —But why the hell should I be humane.
I want it to be merry, merry, merry, for girls to sleep with me, and to cut and slash throats, for the strong to devour the weak.
They'll say: you should be ashamed for that. —Why? And I spit on you.

NB. See November *The Russian Messenger.* The circle in Zurich.[58]

NB. Humaneness is not only a habit, a fruit of civilization. It can disappear totally.
Liberalism is a bad habit.

With the destruction of serfdom ended (did not end) the reforms of Peter and the Petersburg period. Well then *sauve qui peut.*
Americanism will set in for a short while.
The commonfolk are coming. Here are the ideals which Potugin ridiculed.
Having ended the internal period: but meanwhile one has to be ready. The Pope. Emperor German.
In the German Empire the internal disorder will make them, for unity, attack France or Russia (like Napoleon in the Crimea).

There are as few ideas in the German Empire as in France. In France they at least have the communistic ones, but in Germany only: long live German pride.//
/.../

New Time, No. 325. Saturday, 13 December 75. Biography of Pogodin.[59]

Turgenev's pious remark in *Smoke* that in 1862 Rastadt was still an allied

71

fortress.[60] So what.

In *Smoke* Litvinov, a sorry role, he himself didn't believe in the honesty of the flight and said to himself that this was in novels, [61] and in Simbirsk Province out of boredom, —— and when Irina refused, he was the first to be furious with her. There isn't even any passion of the flesh. D/evil/ only knows what it is. He should have been shown realistically and revealing his faults, but in Turgenev it's done idealistically—and it came out junk (show this type realistically, i.e., revealing the faults).

He doesn't know how to introduce the narrators in the story "The Dog," he doesn't know the milieu. In society no one says: my dear sir, and no one says: he ran, he did lancades that Napoleon's ballerina dancing on his birthday could not equal.[62]

NB. Very artificial and invented. People don't talk like that. //

In Turgenev's *Smoke* a terrible decline in artistry is apparent.

He doesn't know Russia. What kind of people are they? What kind of characters? What is Gubarev, what are these women with the latest machines. It's all made up. [63]

Journal literature has been broken up in fragments. /.../ And they publish.

Stock Exchan/ge/ News, No. 344. [64] Sun/day/. 14 December. The Unknown Person's feuilleton—conclusion about Ovsyannikov and the concise history of the School of Law (40 years, opening in 35).

The Voice, No. 345. Sun/day/, 14 December. —In the lead article a few good words about our middle eastern (military) affairs and about the need to increase the number of troops. /.../

The Voice, 15 December, No. 346. Judge Klokachev's report on the Limberg and Morozova trial (indecent exposure! Can we get down to exposure when dealing with such elevated questions!)

Spasovich's speech (the end).

Artistry is ignored only by uneducated and rather ignorant people, artistry is the main thing for it helps express the idea with a rounded picture and image, while without artistry, *presenting only the idea,* we produce only boredom, we produce in the reader inattentiveness and frivolousness, and sometimes also mistrust for the ideas which are incorrectly expressed and for the cardboard characters.

An educated priest's wife and Sedeltse. Mr. Turgenev resembles this educated priest's wife. The remark about Rastadt. So what, what do I care! What do any of us care about that? And for that matter what does anyone care about that?

On predatory animals, monogamy. Turgenev in his transport invented this. We have the nursery home. The mother, let's say, can breast feed, but only to the degree that this does not contradict her civil duties.

Byron's *Don Juan,* Dedication, stanza X. [65]

The main thing is one's tendency—contemporary Westernizing (and nevertheless it is contemporary Westernizing, no matter what you call it)...—is a great causer of laziness: we, they say, are *irreconcilable,* we stand off to the side (i.e., we do nothing). And since there's even honor in doing this, Russia has been left to its own devices [words] for the course of 20 years.

O, scoundrels! All any of you did was laugh and you defamed everyone. That's so easy. You are uneducated, you don't understand anything.

Tendency! My tendency is the one for which no ranks are given.

...In this case it was a simple fist-fight, and the candidate of laws simply punished them for rowdyism, drunkenness and misbehavior—therefore, for Limberg the fist-fight was a drunken one, but for the candidate it was an ennobling one.

Judge Klokachev—sold out and nothing else. [66] //

The meeting with a student from the Medical Academy begging for alms.
The opinion of [one word indecipherable-
Friedrich's house (they live as gypsies).

300-ruble stipends from the treasury for *all* Russian students, with the condition, however, that they are obliged to serve four years in the government afterwards, in any area, at their disgression.

A so to speak slanderous treachery.

The *best people,* in the sense of awareness of national truth, cannot fail to find their positions—they cannot, because most of all a person needs something before which to bow down.

Potugin. The London exhibition. [67] The law of the population: and therefore stupid Potugin is angry at Russia because she has 65 mill. people and not 165. Within 50 years there will be 165 mill., and you will see yourself that we will be, perhaps, first on exhibition. That is as clear as two times two. That is a law. It was not the will of the emperor which built the railroads, they got built by themselves. Precisely by themselves, no matter how much it looks like it was by somebody's will. Everything happens because of the well known laws of human nature. They are unchanging, and therefore only Russian landbarons abroad who don't know anything can deny the Russian people's ability to rejoice that the Germans are superior to us in intellect.

Besides which we could not put our political unity out at the exhibition after all (i.e., the people's idea of the state) or our faith. [dev] That too is a developed thing. Germany, for example, attained political unity only five years ago, well so we developed it many centuries earlier.

So [obscenity deleted] on the Russian people.

Litvinov—should have noted and shown that he was more guilty than anyone else, and he's a comic character from the ranks of the Pirogovs,[68] not a pathetic one.//

He indicated to her, as in 1853 the Sultan indicated to Prince Menshikov [69] the place in the chariot beside him, but if she had taken that seat, he would have been the first to be unhappy, and if he didn't slip away from her at the first post-station it would've been solely from lack of character. But he certainly would've slipped away at night. The characters are completely unclear and artificial. Mr. Turgenev knows reality too little (from the story "The Dog") and makes up a lot out of his own skull.

Specializations of doctors, they have specialized—one treats the nose, and another the bridge of the nose. One says everything's from disease of the womb.

The story of how Lily broke her arm.[70]

In the Russian man (for the most part) from the simplefolk you have to separate the beauty from the superficial barbarism. Whoever is a true friend of humanity, whoever's heart has beat because of the sufferings of the people, will understand and forgive all the impenetrably caked dirt and take the diamonds. (In Russia the commonfolk are a theory, and among those who love them, they will remain so.) However, I'm not going to start talking about touchy subjects.

The story of Limberg and Morozova.

Outline of the issue
1) Tendency. Diseases.
—So, doctors.
—"Impolite Koronat" (especially Golovlyata)
—In the Russian man separate (otherwise lies).
—Limberg and Morozova.
—The Medical student of the Academy.
—Reread *Smoke.*
—Politics.
Refuges. Hospitals and so forth.

Ap. Grigoriev. That eternally declaiming soul.

Ems. Vespers in Ems, and the swindler who hid under the throne at Spas-on-Sennaya. //

The Voice, No. 348. The rotten advertisement of Volf's children's editions. Barrister Yazykov on the role of literature in the Ovsyannikov case.[71]

Where would one get the doers for such a massive reform, lo and behold the [doe] Filonovs appeared.

Newspaper. Advertisement. Stechkina, Tsebrikova,[72] what to fill with. The girl's confession, both legs, they didn't do that with me. Primarily for young women who are not able to get married, yes sir, and no sir. No imagination, fantasy. Now is that advertisement immoral? No more immoral than ba/r/ed shoulders, breasts, dances. And then the more immoral, the better it'll sell. No imagination, or else they could've gotten rich. And they don't even know how to get rich, —the temperance house (Grom). Nekrasov.

Writers have no imagination or fantasy.

The prosaicality of the clergy.

On Russian pride: Gogol, Ostrovsky, I think that statesmen (Potemkin etc.). The Germans corrected. Economy. The vastness of significance corrected (Potemkin).
Great Pushkin—without pride.[73]

Seminarians as *status in statu,* —outside the commonfolk.

A feeling of locale and habit works powerfully on people of weak intellect. Mr. Turgenev in his novel *Smoke* writes about the city Rastadt (and the main thing is so seriously). What do I care about Rastadt, whether it's gone away or not, even if it disappeared into the earth, so what.

We have no feeling for locale in Russia. Well, what is, for examp/le/, Vladimir? and why know it, the way it is we are even ashamed of the Kostromas. But as soon as a Russian goes over to Europe, then [immediately] he feels like a local, and starts to nest, ah, and Rastadt. //

The Russian Messenger. November, 75. The fight of the people [dima] with the aristocracy.[74] Plato's words on tyrants. Tyrants result from democracy (pa/ge/ 13). NB. These are fresh people; this is the first observation of man in society.
Ancient Greek tyrants. Assa, demanding 300,000. Mikhailovsky is angry.[75]

NB. Seminaries must be raised to the level of high schools as quickly as possible, i.e., so to speak turn them into high schools, if for no other reason than the fact that by doing this the greenhouse of nihilist rot will be destroyed (see Eliseev's "Inter/nal/ Survey," *No/tes/ of the Father/land/,* December). Eliseev's ridiculous projects for the resurrection of the clergy (two priests: prayer-book and didactic).[76]

Read *No/tes/ of the Father/land/.* (To Mikhailovsky.) Competent people told me that the Tuilleries were burned by some private person, by some clown who gathered a gang without the communards knowing about it. But what would this mean?.. Don't [deprive] deprive a historical fact of its magnificence, terror (a break with history, a break for all time, and this at the same time as the fall of the communards). This is a commune wounded mortally, raising its head and crying out for the last time: that's how not only you will disappear, but also all traces of you and your history. And you insist on making them innocent sort of like August Kotzebue's heroes.[77] Can they really *descend from.* They must come independently with everything new.

Complain: there, they say, is how we were treated (they shot the communards, the Decembrists)—that's what he went to do, and after all you would've done the same thing yourself—isn't it stupid to shout: o, how they tortured me. What's sad // is not this, but the fact that you don't make peace and there is no way you will end with peace. And reconciliation for nothing is impossible, and—and undesirable. (For only on the basis of Christ is reconciliation possible.) But here on economic calculation, theref. the sooner and better, only our poor grandchildren... and maybe even our children. And, of course, this generation will not pass and not a single one of the now living will see this divine thunder.

But judges look at things in a terribly prosaic way: for him a fight with teeth-knocking and hair-pulling is simply a fight with teeth-knocking and hair-pulling, and nothing more.

Or take the fact that Ovsyannikov is answering for the whole epoch. But Ovsyannikov is a petty, comic charcter, it would be better if he were more majestic. Besides, this epoch always has been and will be, even if some of the people are always going to revolt against. And that's good, revolt, but don't commit injustices: "I like it that Ovsyannikov has been punished for his whole life" (Suvorin).[78] No measure, like Mrs. Morozova.

Now you find this terribly retrograde, because it doesn't correspond to prevailing opinion. You love the prevailing opinion and court it: a plush position and profits. You are like the senators used to be. I do not agree with the prevailing opinion.

General-abstract liberalism: haven't the Spasoviches, publishers, etc. piled up enough money.

And what did Spasovich take from the insurance society.[79] Quite a bit after all, no doubt Turgenev took less for *A Nest of Gentlefolk* and Tolstoy less for

Childhood and *Adolescence.* And maybe they even took less for their whole collected works. //

Cain. Byron lame. He laughed at Wordsworth for the customs house. Orange colors. Wouldn't give up his aristocracy. It's surprising that Pushkin refused so quickly. Lermontov. Byron lame, if his leg had been straight he would have been calmer, Lermontov is vile. Egotism. Stechkina. Advertisement. The newspaper *advertisement.*

Saburov[80] and Adriyanova. Stole 30,000 without any feeling of aristocratic honor.

14th of December there was a mad Westernizer affair, ugly, why aren't we lords? The Russian Tsars also played this game (beginning with Catherine). But Catherine had genius, but Alexander—no. [T] Would the commonfolk have freed the Decembrists? Without doubt, no. They would've disappeared without having managed to hold on for two or three days. All Mikhail, Konstantin had to do was show their face in Moscow, wherever you like, and everyone would have streamed after them. —It's amazing how the Decembrists did not realize this. Lack of education, the demand to meddle, to consider a rascal like Pestel[81] a human being, —the same thing now too: the members of the Agricultural Club. However with the disappearance of the Decembri/sts/—the as it were pure element of the gentry disappeared. What was left was cynicism: no, they say, obviously he can't get by being honorable. An arbitrary kind of honor appeared (Rostovtsev)—poets appeared.

This has so barbarized that when they chewed up Belinsky, —all streamed after him, to such an extent that even now, forcibly, they want to see *from above* the same thing as in the last Tsar's reign.

And, however, Nicholas's personality. //

(After all the petty-comic posturings, [run] take her away or not?) Magnificently, like the Sultan Abdul-Medzhid[82] indicating the seat beside him in the chariot, he points out the seat on the train to her.

And is it for Potugin and him to decide the fate of Russia under the Russian tree[83] in Baden-Baden?

Shut up, you are not competent, you are the infants of Russian life and comical idiots.

And then all will be *"des (hommes) heureux, qui n'ont pas l'air content."*

And then all will turn into happy, but dissatisfied, *des hommes heureux, qui n'ont pas l'air content.*
Il était humble et hautain comme tous les fanatiques.
Il avait la réligion de ses fonctions et il était espion, il l'était espion comme on est prêtre. He was a spy without any malice, *il l'était espion comme on est prêtre.*

Ces gens-là, quand ce n'est pas de la boue, c'est de la poussière.

The Voice. Saturday. 20 December, 75, No. 351.[84]

Father Gerasim's comment *against* Osinin about the *inflated* agreement of the Bonn council with the Eastern church. (NB).

In telegrams too.[85] Numbers finally established by the Nation/al/ Assembly on voting for deputies and senators, and the dissolution of the Nation/al/ Assembly.

Politics.
The political idea of France is not in the election of the Assembly, but in general in its position. For the Assembly can decide something at the very first step, and suddenly a minister will appear and say that this decision is not in accord with the intentions and plans of the marshal to save France, —and the National Assembly will immediately rescind the decision, and if it doesn't rescind it, it will be considered *as revolt* and it will be terminated. //

The student hunts for a place as doorman. *The Voice.* Sunday, 21 December.[86] /.../ //

Mos/cow/ News, No. 324. Saturday, 20 December. On changing the gentry's rights (lead).
On spiritualism. Report on *Mendeleev's* experiments.[87] //

The *"Unknown Person"* says: "True grief is not expressed in banal phrases thought up at leisure, [etc] the value of a man is not expressed in the speeches which are usually pronounced over his grave."[88] O, what a small and bookish thought! Know, Mr. Unknown Person, that very very often true grief is expressed in the most banal phrases and rituals, and thus grave-side speeches are still very much loved (the death of a mother, Saint Barnil's sermon and everyone wept). You haven't learned this yet, Mr. Unknown Person!

Stock Exchange /News/. Sunday, 21 December. //

To Suvorin. —I will tell you that your liberalism is a craft; or a bad habit. In itself this habit is not a bad one, but in your case it has turned into one. You will say that, on the contrary, it isn't a craft, and that you have been warmed by the feelings, etc. And I'll say that you have not been warmed by anything, but quite simply have been carrying on a profitable profession, and that in general it would take a great deal to warm you up...

Witticism. Rurik, Sineus, Truvor and Pogodin[89]—very [disresp] bad.

And there's no reason for you to prejudge Judge Klokachev.[90] That's a threat. The whole point is this fact: was she sitting on top. Prove that this was not the case. But this can be decided only by [court] a supreme court etc.

And about *satisfaction* in Mr. Morozov's letter, it's not for you to speak of this (the feuilleton about the leap from St. Isaac's Cathedral).

Comparison [of the Unknown Person to Bulgarin]. Of a liberal feuilleton with the kind Bulgarin used to do: the same firm support from behind.

To the Unknown Person. Because you cannot allow yourself certain expressions (such as Potekhin's reputation) and you know why.
—Why?
—I'll tell you. Because we are all obliged to be decent human beings, and a decent human being cannot allow himself that kind of relation to another human being. And if on occasion he decides not to continue being decent ([there] for some reason it gets hard), then nevertheless we should apparently restrain ourselves, out of respect for decency, if we wish to belong to civilization. If you don't want to—that's another // matter. Then go ahead and do what you want, [then] but society has police which protect it from such desires of private persons.

There always has to be a measure of decency which we must respect, even if we don't wish to be decent.
(Stechkina)

Aristotle. *Russi/an/ Messenger.* Kutorgi's article. November. Tyranny is monarchy which has in view only the good of the monarch (in contradistinction to monarchy which has in view the general good), oligarchy is government which has in view only the good of the rich (in contradistinction to government by aristocrats, in the sense of *the best* people), and finally, democracy is government which has in view only the good of the have-nots ([in contradis] none of them worries about *social* good).[91]

See the pages inserted in the article.

The opinion and conviction of the *Diary of a Writer:* We have everything to expect from the commonfolk: only they can give us the best men. But for that we need conditions under which the commonfolk can give us their best men. Peter created the best men from the gentry and from the valor of people coming up from below. From the service, in the final analysis, and he tied up all the rest of the people with taxes.

Now Peter's idea has been infinitely broadened, and now it is from the commonfolk we demand the best men. But it is essential for the commonfolk to be in conditions to put them forward.

Notes for *Diary of a Writer.*

(Who are the leaders? And will the commonfolk stand for leaders? They must bow before *education.* But will they consider education. It will acquire only knowledge.) //

Will it take this as education or as the acquisition of knowledge. Is Aksakov correct? Aksakov is unquestionably correct. The ideal is in love.

It is not the Potugins who should turn up as its leaders, or *becalmed liberals* with their lazy program: translate directly from the French. On the contrary, the commonfolk, with the first rays of education, will now immediately see how far the copyists have gone and what they have turned into (i.e., the gentry, the grandee/s/ and the Petersburgers).

The becalmed liberal!
Now the becalmed liberal rules.

NB. On the contrary, a patriarchal monarchy, in which there are more than a republic—is their ideal. In Russia monarchy in its ideal can never be tyranny— only as a departure from the ideal.

In Russia: those who support civilization (i.e., the civil order of Europe) therefore also support Europeanism, i.e., they are Westernizers. And therefore they must support the nobility, for only the nobility have been [sup] proponents of Europeanism. However, our Westernizers (the Unknown Person, Turgenev, the Journalist) etc. They talk and assert that they stand for the commonfolk, and when [the commonfolk] tells them that the commonfolk cannot exist without its individual character, and you are rejecting all our commonfolk principles and laughing at them, then they get mad and say that they are the genuine *narodniki,* but only on the condition that this commonfolk not have anything of their own, but they // are wrong, for they are not *narodniki*, but just aristocrats and young lordlings.

The commonfolk possess two ideas immanently:
1) Orthodoxy.
2) They never consider the monarch a tyrant, the most liberty. They do not understand how the monarch can fear them, and therefore not give them all possible civil liberty.

Its own unified tendency is had by only three nations: English, Russia and America (?)

One has to think a while to get to these ideas. If they do not comprehend them, it isn't because the ideas are stupid, but because their uncomprehending heads are stupid.

Volk's advertisement and the advertisements about Volf.[92] (NB. Besides *The Voice* and in Suvorin's feuilleton. *The Stock Exchange /News/* of 21 December.)

They praise it frenziedly, they present it as if it were a solution to the problem.

Solon split up ownership of land into small parcels in Athens with a law forbidding the unlimited accumulation of land in one person's hands. The convention // in France divided up the big property of the emigrants and church into [parc] tiny parcels and started selling in the light of the continuous financial crisis in France at that time. This measure enriched France and gave her the ability to pay out 5 billion in 80 years. But while making possible this temporary state of well-being, for a terribly long time this measure paralyzed democratic aspirations and crushed the Revolution at its root, which, of course, the revolutionaries did not want, but it turned out that way, for the army of landowners multiplied immeasurably and the limitless sway of the bourgeoisie, the primary enemy of demos, began. Without this measure the bourgeoisie would not have hung on so long at the head of France. Well, as a consequence of this the lower class too was made more ruthless. Nevertheless the lower class goes on, it was not crushed and ends by conquering all, and if the bourgeoisie does not give way in time, some ruthless things are going to occur. But they won't give way in time, they won't ever give away anything, and this is what awaits France... Only France?
Tyrants. Bonapartists. Communism. Bismarck's politics.

Churila Penkovich,[93] Potugin, falling marquises, marquise-lackeys, dancing the polka modern Alcibiades, covering its rear with its skirts and flipping them up in little obscene ways—maybe you like this and you find this prettier than Churila (even Churila [didn't] didn't walk the way that the peasant in Olonetsky Province later redid him in the bylina). —here we have something, Mr. Turgenev, that never fits under any general law, not since the end of the last century. Probably the naked body alone is suitable, and no matter what man dresses in, if he is enchanting in his time, in a very short time thereafter he becomes repulsive. Of course, some sooner, some more slowly. [But] The skirts and frocks of the Empire and the Restoration periods became disgusting faster than the costumes // of our ancient princes and their retinues which are good even now. But they are good for us, but maybe in Athens they would be ridiculed and condemned. I repeat, only the costume of Apollo Belvedere and Venus de Milo has remained stable (in beauty). Meantime there's the bas-relief of Karamzin and Alexander in Simbirsk, and in the ancient style, quite probably that seemed beautiful then if the decision was made to immortalize it in a monument, however it is already ridiculous to us now.
So that even Apollo Belvedere's costume is not always good.

All of this is well known, and it would have been omitted here, but I say this to show the degree to which Mssrs Potugin are steeped in malice against Russia. Even for its dress I'll ridicule with hatred and I'll lie; for having concealed the skirts and the fact that even Churila was arrayed that way only in the village, Potugin was telling malicious lies about Russia. To a person who doesn't think about it it might really seem: "How much inferior Russia is to all other countries even in the beauty of its dress."

Potugin and the nihilist who wept: lies and ignorance of reality. He wouldn't have wept if he had been smashed. You didn't smash Pisarev either, he simply kept silent. The nihilist would answer that the family and feeding the offspring is not necessary at all. The nihilist fantasizes his ideal. If you wish, it's not bad (after all I am only speaking about the ideal). But this ideal is impossible, since it is being fantasized, but, probably a different one will be possible.

Impolite Koronat, good-looking? —But to some it seems he is good-looking.

The ideal of the nihilists of the highest flights, although not today's and not ours. Will society manage to correct itself. Will they give way to demos—of course, much, very much must be given way, but [in] this is salvation to everyone. //

It is difficult to wait for truth from the outside /.../
        The seminarian, as you know,
        In this sense too—is a democrat.[94]

But can a seminarian be a democrat even if he wants to?

Peter had one creation—the nobility [serv], all the rest collapsed. Now the nobility too has decided, what is left, nothing. Now the Slavophiles and Westernizers could be reconciled: both of them expect everything to come only from the commonfolk; but the Slavophiles believe in the commonfolk because they acknowledge that their own roots lie in the commonfolk, but the Westernizers agree to believe in the commonfolk only on one condition: that they not have any roots of their own. And that's why the fight is continuing. But a fight is one thing, love is another, and why can't those who are holding each other by the hair love each other. On the contrary, this is very...

The honorability and honesty of our society in the highest sense, the honorability of our youth, the idea and ideal above all, faith in the idea. Earthly rewards only after. In this our society is similar to the commonfolk, and this is its point of contact with the commonfolk. There are many scoundrels among the commonfolk, but even a scoundrel will not say: that's the way it has to be, but he sighs and respects virtue. And if there are cruel monsters, the commonfolk condemn them. If a young man says: that's the way it has to be, I adore baseness, it is only because he considers this the truth, and not otherwise, if he did not consider this the truth, he would not follow it, even in spite of the fact that many of them are carried away by simple ambition.

Ovsyannikov, profit, from his mat/er/nal cradle, but then he *is* a *peasant,* and profit meant a great deal to him. "The Idea" of *A Raw Youth.*

83

A terrible shock awaits society: the road to Siberia, unification with Siberia, trade can be increased 10 times, and agriculture in the barren steppes, intensified animal husbandry and even factories. Russia, connected to Asia by roads, will say a new word, a completely new one. It's just beginning now.

China.

Turned attention to the article in *The Voice.* //

Malthus' idea about the geometrical progression of population is without doubt wrong: on the contrary, having achieved certain limits, the population can even stop altogether. *La population reste stationnaire,* here, of course, there are multifarious causes (so that given a different social situation even in France the population could increase even more), but nevertheless, it seems, it will be most correct to follow the axiom, true, still not proved, but only foreconcluded, to wit: that territory can support only that size of population which is commensurate with its means and borders, and beyond this *la population restera stationnaire.* This axiom awaits, perhaps, all Europe. In this manner the states with great amounts of land will be the largest and most powerful. This is very interesting for Russians.

Education begins only later with a certain density of population. And all civilization too. Here there should be first scientific [conclusions] rules. But the character of the people promotes this too: with the Germans it's education first of all, and only then political thought, but with Russians it's the other way around.

This itch for debauchery is beginning.

War is an opportunity for the mass to respect itself, a call of the mass to the greatest general task and to *participation* in them (soldier and commonfolk songs). (Be dispassionate, hear this out) You [such] // cannot find another means of participation of the mass on an *equal* footing with the intelligentsia (directing the mass by rule) in *higher deeds* (for participation in higher deeds). Except for war—everywhere intellect, science, cleverness and talent rule, and the mass must obey without objection, i.e., sacrifice its initiative. War suddenly raises everyone up—and no longer through the intelligentsia, but through magnanimity. By the right to die for the good of one's country, of all, the lowest are raised to the highest and become equal to them as men. Apart from war, I simply don't see any places where the mass can show its worth, for everywhere there is talent, intellect and the best people. Sometimes the mass is left with nothing but revolt to assert itself. Sometimes it does assert itself, but this is ignoble and not very magnanimous. Education, which the commonfolk do not have, wealth, protection. Dying together—that unites. O, civil war is another matter.

No matter how you equalize rights by means of revolutions, you'll never equalize to this stage of satisfaction.

I do not consider you an honest writer, Mr. Su/vor/in.

It's not that he is stupid, but there is not so much intelligence in him.

The critic Mikhailovsky citing the poems of his patron Nekrasov in his articles. Know that I would not do this.

In *Russ/ian/ World,* No. 262, Wednesday, 24 December 75. V. S/oloviev's/ article about me.[95]

Smoke. Here some guy riding in a railroad car condemns everyone, and decides that this is all smoke. It vexes me that he is given this right. He is worst of all and has nothing to say about this. Even if he condemns himself, but it doesn't occur to him to condemn himself.
The author should have put him in the proper light, the author did not do this. //

In the *Mosc/ow/ News.* December. Wednesday 24, No. 328. About the Ovsyannikov case and the role of the press—a fine lead article.[96]
The news report on the monks who strangled the Vereshchagin girl.[97]

The Voice. Thursday, 25 Decem/ber/, No /30/ 356.[98] The news report from the *Kiev Telegram* about the secret murder in Uman. Crowbar. Pavlusha.

(Hamlets and Don Quixotes.)[99]

Such Rastadtenizing of the former gifted Russian writer.

Turgenev lacks knowledge of Russian life *in general.* And he once learned about the commonfolk's life from the house lackey with whom he went hunting *(Hunter's Notes),* and he never knew anything else.

How much of the form of the French novel went into your work, Mr. Turgenev?

I was at the child/ren's/ ball etc in [artis] the Club of Artists 26.[100] Didn't see the Christmas tree. Mountains Children. Very unbashful, richly dressed, Petrushka, his character. The bear with the cup for the Herzogovinians bears witness, aside from inventiveness and unquestionable wit, to the constant desire of the club to entertain its visitors. The crowd, sun, crowd (get some air). Tableau vivant, the donkeys. (Arrangement of the buffet, the servants.) People afraid to say *oui et non.* The society is not competent. If each one knows how much ingenuousness, honesty, good and magnanimous feelings he had in his heart, —if they all wanted to, they would make everyone happy. Now everyone thinks: Ah, well, // won't they call me a fool? Try to start talking, and the man will get confused, lose control and look at you furiously [And meanwhile, if] True, in order not to appear to be fools they yawn and say that it's boring, out of fear that they'll be considered fools if they praise anything and if they risked saying that they were having a good time. This, of course, is intelligent, but it is an old trick, and therefore it must be getting stupid. Now the first person who thought it up was intelligent. But if all these gentlemen knew who, they would suddenly get more intelligent and intelligent in the full sense of the word, if they would suddenly wish to become ingenuous, honest and loving. Such treasures of intellect, talent and wit would open up in a certain general quite unexpectedly. Civil Servant. Art, *Petrushka* (Gorb/unov/: does not go). Does the golden age really consist of porcelain cups? Dances, it's not for the wives to dance. The young generation is pushing (*not all,* but very many. Of course, this is liberty, but...). The rest are polite, and the audience is magnificent. Description of the dances, the spinning polka, costumes (Potugin. Costumes, Churila Plenkovich, Alexander and Karamzin). I because I reread *Smoke.* A few words about *Smoke* (easily comprehensible ones). The younger generation. Pavlusha, whole people.

A colony for the under-age (sister without a place).

Lord, what [thi] was it like in Sodom? Babies in cradles, bassinets. This people was wiped out. You are looking for guilty ones.

Man forgave Margarita—Faust.

Job and God.

...For oneself, one's own rights; for people, the rights of people. That's the difference between the word of Christ and the word of socialism.

Kind people gave me the opportunity to see this. Kind and true citizens.

Besides it's not enough to live there—everything will suddenly change!

Koronat—well isn't this slander on young people? Are they really that crude, stupid and dull? //

I to Gorbunov, let's suppose, to an artist (and a complete artist) about the Alexandrinka.

O, where are the vaudevilles where one person crawled under the table and the other dragged him out from under the table.[101]

And now the *Dead noose.*[102]

Let's go to Petrushka.

Pushing (and it promotes a feeling of liberty in the younger generation), but, for example, it would mean even more liberty if one were to fist-fight. It has always seemed to me that civilization in Russia consists only of one form, and if the form were not here, —everyone would start punching each other at balls, because we have no internal need to respect the human being in another person, in the way that it still continues to exist in Europe, and that we were taught this only mechanically, and *grattez le russe* always remained.[103] But has the nobleman, even with his external civilization, destroy/ed/ himself by liberating the serfs.

That's why it's good that they dress in clothes which delight the eye. Here we have insincerity, hypocrisy. Hypocrisy is the price... But the forms were essential, they have to be maintained. This is potentiality. Now, what is a dance? it cheers one unconsciously, the choice of fiances, a lady cannot dance.

The lawyers condemn Ovsyannikov in advance.
But can that be so?

Not all, but very many. I write very many so as not to write at all. //

The Unknown Person finds himself in a false position, because for some reason he suddenly imagined himself a genius, and, the main thing, he did it alone: absolutely no one helped him in this. Now in every feuilleton one senses the most repulsive falsehood: [everyone] they want to talk playfully and simply, but [and everyone] they also want to say something extremely sapient, so sapient that it would never occur to anyone, they want to knock us over with their wit. But then, to our surprise, no playfulness is visible, no sapience observable. But some sort of pounding, some kind of puffing up of the God-given portion of intellect and talent, in order to blow them up as big as the Sukharev Tower. Some resemble [the last words] Mr. Turgenev, who has been writing himself out for the last ten years and who keeps on pounding his tiny talent annually in *The Messenger of Europe* and milking the humble [dried-out] cow of his wit, with its dried-up teats.

The Unknown Person in his feuilleton No. 357 of the *Stock Exchange /News/,* speaking of spiritualism, says that Christian teaching about immortality is better, while here the *spirits are stupid.*[104] The Unknown Person is mistaken about the stupidity of the spirits. If they are devils, they couldn't do anything cleverer and [deeper] more intelligent than present themselves as stupid and petty jokers and tricksters in the start, in the first period of spiritualism. And already, of course, they are ruled by some kind of vast unclean spirit, with awesome power and more intelligent than the Mephistopheles made famous by Goethe, Ya. P. Polonsky[105] assures us. This main hellish spirit is more profoundly a politician than Mr. Suvorin supposes. [if] Spiritualism is an important thing, and the devils must have spent a long time waiting for the epoch when people would get to the tables. (I repeat: all of this assumes that they are devils, i.e., spirits.) Now, even Mr. Suvorin doesn't want to believe precisely because of the stupidity of the spirits. If devils appeared with revelations about the laws of nature and the secrets of the earth—and the life of people would be stolen away, and the people, showered with benefits, would stop being melancholy, and at first they would cry out in ecstacy: Who is like unto this beast, he brings the light down from the heavens. And what is the Unknown

Person did believe? Here—on the lack of consolation in a teaching which has con-
fiscated life. Later on people would start to rot, be covered with sores and start
to bite their tongues, in torment, seeing that their life had been stolen for bread,
for stones turned into bread for these secrets of nature which had been announced
for free, revealed without any labor, just by the table-spinning knock of the spirits. And if they started right off with this, who would withstand them. I think
that even Mr. Suvorin would surrender in the beginning and shout: Who is like unto this beast? But the sly devils, they don't need a kingdom which forms easily and
accidentally, they need one which will form solidly and stand by itself without
their work. Perhaps a kingdom in the mind and revelations communicated from
the other world would collapse in the end. Maybe people would erupt with abuse
and shout: "We're rotting! Man does [will] not live by bread alone," and stop playing at being Magi. And so that is an unstable kingdom, but the kingdom built on
discord, or, perhaps, on blood—is more solid. And the discord is already beginning.
Intelligent people are turning away precisely because the spirits are stupid, they
are turning away and laughing at people who are very much deserving of respect
and who are intelligent, but who believe in the tables. From the crowd the matter
goes over to science, the disunity and ridicule intensify, more // serious abuse and
discord begin. But so as not to lose adepts, but acquire them in geometrical progression, the spirits use new cunning: they shamelessly pass before seriously dis-
believing, before people of science, before critics and inspectors. The seances are
not successful, the discord and ridicule intensify, and when the inspectors turn
away slightly, in the circle of true believers which is left unthinkable phenomena
suddenly begin (the photograph in Paris). The tables dance, knock, speak, sometimes beautifully and then even raise up on all four legs, and then come shades
from hell [in the form of]. It is impossible to doubt, the adepts rush ahead, but
the skeptics cannot be convinced: discord. Then the devils are cunning: they suddenly choose a skeptic, an enemy, a scientist who has written and bellowed against
them all over Europe, —they choose him and they all appear to him like two times
two; a new scandal, new discord. And thus aggravating matters and gradually in-
creasing their power more and more, the devils, finally, achieve such discord that
blood starts to flow. This, undoubtedly, will start, if, for example, they start curb-
ing spiritualism in an external manner [I am convinced] because it is catching on
among the commonfolk. Then it will pour out in an instant, like lighted kerosene,
and set fire to everything. Every forbidden idea, immediately, as soon as it is forbidden, is placed on a pedestal by the forbidders themselves. If Strauss[106] and Renan hadn't been forbidden, who would know about them in Russia, for example?
Every forbidden idea is like that very petrol can with which the incendiaries doused
the floors and tables of the Tuilleries before the fire. You forbid some idea, that
means you have already poured on a cup of petrol into the edifice you are protect-
ing: rest assured, it will soak through and in its time burst into flame. People don't
// want to see this, but the devils see it clearly and they see that they cannot forbid; with all his intellect man really is weak before fact. Well, what happens, for
example, if spiritualism pours into the commonfolk, and [they] 9/10 go over to
spiritualistic faith in the absence, it would seem, of almost any help from their spi-

ritual leaders. It would be too bad, right? They won't rebel, but then it'll be too bad, too bad, right? How enlightenment, development will be delayed... The whole problem is: are the devils really involved in this, or is it simply a trick? From the other world Gogol asserts that they are devils. He sent a letter, you shouldn't tease devils. The great holy leader asserted that the devils are a terribly difficult question. terribly difficult, especially if you bluntly assert (put the question) that the devil has never existed.

I am joking, gentlemen. //

If it's not the devils, then of course it can turn out to be trifles, too bad even. But if it is the devils, they are acting in such a cunning way that one can even admire it.

But they'll all go brother against brother, and only through discord will the idea take root. How did Lutheranism and various sects in Europe take such firm root—by the fact that blood was spilled for them. //

About censorship—forbid three things, forbidding the rest is dangerous and unprofitable.

Spiritual leaders, priests who refuse to teach. The priest-prayer-book and the priest-preacher of Eliseev.

Don't worry, the devils know their business...
Only, are these devils...
Now with us, for example, how many people have quarrelled and offended one another because of spiritualism.

But then suddenly: you have the electric telegraph (if it wasn't already there), the swarm is there: you'll find a treasure and you'll find coal deposits (fire from the sky, especially if they cut out the forests). But then it would be too simple that way. How is the religious idea of spiritualism vile: the theft of your freedom, and they say it is a coming of the holy spirit! Never will God allow such a terrible thing (trick) to be done to man. But nevertheless in the beginning there would certainly be adepts, they would shout and holler, they would say: // an end to material needs, now only spiritual life! [But] And they would shout, and there would be adepts, and what intelligent people would shout this! But then they wouldn't notice that spiritual life no longer existed: stolen, the source dried up, for the source of spiritual life—is work and [free thought] free examination of stored-up riches which have a goal [giv] and ideal: [give everything to your neighbors] not one's own flesh, but [one's own flesh] the happiness of one's neighbor.

Even if he were resurrected from the dead, they wouldn't listen to him. A terrible truth. Thomas.

And that's why the devils speak stupidly and mysteriously and, mainly, they don't say *anything new,* —and this shows vast intelligence! Such intelligent ones!

True, they laugh and lie, but then that's why they're devils! Only, are they devils? If not devils, then of course [the result is not] infinite stupidity is the result. This is on the spiritual side of spiritualism. Practice is another matter: here, it seems, no one can say anything yet. In fact, if the matter were decided already, wouldn't investigative commissions (Mendeleev) convene?

Are there devils? I could never imagine what satans would be like. Job. Mephistopheles. Swedenborg: bad people... about Swedenborg. // Criminals: the system of punishment by deprivation of freedom. The vileness of penal labor and the gaiety of labor *attrayant.* They'll say, the prisoner's standard of living will turn out to be better than life at freedom and man will prefer to become a prisoner so as not to live in some hellish life at freedom?

But the very point is that deprivation of freedom is the most terrible torture, which almost no man can bear. I saw this (Orlov),[107] they didn't fear the lash or the gamut. Only the deprivation of freedom is terrible. It's on this principle that the system of punishments must be based, and not on the principle of tortures. //

I was assured that it would be unclear: what is the *Diary*—I'll explain what the *Diary* is.

The cook cut off the yardman's hand. *The Voice.* Sunday, 28 December, No. 357.

About Koni and Kovalevsky's stories about insults from police officers.[108] No one is to blame for this, it's a matter of morals.

MacMahon.[109] An honorable soldier, a brave soldier, but all of this so as not to say that he's an intelligent soldier. Nobody said anything about the intelligent one. The whole politics love for one's country. Disperses the assembly. The future is pregnant. The Republic is essential. All dynasties must certainly be enemies of France and strenghten their authority. Napoleon. Honorable Chambord. The Republic is the only salvation from the Commune. Neighbors hate one another all the more, but Napoleon would ally with the communards. —There's no peace. The future is pregnant. Something uncompleted in the world. /.../

Until Christ war will not cease, this has been foretold.

If only they are devils: now if only we could find that out more certainly. //

depictions in poems.

In Job; it's because you gave to him. Didn't you hear that *voice,* gentlemen? Does it not ring out even now. Socialism, Proudhon. What an everlasting voice!

The Voice. 28 December, No. 357. Sunday. *Potekhin's letter.*[110] (NB. Await an answer from Suvorin.)

If when the earth disappeared, of course the Bible. All characters. Read to children.

This is criticism from nature, or even better, *through nature.*

I don't believe in *The Voice's* hate for the *Stock Exchange /News/,* the former *Not/es/ of the Father/land/* for the form.

They are men of quick but not of durable hate (in/contradistinction/ *pendant* /quick/ eternal Great-Russian kindness: Pushkin). When they appear men with very durable hate have been very highly esteemed (Sylvio, A Hero of Our Time),[111] they were esteemed as highly as foreigners (Kotlubais etc.)[112] and as un-Russian people and they are people whom one must respect, if only for the reason that they aren't Russian.

In Russia anything can be done (NB. Koni's stories etc. News report on the [lawy] attorney who discovered 1000 r. *The Voice,* No. 358. Monday).[113] Catch them, they'll start to lie and say nothing like that ever happened. Cashiers from the cashier's windows... No honesty, no concept of duty. How can one live here and can one live?

The Voice, No. 358. The priest shot himself. His superiors paid no attention. And why do so: sleep and peace there. //

Everyone wants to seem noble. Do something base with nobility... This must still be good, it means they still [value] fear nobility, [still] if they resort to it. And "hypocrisy is good, [once there's no] because it is the tribute which vice pays to virtue."

The Voice, /No./ *358.* The article about domain registery (note on Markov's article) (state serfs *are permitted* to divide it into separate plots if 2/3 of the votes [village] of the village commune so desire.) A supreme *ukaz* of 24 November 1866. //

Pseudoclassicism is still raging in France to this day. France gave in during the epoch of the Restoration, while Germany and England were more inflexible. During the Revolution any triquotez was called the mother of Gaius Gracchus.[114]

The pious man reported the licentious desire, but the consistory paid no attention. Such zeal for faith, just think.

The Northamerican States started out on a firm foundation of reform. But the spirit disappeared, and one of the indications of this is the great widespreadness of spiritualism. But the development of a people and its future life is determined only by what this people believes in, what it considers an ideal of good and truth.

The French squandered their faith for the sake of the encyclopedia, and to this time they are using the law to crush disenfranchised little people. Nothing came out of it. We can still // hope! In Russia the people still believe in the truth... if only our "batyushki" don't squander our faith permanently.

Aristocrat-writers, proprietor-writers. Lev Tolstoi and Turgenev are proprietors.

Polevoi put (appended) a picture of Turgenev's house in Baden-Baden in his history of literature.[115] What does Turgenev's house in Baden-Baden have to do with Russian literature? But such is the power of capital.

The Voice, No. *359.* Article on how it's impossible for secular teachers to teach the law of God (theology). (NB., of course teachers can't, the devil knows what they'll say, it's a matter of conviction, but where are our priests? Belly, food, and *The Voice* talks about insecurity.) *The Voice* says priests can't preach because they aren't secure financially. But this is what matters. They should be made secure, but it would be also desirable to see them perform feats of self-sacrifice, for where else will we see any?

(and without nihilism and without the law of God one can teach the vilest kind of freethinking).

But meanwhile 10 priests in the south refused.

The priest shot himself, and what is going to happen now, in the monasteries? They do exist, they do, and I know of some like this, but we need more of them. It is essential that the idea not die out in them. There are some (let's suppose, and that's sufficient, that there are).

And here we have Eliseev's projects. //

Plan of No. 1
—Doctors.
—Ball.
—Colony.

In the same No. 359 of *The Voice* the *session of the society for the prevention of cruelty to animals.*[116] It is splendid, because it has a morally educational goal and will certainly become part of society. The peasants beat them on the eyes. Sits on calves (vile). The state messenger in 37,[117] on the back of the head—that's viler. This society could not have existed then. [Now] But now it can, because now no one gets beaten on the back of the head; or do they? The woman and four children begging. Breast-fed babies in their arms, walking with a cane. Either they stick away their wives in the provinces, but here they meet about this—a stray dog, if he must be killed, then with some kind of chloroform! *This is fine, and chloroform is fine, but how can this be done with measure and in balance with everyone else.* But now if you think about the little ones in the orphan's home, and compare their fates with the doggies and chloroform. The peasant is compassionate; I'd say that the peasant can even teach the members of this club, but there are moments when he

92

loses patience. I'm not just talking about the backs of heads. Well, remember Anton Goremyka.[118] Remember the fact that he took his children out in a field and let them all freeze to death.

Also feed for livestock: now // they're selling their horses for 2 rubs. each, because they don't have anything to feed them with. And if they don't have anything to eat themselves? //

And therefore it's all fine, and therefore how can this be arranged with measure...? And still, a morally educational goal, and it's really so, really, so long live the society.

And the peasant, as we read about five years ago, sentenced to a 15 r. fine, and isn't 10 r. terrible for a moment of impatience.

A dog dies without consciousness. This is not the guillotine and the preparation for it (6 weeks) ([Victor] see the immort/al/ work of Victor Hugo),[119] not the gallows—in those countries where the societies for the prevention of cruelty to animals especially flourish.

And generally the last conclusion: It's clear that there is a limit to the society's activity, a fence against which it will bump and stop. This fence is the moral condition of society, firmly united with its social structure which facilitates their work. When society itself becomes more moral, it will automatically love animals more and become more humane. Now then's when it's necessary to go after the cruel people, to tie their *hands* and reeducate them as much as possible—because they will no longer have any excuses, or very few, to be cruel. If we don't keep this in mind [and go] now and go headlong into the fence, punishing the cruel wholesale [with a fist bringing morali], this means using fists to instill morality, and therefore knocking one's head against the fence. And because of this may the Society's forehead come out whole and long live the Society, for the morally educational goal (see above). //

The Voice, No. 359. Tuesday, 30 December.
Article: Foreign news. Dates and deadlines set for the French Senate and Chamber of Deputies elections.
16 Jan/uary/—election of delegates for the selection of senators.
30 January—election of senators.
20 February—of chamber deputies. Probably New Style?

Tacitus, revolt of the legions in Panonia,[120] the soldier, Vibulenus, wept and sobbed genuinely, give up my brother, but there was no brother. He was silent his whole life and only once playing a comedy—expressing his whole self, that's all it took. He was an actor.

NB. Apropos of the theater: what is an actor, Vibulenus. Actors are born. Vibulenius could not gain anything and was not seeking power. In Tacitus it's not explained objectively. In Russia people would immediately cry out; incomprehensible because of our minds, dullness, and what is considered comprehensible in Russia, they will make a heap of rubbish, and who: the very leaders!

There are everlasting types. But [you] all you have is: the environment took its toll. (...*tout autres que Dieu ne les a faites et qu'elles ne sont réellement*).

1793, that was the time of the mothers of Gracchuses.
I have Tacitus of that year.[121] Quai des Augustins. //

Ivanishches are harmful.[122]

But how strange: we, perhaps, see Shakespeare. But he is riding a cab, this is perhaps Raphael, but he's in a smithy, this is an actor, but he's tilling the soil. Can it be that only such a small upper crust of people make their marks, and the rest perish (a submissive class for the preparation of the cultured level). What an everlasting question, and still no matter what it takes it must be answered.

Shcherbinskaya's reading for children.[123] *The Voice,* see below.

Only the mediocrity cries out; now it's money, not talent; only the mediocrity is afraid and despairing, but finally ends in respect and devotion. A decent man cannot share these thoughts.
Saburov.
But maybe there are more decent people than we think. Now there's that feuilletonist, if Ovsyannikov bought him, would he take 50,000 or not take it. Maybe he wouldn't take it, knowing that it might get out, be revealed. Well, if given that way, what is there that would never be revealed? You know what, maybe he wouldn't take it. He's a braggart, he's a rascal, he's a Vibulenius, but maybe he wouldn't take it. It follows that aside from the rascality and acting there is nobility too. Yes, there is that and maybe much more than we think.

Lermontov, an ugly face,[124] in the mirror. Byron—a pitiful clubfoot. Guaranteeing honor and personality. Besides the anecdotes about Koni—about the learned cabby who was thrashed: "Nothing will happen!" and went away. The civil servant did not complain. And what would he have done when he ripped off the helmet?
And by the way, how is honor guaranteed and what is there that can replace the duel? Best of all would be not to have honor—as the authorities of the 30s and 40s preached. But while they brought the sword in, they also brought Europe in. And the duel is by no means a stupid thing: those // who reject it are only asserting an idea, but *not a completed one,* and the duel has been a fact since the beginning of the century. When saying the sword was given to you for the protection of the fatherland, the generals did not know or forgot about the fact that those who bared it to protect their own honor, were precisely those who were able to face the enemy honorably, while the calm people and Pirogovs[125] turned out to be warrant officers and "skeptics."

How the 8th of September[126]
For the faith and Tsar we etc. etc.

Christmas tree, the child at Rückert's Christ, ask Vladimir Rafailovich Zotov.[127]

Those who had no crosses on their necks or at least in their buttonholes, in case of danger, naturally perished without a trace, but [already] such was the law of nature, and no one complained. It's not like that *now*. Crosses won't save you, nothing will. Suddenly it turns out while on a walk on your grown-up girls: examine them...
   Let's grant, he was punished cruelly.
   But in Moscow too.
   In the *Russ/ian/ World* the pinnacle of improbability.
   But I took that from nature!
   And if they had a flaw?
   The church—Koni etc. //
   Ab ovo.
   Moscow News, No. 329. Tuesday, 30 December. The report in the *Times* about the absence of spots on the sun with intensified cold on earth.
   The cabby beat up the barin. History. The barin has the look of a professor. He didn't complain. But what if he had complained. Nothing would happen. At home they flog their wives. A bucket of vodka, three silver rubles. —They were given the power to try themselves. But if they were so mentally crushed and humiliated by their serf status, then how did they suddenly turn out to be so mentally sober that they were given the right to try themselves. A court is not an emphemeral present-day thing. As an idea, a court is above the peasants, above the contemporary generation, the future is in it. The future should not be spoiled and besmirched, or is this generation already so condemned? The broad view, I'm agreed, but painful. True, we live far away, in Petersburg. They'll whip their wives, after all, we won't hear the screaming. But among us the peasants themselves fist-fight too...

Why not issue another call across the land in memory of the great Russian man *Alex/ander/ Pushkin.*

Why shouldn't *The Voice,* which has 15,000 subscribers, use two lines to open such a subscription, renewed the first of each month.
   In the newspaper *The Voice* a constant subscription for the Pushkin monument has been opened, to continue until the sum required for the erection of the monument has been reached.

Why shouldn't all the other newspapers come out *with a hand:* we, they could say, are so retrograde.

95

Who was it that subscribed one kopek for Lermontov, why hasn't his name been published, if he himself put it in. *Il faut avoir le courage de son opinion,* and all Russia would remember his name. After all Greece remembered the name of Thersites.[128]

The constant alms, the constantly out-// stretched hand would shame our fools.

Maybe many would like to give, but they don't know where to give. Now a new generation is coming, now maybe they'll give.

117 students—who didn't pay their tuition. Seminarians, poor people. But where are the nobles?

!The train crash![129]

The train crash with the cars full (recruits) is a government matter, and not just a matter for the stockholders of the line where the accident occurs. And not just for the stockholders: if just the stockholders then one could get used to the idea. There are a lot of them, they stuff their pockets, so I'm supposed to like it that they are stuffing their pockets because of the government idea that this adds to the number of capitalists, and even though my leg is broken, nevertheless I'm supposed to like it: I facilitated, *with my leg,* the stuffing of the capitalists' pockets. But the point here is not [capitalists] stockholders at all, but simply a few triumphant Kikes, Christian and un-Christian, now they are the ones I can't abide, and I'm sad.

Golubev?[130] In the beginning I was indignant with the Unknown Person.

No matter how they twisted and turned before the court (i.e., their lawyers, and nevertheless it was unpleasant to me).

After all, how far is this going to go? said Saltykov.

But not now, now I can justify that, i.e., not exactly justify that they insulted Golubev, precisely Golubev, What do I care // about Golubev? The notorious Golubev, the widely-publicized Golubev! I don't care anything about him. But no matter what his name is, Golubev or something else, that man, or those men, is sitting there, doing in recruits by the hundreds (the [3] killed, but 65 were *only* burned!). What do I care what his name is, Golubev or Not-Golubev? Golubev wasn't an individual person in this, but a symbol, a source of arbitrariness, of egotism, of slavish servility and the most arrogant of all arrogant relations to anyone who has no *special* protection.

I am talking of special protec/tion/.

Russian World, 1st of January. The report from Samara in *Contem/porary/ News* about driving the stake through the corpse. The jurists an *acquittal.* Such sentences only make superstitions take root.[131]

Local press. The newspaper *Siberia.* Check in *Notes of the Father/land/* ("Profane") (? in *The Citizen)* etc.

96

Tacitus, Annales Liv. I LVII, *Car chez ces Barbares le plus déterminé est celui sur lequel on compte le plus. Bismarck* (said about Armenia). True to this day.

Tibère: il versait l'amertume sur ses meilleures actions (Tacitus, Liv. I, p. 189).

Ostrovsky and Shakespeare, and there was a time when they believed him, however, only one person believed, and that, they said, was the author himself. But he did believe, after all Shakespeare's word had been said, and suddenly such dessication.[132]

Gusev's pomposity[133] would suffice for two Avseenko's, sorry, half an Avseenko.

There is nothing so beautiful that something more beautiful cannot be found, and there is nothing so trashy that something more trashy cannot be found.
A cabbie driving along:
—Your horse is probably the worst one anywhere.
—No, there are worse.
Great consolation.

Berezin's Lexicon.[134] "Dostoevsky was editor of the *Russian World,* and by doing this he completed his fall in the public eye." I herewith declare that I was never an editor of *Russian World* and that I never participated in this esteemed newspaper, and that this is a fantasy of the esteemed publisher. I know, incidentally, that this news comes from one of [his] the colleagues of his publication [the esteemed Mr. V. Z/oto/v]   the same of whom back in the 60s I was told that even when riding in a cab he read a book, so much in a rush was he to acquire all kinds of knowledge without losing a minute. This writer, however, did not go far. [But] On the contrary the excessive acquisition of too much of all kinds of knowledge, perhaps, caused a certain (temporary) disorder in his mind and reasoning powers, and NB at precisely this moment I happened under his pen. I wish him good health.

Separate criticisms. Why is it that they almost never write anything about architecture? //
For some knowledge is necessary (the classical age. Ionic order. This column—represents the body of a beautiful young man in his prime, while the Corinthian column represents a shapely girl's).

How did I completely fall. For a year I was the editor of *The Citizen,* and having taken on a journal with 1000 subscribers within a year I left it with three thousand. This alone is a sign that I didn't fall in the public eye. And if you want to indict me for something, at least let them find one ignoble line signed with my name. Is the Slavophil movement ignoble? You can call it anything you like, but dishonorable, Mr. Reader in cabs. This is precisely the way in *New Time* they were turncoats for money. Lev Tolstoy's article, [135] not a word about him, but useful for me. No, on the contrary, Lev Tolstoy printed only the very essence of his convictions, and I only a novel, a poem, an invention of images. And how do you know my tendency (I didn't come there, but *Notes of the Father/land/* took my spirit). [136] Do you know, Mssrs. Liberals, that I am more liberal than you. Or do you think that Slavophiles are not liberal? But you are all so abstract, so lost in space and the clouds, and on the contrary if we were somewhere under Tiberius or Metternich, you would be encouraged, you would be given crosses, and your fat journals would flop against us every month like... The Slavophils are another matter; they demand a great deal, and they are implacable [their]. They demand firm foundations. They under Tiberius or Metternich they would never be liked [more], the censorship would suspect them and no crosses would be given... And they wouldn't accept them anyway, because of their convictions... Things are clean there: they don't buy and sell convictions. That's the way it is, Mr. [Unkn]. You don't understand what you're saying. And you're not going to understand it for a long time. //

Take the report on the Society for propaganda, [137] to which I had the misfortune to belong, there it is all too clearly noted how I was able to conduct myself, not giving in for my own sake. It's not Fyodor Dostoevsky that you can reproach for changing convictions.

But you'll say the present Dostoevsky and the Dostoevsky of that time are not the same, but having assumed [Slavoph] different (Christian and un-sla/vo/-philistic) convictions and joining with our commonfolk as much as possible (while still in prison I felt my separation from them, a robber taught me a great deal) [I somewhat] I did not change my ideals in the least and I do believe, but in the Kingdom of God, not in the commune. [I'll argue about this not only with you.] You cannot understand me, and therefore I will not explain any more precisely, but know that I am nevertheless "more liberal than you" and even much more. [To you] For even the liberalism of such as you is senseless retrogradism. I belong partly not so much to the Slavophil convictions as to Orthodox ones, i.e., to peasant convictions, i.e., to Christian convictions. I do not share them completely—I don't like their supersti/tions/ and ignorance, but I love their heart and all that they love. When I was still in prison.

Not in the eyes of the subscribers, but fell in those of honest people [well this argu] i.e., that the subscribers of *The Citizen* belong to the class of the dishonorable. But I do not in the least accept this kind of argument.

He can deny that I have any talent (this esteemed man), but find anything that would humiliate me in any line I wrote...

But in Russia we don't have Tiberius and not Metternich, and Glory to God, we are still breathing strongly//

On censorship.
We are an unlimited monarchy, and, perhaps, the freest of all. There are only

three peoples (i.e., similar) such as we. Given such a mighty Emperor, we cannot be free. Near the end.

Tyranny and freedom.

Napoleon III used power to strengthen a dynasty, but we don't.

And how this peasant Marey[138] pinched my cheek and patted my little head. I forgot this, i.e., didn't forget it, but only remembered it in prison.

This recollection gave me the strength to survive in prison.

I wrote all this because, finally all of this began to bore me.

But enough, enough, although this is precisely part of the *Diary,* because all of this disturbed me.

> He comes to people's holidays gloomy,
> To their graves he comes with a smile.

NB. At the altar in Spas.

Pavlusha.

The Christmas tree. The child.

I begin with unnatural and fantastical stories. (I used to ride to their place— wait, to two places, the ball and the colony.)

The child with the hand.

The Christmas tree in the club.

Dance. Married peoples' dances.

Trip to the colony.

All about children, all about children. [Conversations] And about Ovsyanni- kov.

Conversations about cases of security. Train cars, Police stor/ies/. Golubev.

Tendency.

Criticism.

Politics.

(Fears of the provincial press.)

They don't do anything.

New generations.

Gusev. Pavlusha.

Koronat. Filonov.

Commonfolk. Gentry.

1) Doctors. Meetings of the Humane Society.

The future of Russia;
future of Europe. War

About the commonfolk—the wolf. //

Vl. Zotov. I admired such learning, but hadn't the least suspicion of such thoughts toward me.

Lo-ook! And the corner of a trembling lip touched me on the tip of the finger (I stopped the animal).

Belinsky in prison—I worshipped him.
Nekrasov (hang in Belinsky's hut).[139]

Apropos: bookish people. Eliseev's project for two priests.

The American duel; what baseness, what vileness![140]

The duel. There is in man, besides the citizen, the person. A judge judges the citizen and sometimes doesn't see the person at all. And therefore always possible is the impression of this unseen person, which remains only with him, and the judge will not see anything in it. Even the law does not foresee all nuances. But one cannot take away the person from a citizen and leave only the citizen: the result would be something worse than the communard herd.
There are crimes and impressions which are not subject to judgment on earth. The sole judge is my conscience, that is the judging God within me; but this is already quite a different thing.

George Sand's daughter got married, the husband was (didn't fight), at Belinsky's: why what kind of children do you expect from your base, stinking marriages? But George Sand's daughter blushed for her mother. //

Introduc/tion. Limitless self-love and conceit are not signs of a feeling of personal worth.

"Ovsyannikov in the defendant's box." Ovsyannikov is unquestionably guilty, but this is civic zeal which has grown beyond its true measure. There have been many things which could awaken this civic zeal but they passed without notice, people didn't want to notice them, but there was the million. [How much zeal] It isn't a matter of Ovsyannikov's arrogance either, civic zeal isn't offended by arrogance either. But the million, simply the million—that's what's too bad. People'd say, Ovsyannikov has a million, why shouldn't we. Crush Ovsyannikov.
How do millions dare be his, why not ours, crush Ovsyannikov.

Now we have Lev Tolstoy,
That Leo of Kingly breed.[141]

Two extremely strange poems, and against which no one protested. Printed in the December issue of the *Russian Messenger* in which the public is informed about Count Lev Tolstoi's continued contributions to the journal.

Or—two extremely stupid poems. I make so bold [about] as to think that making this remark in absolutely no way detracts from the great significance of Count Leo Tolstoi's great [talent] gift. These two strange poems were printed in the December issue of *The Russian Messenger,* in which etc. But this is not advertising, it's naivete. That's why [especi] it's remarkable.

Count Leo Tolstoi—a treacly [talent] talent and not over anyone's head. //

Introduc/tion/. Ah, God, and why live then if not for pride.

The Republic is essential to France simply because it is the only thing that can save France from the two calamities which she fears most of all: from war, German retribution, which only the Republic does not [under] risk undertaking, and from communism, for [neighbors] the Republicans are neighbors of the communards, and political neighbors are always each other's enemies even [in friendship] during friendship, etc. It's essential to explain this.

The Voice, No. 4 Sunday.[142] A characteristic murder in Semenov of Nizhegorod Province (in contrast to Pavlusha, who wouldn't even be haunted). One must observe human nature in all its forms. I love those who are haunted.

Ibid from Vyatka about the peasants' suit against Kalinin.

On the cut-back of vodka in Samara and the correspondence of Paris about political affairs (for precision).

But one sensed in this raging against Ovsyannikov not indignance against the millions, but rather worship of the millions. In that case they wouldn't have given them such superstitious import.

The Moscow News, No. 3. Continuation of the political survey of Europe (the facts are explained in more detail than anywhere else).[143]//

A-ah, and why live then if not for pride! I captured this simple-hearted exclamation, of a man who, albeit rarely, does pause to refl/ect/ [once] sometimes.

Typical and characteristic. The whole epoch!

And who fears the socialists, communists and communards—not one of them sacrifices anything for the general good, no one.

Oh, they'll sacrifice in the beginning, all in a rush, like a herd of sheep, but solely to avoid lagging behind the others, i.e., from pride and vanity, but after a bit they'll come to their senses and loot and destroy each other with all their strength.

And therefore, although communism will surely come and triumph, but after a bit it will fall. But then there's not much consolation in that.

For this another tribe is necessary.

The idea of Communism and Christianity.

"Ovsyannikov in the defendant's box!" In Paris they'd make a bigger fuss and they'd forget sooner. Frivolous? No, with more taste. And our life does not catch fire so rapidly. The people and the peasants learning and talking about Ovsyannikov on a mass scale at the end of the trial.

The commonfolk—are not all cabbies. And maybe, unjustly? Some of them reflected.

How is it possible? Jurists, open court. a-ah, he reflected [but], without cussing open court and without any doubts, and about life he thinks: "I was a man, he says, and then!" And to be sure, if Ovsyannikov needed sheep or breadrolls, how many they'd drag in to give him. I'm not laughing. The commonfolk forgive with terrifying readiness, and not just the simple people. Such a thing exists nowhere else. Jean Valjean, Germany, all bear witness. O, while a robber has a knife in his hands, he fights with them, won't hide him, will betray him and search him out, but as soon as he is convicted—forgives him. Prison. Rejection of society, of peace, of freedom. //

Not being surpised at anything is a sign of stupidity, and not intelligence.

Educators, independent-look. I would like this look of self-respect much more if there were more simplicity in it... and real respect, otherwise—

Extraordinary shamelessness, but little affectionateness. I'm not saying unctuousness. Affectionateness is just honesty, and even the most wicked child can be affectionate... and an adult criminal. But the adult criminal has seen more than the little child, he values kindness more than some kind? He has just seen the world upside down, in a new way and light.

All are devoured by self-love and even not excluding the writer Grigory Danilevsky, L-ko.

The Voice on the actions in Central Asia, the new defeat of Avtobachi by Skobelev.[144]

Don Quixote, people made of jelly. Several thousand enemy killed and 1 kil/-led/ of ours. Erevan. The marvelous tambourines on the other side of the mountains (put it in the opinion about the expansion of our means in Turkestan). Kaufman is still riding around.[145]

On the clergy, on the project for a prayer-book and a preacher. Pri/est Pereverzev seven children, in the same issue of *The Voice*.

The Voice. Tuesday, 6th of January, No. 6.

It would seem three companies would be enough in Turkestan instead of 27,000. Send 5 men to the Khanate, and they will "bravely" carry out the commission. // /.../

Rejection is essential, otherwise man would just remain closed in on earth, like

102

a bedbug. Rejection of the earth is necessary, in order to be infinite. Christ, the most elevated positive ideal of man, bore in himself the rejection of earth, because a repetition of him turned out to be impossible. Only Hegel, the German bedbug, wanted to reconcile everything with philosophy etc.

The Citizen, No. 1. Petersburg.[146] Chronicle. Train wreck. Petty little people—come out of the car, carry out onto the rails, if there had not been anyone to intercede, and nothing would happen. Golubev. The railroads, well it's a public matter, general /.../ O Peter the Great, is this what you wanted. But, of course, it is! Of course it is! For if you were a genius you must have understood that the thing [this way] would end precisely this way and no other. But nevertheless why must my wife, my children perish on trains, and if [if] I cry out that they perished, immediately the requisite authority appears, and not a simple authority, but a state authority, and they put you on the station platform, and the train moves away, and no matter who you are, the boss of the station shoves you, with all your woes and insults, into the lock-up until the next morning... Devil take it! Never has there been anything like this in Rus before! //

The bankruptcy of the conservative party, Katkov and Leontiev were the warriors—they've grown old. N. Danilevsky, having written the true book *Russia and Europe* went off to enjoy the pleasures of botany instead of becoming a fighter for the truth.[147] The Slavophils in Moscow have disappeared. *Russian World* is a scandal of flabbiness and incapacity to conduct the struggle.

Generals' funerals, 6 copper buttons. What there was during life. Velvet pillows, medals. Plant a thought about oneself, leave a good memory, sound.

St. P/etersburg/ News, 7th of Janury No. 7. The article on universal military obligation in Japan. The Mikado's manifesto (curious to the highest degree) and... China, politics.

—the review of a certain brochure about what will happen in the spring of 1876. The liars of *St. P/etersburg/ News,* for, without doubt, the Republic, if it is set up, has the strength to repulse Germany. An attack is repulsed only by unity. The enemy is repulsed only by accord.

In Russia civilization began with depravity.
Every civilization begins with depravity. Greed for acquisition. Envy and pride. Peter the Great's reform succeeded because of depravity.

Moscow News. January 6, No. 5. The declaration about the Voronezh station (from the newspaper *The Don).*[148] Rostov on the Don. Voronezh railroad. (List of events of last year.)

Do whatever you like and, maybe, even entirely out of carelessness, laziness, indifference or piggishness, and people will live even out of mockery. Do they clean the shit out of the railroad car? Do they get there this way? They do, Ivan Serge/-ich/?

—They do get there, sir, Sergei Ivanych, why shouldn't it get there.
Iv. Serg. smiles. And really don't clean it, now I'll just have a look. //

And what do I care about Golubev? Mr. Golubev I [don't know] don't at all know; I am talking only about the idea and therefore we call him Vorobiev. And so, Vorobiev revolts, Vorobiev feels insulted, Vorobiev robs...
Lembke Rosenbaum.

But Vorobiev walks away, under-Vorobiev wishes to revolt a bit, a somewhat lower civil servant.

Why with a maneuver like that "you'se can kill as many as you likes," as the goose herder said in the commune court about the geese when a driver intentional-ly ran his wheel over his goose [neck] his long neck.

Anger at our railroad rules is growing more and more intense.

There is a kind of artificial implanting of socialism (in Russia too)—our youths already 30 years old go (for this) into exile for this delirium. For if there, in Europe, it's a question, here in Russia it's delirium. We have many of our own social questions, but not at all in the same form and not at all about the same things. Secondly, in Russia there is terribly much that is quite new and unlike Europe, and thirdly, in Russia there is an ancient moral idea which, perhaps, will triumph. This idea is our own concept from deep antiquity of what honor and duty are and what genuine equality and brotherhood among men are. In the West the zeal for equal-ity was different, because the kind of dominion was different.
The cabbie—*with a penknife.* The infection of disorder. I saw him.
Ball, they gathered to be merry, no, they are not merry, and that's all there is to it.
Diamonds.
Dress is superior, beauty.
To seem more beautiful. This means showing how I understand beauty, how educated I am, how I adopted this.
No, going to a ball is a chore for a woman.

Potugin says that he loves Russia. Well, nonsense. You can't fool us. //

The ball, the generals have gotten smarter...
But this is very, very hard.
The Petrushka type.

Vuiki,[149] don't get married.

Petrushka with interpolations (the theater is alive).

Ovsyannikov's trial. Condemn balls.
But how many marry—

Yes, if cabbage grew.
It'd be a garden, of course!
What to say.
We parted.

It seems that actor Grigoriev[150]the 2nd (caricaturing the merchants, but extremely poorly) allowed himself other interpolations (with whose permission I don't know).

A seamstress can get even more stupid.
At home—they eat. Debts.
Digestion is [seam] the dues...

—But you understand much better... Your excellency.
On ads, on *Kitty Cat.*

No, sooner the Assembly will go than MacMahon.
And throughout the whole history of its revolution (except for the first assembly of 89) France has never respected the assembly it has chosen, and always preferred and supported anyone who bridled its assemblies, and dispersed them, products of these very assemblies, constititions and laws which they themselves had promulgated, all went off to the devil (France did not respect her own assemblies). She always heeded the rebels who seized power. That's how it is now: [assemb] the assembly will disintegrate, but the soldier will remain.

The Voice. Thursday, 8 January, No. 8. The critique of *Kitty Cat,* the writer lacks only literacy.[151]

Life is boring [for] without a moral goal, it's not worth living just to eat, even the worker knows this. Therefore, life must require some moral occupation. //

Liberals. They have tied themselves up as if with ropes, and when it's necessary to express a free opinion, their first worry is: will it be liberal? They all worry, to the last man they sometimes utter liberalisms such as the most terrifying despotism and coercion would never think up.
The main thing is that in Russia liberals sometimes haven't the slightest idea what is liberal and what is not.

War. Paradox. No, war is better than the current state of society. —I in the sense of not forbidding it.

Ball. They'll fight. Petersburg. The newspaper about the fights in Moscow, [152] they can be called Slavophils, only practically they believed that you can, in the final analysis, throw off European forms, that they already allow that, that it is good.

Chichikov—Skvoznik-Dmukhanovsky[153] also loves forms, and he (al) knows that this form is good, even though in everyday home-life he uses his fists—and good. —and good precisely because it is not like him. He loves and respects it because of this. In general at a ball there is much ideal. This is good, the more ideal the better, but the ideal is not complete. —*If there were simple-heartedness.* The young people dance, but the grown-ups play at nobility.

The Voice. Thursday, No. 9. January 9.[154] The news about Chikhachev, the director of the Russian society. 1) About how the minister of transportation—extreme dissatisfaction—because of the train wreck with the recruits. 2) The news about the *wife* who was dragged out of the car by the station master (he considers himself all-powerful, he is so arrogant and uneducated that he considers himself competent here). 3) About the theft of 180,000 rubles from the cell of Archimandrite Viktor. //

Lord, I thank Thee for the face of man which Thou hast given me. (In contrast to suicides.)

You feel that this (the world, the stars) is not above your understanding, and for the happiness of feeling this you have to lose nothing more than your human face.

Pref/ace/. It's desirable for our bosses "to have a raise in spirit even before a raise in salary."

I could never understand the sense in having only 1/10th of the people receive higher development, and the remaining 9/10ths serving only as material and means. I knew that this was a fact and that for the meantime it was impossible to be any other way and that ugly utopias are only evil and ugly, and do not withstand criticism. But I never have stood for the idea that the 9/10ths must be preserved and that this is precisely the sacred thing which must be kept. This is a terrible and absolutely anti-Christian idea.

Mr. V. Z/otov/ is a man overloaded with books.[155]
But finally in his work everything got mixed up and therefore the nebulousness was revealed.

When *Poor Folk* appeared, Mr. Z/otov/ had already made a splash in literature, he had written *The Daughters of Charles the Great,* novels, stories, all this had passed without a trace, but I suddenly attained fame: right then Mr. Z/otov/ got envious, and now he is taking revenge on me with the news that I was born in 1818. The *Russian World* has humiliated itself. I have many enemies because of that sudden fame. He talks to me about nebulousness (without supporting this with anything, without a single example). To this I will make only one comment: nebulousness does not always come from the writer, but because that which the reader himself [in] has in his head [occasionally] is nebulous. Mr. Z/otov/ is a man overloaded with books, but now it's all got mixed up, as a consequence of which his nebulousness could be revealed. Nowadays, however, people are proud even if they don't understand something: a person looks at the work of an artist and suddenly says proudly: I don't understand it, and walks past [they don't consider]. But this incomprehension, again perhaps quite often, results not because the artist is incomprehensible, but because you are dull... Of course, I am not applying these harsh words directly to Mr. Z/otov/, I am just asserting that he is nebulous. //

He, as they say, is a man overloaded with books. Now in the final analysis a certain nebulousness could be the result of this overload. So that in the final analysis in his work everything (of his) got mixed up. I just about the source of the nebulousness.

A few of my works. "A Weak Heart"[156] (the very first) [and written] placed [one] in the last period of my literary career, much later.

True, he can say with contempt: well, what difference does it make when you were born? Well, that's so, but nevertheless for accuracy. —Sloppiness.

A little page, and so many mistakes.

I say this, of course, in the sense most respectful to him, but nevertheless he is one of the overloaded ones.

Lexicon. And if the other articles contain the same nebulousness, one cannot make a favorable conclusion about Berezhin's publication, but I suppose that the publication is better nevertheless, and here's why: Mr. V. Z/otov's/ article is a prejudiced article (envious). Why, finally, not speak the truth? I seriously want to write my notes, but to write them telling the whole truth, but so far I have feared wounding self-esteem (Mr. V. Z/otov/, I never had the pleasure of meeting him).

But why, finally, not write them?

This Mr. V. Z/otov/ wrote innumera/ble/ dramas. All this passed without a trace, flowed past like spring waters, although without the usefulness of the latter, for they didn't irrigate the scraggy plain of our belles-lettres. Precisely then *Poor Folk* appeared. I know that its appearance stung and shook the self-esteem of a multitude of people, for with *Poor Folk* I immediately became well-known, but they flowed past like spring waters... Since then some people (in literature) have taken a terrible dislike for me, although I didn't know them at all personally. Incidentally, Mr. V. Z/otov/ I never had the pleasure—

I seriously want to write my notes. Incidentally, Mr. V. Z/otov/ *I never* knew and did not have the pleasure to be acquainted with him in the slightest.

Of course, I am using the word "overloaded" [usi] in the sense most respectful of him..., so to speak, as a scholar..., so to speak, speaking as if about a scholar.

So that in the final analysis in his work this all got mixed up.

"A Weak Heart" toward the 60s.
While to the very first period, to the forties.

But after all if these people (the Zotovs) are worth it, for the petty envy which has lasted for thirty years. But after all, this hatred won't make them more talented.

And this alone should have restrained them, that this hatred would not make them more talented. //

To F. I. Tyutchev, on the contrary, *Crime and Punishment* seemed superior.[157] I warmly defended my opinion.

In Victor Hugo there are many terrible artistic mistakes, but then that which came out without mistakes in his work is equal to the best of Shakespeare. A writer not without talent. However, Pushkin could say that.[158]

What a terrible genre the French lyrical poem!

The Jesuits—war. I.e., let him be a brother, or be a brother to all, or off with his head *(ou la mort)*. An infinite difference.

Railway cars (at least something).

The Society for the Prevention of Cruelty to Animals.

The cabby who beat the *barin* (nothing would happen!).

Turgenev. The dog. An etude of the mysti/c/ in man.

In Potugin: the Slavophils and the Westernizers could be reconciled.

War.

That's all. About spiritualism later.

Gamma.[159] —But can you really think that the death of these 200 men has no revoltingly-harmful influence on the commonfolk because of its cynicism: you can do anything if you have money, strength crushes anything, money buys anything, only in money is there truth. Ovsyannikov in the defendant's box. //

The Moscow News, January 10, No. 8.[160]

Survey for the last year (courts) etc.

The case of the rape of the noblewoman Rosenfeld by the police medical supervisor Fedor Ivanov (the testimony of an honest woman). Sentenced to corrective incarceration for 2 years 9 months. The details of the train wreck with the new recruits.

The Voice. 11 January, No. 11. Sunday. —Gamma's feuilleton on the self-government of the railroad companies.[161]

Status in statu.

O if this (Litvinov, Sultan Abdul) were a psychological etude. He decided to loom over the poor creature. Brutal cruelty.

How will cases of kerosene lamps end.[162] You cannot read a single newspaper without... children burning up, adults...
floors and so forth.
more precautionary and nonflammable.

No, war is more noble.

The Mos/cow/ News. January 14, No. 12.[163]
—Preaching against spiritualism.
Correspondent from Petersburg on compulsory education.
—Lead article from Petersburg on compulsory education.
—Lead article on the Bessarabian *zemstvo* which forbade Latin in a woman's high school.

The Voice. Friday, 16th January. On the fall of our exchange rates abroad with a cursory enumeration of the reasons.

Slavdom and the role of Russia alma mater. Bozhidarovich's response.[164]/.../

Long live the Great Russian, but let him think about himself more.

Conquer with magnanimity. War.

Russia, since she entered the entity of Europe, has caused no damage to Europe, but only totally served Europe, often at the cost of terrible damage to herself. One must admit that our entrance /into/ Europe in many ways knocked us off the track, from a genuine understanding of our goals, and to such an extent that now there may be no returning to a genuine understanding.
The future of Russia is clear: we will go on, perhaps, without war with Germany—we will go on until terrified Europe rushes to us and starts begging us to save her from the communards. She will start not begging, but demanding: for—she'll say—you are saving yourself, you must save yourself too. And here we, perhaps, will see too graphically for the first time how unlike Europe we are and how different our essences are... [such] and what a political mistake we have been making until now, so slavishly enrolling ourselves as Europeans. And the communards have a future. It is the only European idea which has a future there: conservatism.
But about this in the next. Rus/sia/, on war, on China.

The article in *The Voice.* /.../

We won't be drawn into war right now.
I am talking about the future, more or less distant, well, roughly 1/4 of a century—

109

Russia wouldn't even exist, we'd turn into a pitiful Armenian—Gregorian heresy.

Did Russia gain a lot.

Even her European borders became less strong at the beginning of this century than they were at the end of the last.

The final program. Colony, Fathers.

> Spiritualism. Devils. Censorship.
> On protection of animals.
> On protection of humans.
> Zhivio and Slavdom. The article of *The Voice.*
> The promise about war. Berezin.

Spiritualism is the turning of stones into loaves and the killing of idea and spirit.

On prevention of cruelty to humans.

I am not saying vodka, but something suggests it.

Railway cars—can it be they have no influence.

Nothing will happen.

The courier is one of the pictures of my childhood.[165]
Marey.[166] A picture from childhood, I was not thinking about it, that is, I had not forgotten it, but once later, long after that—oh, what it was like, I dream, and often—and suddenly I recalled Marey, it is true, some childhood pictures give one an opportunity to look at things quite differently. //

Nothing will happen.
...He whipped the horse and drove off
Of course the policeman...
And this is so strange; where is the policeman.
He passed by just a minute ago. About the police
2 millionth and something or other time, but...

Prevention of cruelty to animals. Abstractness and impracticality in an excessive and rushed fervor.

Long ago I read about the driver condemn/ed/ to an awful sentence.

I would just like to note the unrealistic and unsettled nature of our society in any practical application whatsoever. Alas, for 200 years we grew unaccustomed to action, by the wardship in which we had been held; and now we can only save ourselves by slavishly copying foreign things, in spite of the obvious inappropriateness of the foreign things to our country (about the Slavophils).

Apropos, I will tell a story from my youth.

The courier. Right here is where humaneness should be preached. The main thing is that this is not a picture, but actually a symbol. In fact: he is a barbarian for having lashed his horses like that, but then his every lash was caused by a blow on his own back, without these blows he would not have whipped the horses. I repeat: this is not a picture from my reminiscences, but a symbol, a symbol to be engraved in print for society, that the picture is real, I swear. Teach first how to be humane with humans, and then the Russian man will understand that he has to be humane with beasts too. But now there is no longer what there was in '37—true, '37 was a long time ago, but is it really? However, the courts, there is no landlord, don't they take whatever they want. And won't his help sow the seeds of lawlessness.

Worship of money, coarse ideas are in the air, destroying faith. During a fire the peasants protect the taverns, but not the churches. The railway cars— [the boy] . the penknife. And we ourselves, our daughters to the police.
Nothing will happen.

We must take hold of the matter closer to the roots or consider what the situation really is. The Samar/a/ famine, and the dog from chloroform.
Nothing will happen.
Nevertheless. God grant the idea of all possible happiness. All the more that the Russian peasant is humane. Marey.
There is no courier now? You think not? Let's suppose I grant you that about the courier, even though in myself I know that he is simply wearing a different uniform now and has not disappeared at all. But instead of the courier there is something even worse, there is good old vodka, there is a 200-million revenue from the vodka and right alongside it—lynch rule.
Besides this, there is the disorder of ideas, materialism—what do you [the commonfolk] think, doesn't Vorobiev have an influence? What kind of humane ideas can be inculcated here? //

Spiritualism, Berezin.
A certain liberal newspaper of ours is that vainly rushing captain who pushed his way into the center of the hall at a Moscow ball and barked in his national tongue. [Alas] Poor fellow! Why in fact, he thinks that he is in Europe. My dear sir, you are only a captain, not a liberal, you are a nationalist, and they will throw you out. Throw you out, my dear sir, throw you out! [Soon, very soon, just you wait.]

The *generation* which will take your place is now growing and will inevitably

111

grow up. It is only in the fifth grade now, but it will grow up and come forward, and then no trace of you will be left.

You, you are just hindering [liberalism] a good cause.
It will happen soon. The generation which will be humane, humanistic, and magnanimous is already growing up.

The Bible belongs to all, atheists and believers alike. *It is the book of mankind.* If the whole human race ever disappears
Besides this, we have a great school of theology, it is our Mass, open to all.

What is prayer? Prayer is a lifting up of the mind.

Well, who among us, for example, is strong in doctrine?
Even our specialists in this area are not always competent. And therefore we leave it to the specialists.

And the press is bursting to write an exposé of the railroads, but they are the ones who are laughing, they are the ones who are laughing.

Marey.
Society for the Prevention of Cruelty to Animals.

As for [mind] the worries about chloroform, at the present time this will strike the peasant as absolutely incomprehensible, perhaps even ridiculous, which is the worst of all. But if he happens to understand, he will point out to you his Samara children who died from hunger at their mothers' withered breasts, while here ladies and gentlemen were getting together and discussing chloroform. He doesn't care about chloroform yet. But then I myself am for chloroform, the idea should not die! I just [out of place] wanted to say, there is just no reason to rush it [too much], or it will come out too abstract and the peasant will not understand.
1) The penknife.
Helmet and professor
2) First it is necessary to at least bring a little order here. //

Something is in the air, lawlessness, the peasant has been infuriated by something.

And over everything, Mammon /.../, but the main thing is that everything /.../ has suddenly bowed down.

So let it not be Golubev; I will not use the word Golubev, Mr. Golubev is pure [and sinless] as a dove, and sinless, but to make up for that, Vorobiev is guilty! What Vorobiev is this, who is he anyway? I don't know, gentlemen, and it makes no difference to me, but there is a Vorobiev who is going on a spree and causing an uproar, ruining the goods.

Do you really think that it has not gotten through to the commonfolk, after all, they do see what can be done with money.

Chloroform. Don't turn a beautiful idea into an abstract matter, and spare both the idea and yourself.

After all, the main idea of society is what: surely not dogs [and cows] so much as people, coarsened, inhumane, half barbarians, waiting to see the light. You want to illuminate them, inculcating in them humaneness even toward animals, isn't that so? So isn't it better to first think about their position and at least to discover whether they have been prepared or not by circumstances to accept your beautiful preaching. Be a little more humane yourselves.

But people are humane, I've known that from the time I was a child, and again I will tell one childhood story.

NB. January 19. V. V. Gri/gorie/v's opinion.[167] They have banned corporal punishment in schools everywhere, fine; but just what *among other things* did they achieve? That in present generation of our youths many terrible cowards have appeared, they are afraid of the slightest physical pain and so much so that in the face of the least little danger, threat, or physical suffering, some now hang themselves. [There are many examples of this] They have gotten terribly unenduring. [their spirits fall quickly, they shoot and hang themselves]
Really it is most accurate to explain certain cases like this among our youths exclusively as cowardice. But a strange point of view on the subject nevertheless.

NB. He will be expelled from the fourth grade of the gymnasium and—where is he to go? He goes straight to the commonfolk. Nowadays so awfully many go to the commonfolk and they act // effectively—not with their former utopias and social [abs] absurdities which were incomprehensible and ridiculous to the commonfolk, but by a direct call to revolt: "you do not have to pay the tax," they will say, and of course. That the commonfolk can understand.

An Eastern (Turkish) proverb. If you set out for a destination, and along the road you keep stopping to [throw] toss stones at every dog [that chases you] that barks at you, you will never reach your destination.

The Voice. Sunday. More about Perova's fate.[168] No. 18, January 18.

I will end with one indicative and amusing Turkish proverb which is somewhat relevant.

The Bible. This book is invincible. Even the children of the priests, who are

113

writing in our liberal magazines, will not shake this book.

We already had experienced what [repressed] ideas turn into that have been repressed when there were demonstrations in the universities, and how revoltingly they are vomited up afterwards.

God grant everyone health. But it's too bad if you get sick, our doctors are fine, but they have all specialized—the nose, and another one the bridge of the nose.

Golubev, and besides, with such details of his mental and spiritual feelings [and besides with the minist.] before the insulted minister. But I have changed my view, let Golubev be as innocent and pure as a teardrop, but in return Vorobiev is guilty, so in return, go after Vorobiev.

Who is Vorobiev? I don't know, a mythical character, but an extremely powerful character. //

Animals. And in order to "shape up," to humanize, so to speak, the Russian man.

My whole trouble is that I simply cannot believe in these devils, so even that is a sort of pity: after all, they are [not] too intelligent.

Svistunov and Nazimov. About the Decembrists.[169]

Happiness is not in happiness, but only in its attainment.

Well, who cares when you were born, and does it make any difference anyway? I [agree] am willing to agree with that, but still for the sake of precision and if only for the sake of the word in the dictionary. Otherwise they will think etc.

...The taking away of all personal and spiritual freedom from people, the killing of the individuality. In this sense spiritualistic teaching is a terrible teaching. No satan except the real one could thing up anything to compare with this.

Over the Russian commonfolk stand two things in place of the courier—vodka and Mammon, how will vodka replace the courier?
It coarsens and brutalizes him and debases him. A drunk has no compassion, even for his own children, let alone for animals.
Vodka poisons the source of future strength, [to strength ahead] poverty, and the moral condition of the new generation.

The writer Apollon Grigoriev. //

"To shape up" is a commonfolk expression: to give shape, to reestablish in

114

man the human shape. "Shape [him] a man up," "you should at least shape yourself up," they say, for example, to someone who has been at a long drunk. It is
heard from the convicts.

2nd money—the courier was at least understandable, even if he was ugly, even
if a usurper, he was a representative of a certain power which it was impossible to
avoid submitting to, otherwise the earth could not stand, and everyone understood
that.
    Nowadays money. And the commonfolk say: Ah, so money is everything, so
that's the way it always was, and we didn't know that. [nowa] (Vorobiev). *So,*
there is no strength or power other than money. Now that is the hardest thing of
all if the idea runs like this.

    I do not want to think and to live any other way than with the belief that all
of our ninety million Russians, or however many of them there will be then, will
be educated and civilized, humanized and happy. That light and the higher bless-
ings of life are bestowed upon only 1/10, according to Potugin's civilization. With
this condition of only 1/10 of the people being happy, I would not want civilization then. I [want] believe in the complete Kingdom of Christ. How it will be done,
it is difficult to foresee, but it will be. I believe that this king/dom/ will co/me/.
But even thought it is difficult to foresee, signs in the dark night of conjecture can
still be envisioned mentally, and I believe in these signs. (The Slavophils and the
Westernizers.) And the universal kingdom of thought and light will come to pass,
and it will be here in Russia, perhaps sooner than anywhere else. And therefore
any such society, in spite of chloroform and dogs, is precious and joyous for me,
and I love it with all my heart. But there is no need to break the chairs, one has to
be at least a little bit more practical and realistic. It would be better to study the
reasons why the commonfolk are animal-like, [and surely not really] and to act
accordingly. Surely they are not really for the sake of the dogs.
    And you will certainly do this, for if this is not an aristocratic whim, but true
zeal, you will certainly arrive at the idea that it is better to have an effect on the
commonfolk. And our commonfolk are compassionate. Only they have to be
shaped up.
    Did I correctly understand your beautiful idea, worthy of the highest praise,
a society by subscription. If I do not belong to your society, still in my soul I do
belong to it. I love animals, but I love the Russian man most of all. //

    Marey. He loves his mare and calls her the one who feeds him. But if he has
moments of impatience and the Tatar in him breaks loose and he begins to lash at
the eyes of the mare who feeds him as she is stuck in the mud with her load, then
remember the courier, here you have upbringing, habits, reminiscences, vodka, Vorobiev.

    The impressions, the description of which, hour by hour, minute by minute,
V. Hugo gave us in his immortal work *Condamné à mort.*

115

This morass of depravity begins.

But the Russian commonfolk are kind, and the society has placed its trust in the Russian commonfolk.

Our age is not interested in the prevention of cruelty to animals. I myself reject this position, as an absurdity and an impossibility.
If this is the reason.
Draw water not where the spring ends, but where the dam begins.
A conclusion about society.

If more people would take into consideration the main reasons.

Otherwise it would be drawing water from where the stream ends, and then killing by chloroform will be ridiculous. Draw water where the waters run deep, and the commonfolk will not understand this for a long time.
About the 9/10 at the very end. //

Devils.
If Catholicism were destroyed, then of course Protestantism would immediately be destroyed too, for what would it then have to protest against. And really, Protestantism, as we see it, borders on pure atheism and would gladly go over to it immediately, and if it is still hanging on in the form of a religion, it is *solely* because it is still *protesting,* i.e., fighting and struggling against the Holy Pope.

O, the devils know what a forbidden thought means, for them it's a veritable treasure. The devils know perfectly well that any forbidden thought it is the very best fuel for the fire etc.

A society consisting of 750 influential members, if it wanted to assist even just a little in the elimination of the causes, would make things easier for itself and for its propaganda, would prepare the ground. Otherwise Danaid's barrel—what do you think, like a stream? By eliminating the rights of Mammon and the Kike, Orthodox or non-Orthodox.
That is what I call the equilibrium about which I spoke above. And your propaganda will work, our commonfolk are good people. I have come to know this all too well. I will tell another story. Marey, the Pole.
Thus, on the way, a society, on a good road, to humanize people, from the other 9/10—that doesn't bother anyone if everyone is kind, educated, and rich.
I just wanted to say something on the topic, but I am a zealous member of the society.

Devils. A split—but of course this is almost a preoccupation, in a split there are philosophers and savants, and this preoccupation is precisely what man will

116

need.

Devils. The other side is starting [to erad] to persecute them, to forbid them, but the devils know the power of this forbidden idea.

I offended you, therefore I must get revenge. //

Biographer V. Z/otov/.
All this gives me the idea to write my literary reminiscences. I do have a thing or two to tell, after all, I have been a writer for exactly 30 years. I have long been thinking, perhaps I will start putting it in the *Diary,* chapter by chapter, but for now I will conclude with a Turkish proverb, a real Turkish one, not one I composed:
The proverb.
I'll put this in just in case.
F. D/ostoevsky/.

You see, in feeling sorry for the offender, you thus do not feel sorry for the offended, can't you understand this simple thing.
Rotted—a humane time.
[Se] The ideal of liberalism and the legal profession. I do not want to get involved in the secrets of family life and I am not entirely familiar with Mr. Kroneberg's character.[170] Any man is complex and as deep as the sea, especially a modern, nervous man. But all the same, an affair that has already been publicized, brought to court, and discussed in the newspapers has become a suitable topic for public debate and so it is impossible to be silent on the subject.

Slander of me in *The Illustrated Gazette.*[171] *Russian World,* No. 23. Saturday, January 24.

Potugin shouts that Russia has never invented anything original.[172] Russia [ser] did invent the abolition of serfdom, but in Europe, in your civilization, the peasants everywhere freed themselves through revolt, with weapons in their hands, and blood was spilled: it is being spilled even now and it will go on being spilled. What have we invented? you ask, we have invented the abolition of serfdom without blood. And you are throwing mud at yourselves, you have no shame at all! //

The Voice, January 24, 25, 26, 27. The case of Maria Kroneberg.
The Voice, Jan/uary/ 28, No. 28, the Kroneberg case.
Mos/cow/ New/s, No. 25, January 27. (About church elders.)
Stock Exchange New/s/, No. 31. Sund/ay/, February 1. Suvorin on Kroneberg.
Suvorin. There is dishonesty and declamation here (abusing him for almost every feuilleton and being terribly fond of reading his feuilletons).

Program. The Kroneberg case. (Pob/e/d/o/nostsev's/ idea: disgraced for a century.[173] My idea: a word about how the family cannot stand to be preserved for such villainy, and that this is slander on the family.) (About what went to Suvorin.)

—Reply to *The Petersburg Gazette*[174] (about Zotov's *Illustrated Gazette,* the slander).

?—Potugin and beauty.

?—Genius of pure beauty.

—China, Japan. The stirring up of the nations of Central Asia.

—The Slavophils and the Westernizers.

—Slander of me in *The Illustrated Gazette.* "Vernal Waters."[175]

NB. NB.—(Definitely describe two or three incidents; *walk around for awhile* here and there.)

—The story about the rearrangement of the heads.

—The coachman who beat up the professor.

—Marey.

?—(Slavdom and the role of Russia. *The Voice,* January 16. Friday.)

Definitely.—About how *war* is better than the current condition of society.

—About how MacMahon will go.

—Petrushka and Gorbunov.

—*Pavlusha (The Voice,* No. 4) and the murder of the nuns.

—About American-style duels and about duels in general.

—Vibulenus.

NB. NB. —About the local press. Definitely examine the newspapers. Mikhailovsky's shouts in *Notes of the Fa/therland/* (December).[176]

?—The monument to Pushkin, monument to Lermontov (he subscribed 1 kopek. Who is he?)

—*La population rest stationnaire* [Poli] . Experience (fantasy) about future political fates in Europe.

—About the Decembrists.

(See at the beginning of the notes.) //

NB. ? (With Ivanova about the boarding house.)

—About why Mikhailovsky is getting angry at the comments about the burning of the Tuilleries.

—About the specialization of doctors.

—Potugin. With the abolition of serfdom, the reforms of Peter the Great ended (Pobedonostsev's book).[177] —The commonfolk are moving, will they say anything? (See the notes *at the beginning.)*

—Baron Delvig, who stole the watch in Moscow. *The Mos/cow/ News No. 32, Febr/uary/ 4.*

—About the provincial press. Does the government want and *does it need* the development of the provincial press.

—University towns (Shram etc.).

—About the diplomatic note to the sultan from the heads of state. *Mos/cow/*

Collective action as the beginning of Europe's interference in and overseeing of Turkish affairs. /.../

Prediction.

The Pharisee. *Olonets/ky District/ New/s/.*

/.../

We should live only for ourselves, don't be afraid of this: for a Great Russian to live for himself means to live for others.[178]

/.../

Pobed/onostsev's/ comment on passports.[179]

Have a talk with Vas/ily/ Vas/ilievich/ Grigoriev about the provincial press and about our Eastern outlying areas. About Slavdom.

Spasovich.[180] *Ce n'est pas l'homme c'est une lyre.* This was about Lamartine. But also about any poet, about any artist. The physiology and psychology of the poet as a liar. That's what kind of talent he has. And, so to speak, *plus de noblesse que de sincérité.* —Vibulenus.

Fireworks and Zhemchuzhnikov.
About Bazunov.[181]

People at the ball—superior to Shakespeare's types. Corruption could vanish in an instant. K. Aksakov. The commonfolk will become the same and just as corrupt, they will reach the same point. Although, of course, you must expect everything from the commonfolk. Although those who expect everything from the commonfolk, by so doing, reject Peter and his reform.

A reply to the *Stock Exchange /News/.* The ball, better than Shakespeare. Why not cast a *magnanimous* reproach at these people. This is not the adulation of these people before the commonfolk. It is just a word about their having been spoiled and that, in essence, they are fine people.

But the commonfolk and the public // are one and the same. Except that the commonfolk, perhaps, will go even beyond this phase of depravity and falsehood. They are depraved and false themselves: not so much so yet, but now they will be just as, with civilization. Is that how it is, in your opinion? I would hope I am mistaken or that you will tell me something more comforting. But if this is actually going to happen to them, then let's both contribute to making things proceed more easily and directly to the goal. You hold your hand out to me, all right, we'll go together. By microscopic action, like the hero who paid the ransom for freedom. But as for the Shakespeares and Homers, art, no doubt, is inferior to reality. (The artist and the synthesis of his view: types and so on). And if each *individual* could reveal itself fully, but it cannot, for a thought when uttered is a lie.[182]

I have great hopes that the commonfolk will preserve their nature and will not begin civilization with depravity. Even granted that we have gone beyond this phase.

Civilization will spoil the commonfolk: this is the way things happen when, along with a radiant and salutory idea there is the intrusion of so much that is false and fake and so many wretched habits, that it is doubtful whether radiant seeds can be nurtured in the generations ahead at all, while falsehood and darkness will be in the forefront. We ourselves have drunk our civilization away, we began with depravity, and only after a very long time did we get some sense. Nesterov, cavalry guard, illumination—all of this is as it is in Europe, but can these really be cavalry guards?

Or limit it to just a cursory remark, to Avseenko; about the *possibility* of the scene in the brothel, two ladies of the gentry, true fact, but two virgins examined in their innocence?

NB. *Visit to Petrov.* See the antiquities of Petersburg. Article.

The Alexeevsky Rampart.[183] —Rostovtsev, Filippov. Finished pondering. Dreamed of those who have children. Whose blood is this? Filippov *escape* (the fencer cut through).

Why to the *Diary of a Writer?* What do you mean why? I am still dreaming about it.
In *The Peters/burg/ Gazette* the evaluation of Adveev is taken literally from *The Voice,* without any indication. In the same issue railing against Gamma.[184]
An/na/ Karenina. Heroes. These people are strangely interesting.

Well my sickness is more healthy than your healthiness, doctor and sick people.[185]//

The Voice. Saturday, Febr/uary/ 7, No. 38. About the Siberian university and about the captain's affair (irritation, a leader with his subordinates, they stick out their tongues). The Decembrists, why we are not lords.[186]
One of the local Vagners, an expression of *The Voice.*

About the ballet *Don Quixote.* —About Don Quixote.
The fine things of the century: Pickwick, *Notre Dame, Misérables.* George Sand's first stories, Lord Byron (lame leg), Lermontov, Turgenev, *War and Peace,* Heine, Pushkin.
Walter Scott. Walter Scott is not a legitimist, but [reached] a well reasoned, supremely sincere reconciliation with his hatred of the past. *Notre Dame* is not it, hatred etc. (Music.)
Our concèssionaires; after all, you swine, you are the ones teaching your children Walter Scott.

The Poet: And among the worthless children of the earth etc.[187] I am just afraid that Mr. Spasovich might take this upon himself.

Insult. Gustav Khristianovich.[188] He was a cog in a machine's wheel, but are these cogs really worthless? Now, they would not necessarily have been *worth* anything or doing good things. They could be doing bad things or any kind of things, but they are still living and are still part of a machine. The machine would exist.

What a mistake! And this is here in our country, where there aren't even any doubts about power in the first place.

But there was also naivete in our country (Nikolai /?/).[189] They demanded honor, honesty, and fulfillment of duty, they did not have the slightest understanding of the actual conditions, that good could not exist at all except in isolated instances, and that the whole could never work.

And it is no wonder that they never suspected how it had to be done, when the very negators were even more stupid and did even worse things (Decembrists).

"The Writ"—i.e. the French constitution, MacMahonism.

The Russian World, No. 38 (Sunday, 8). 1) Poletika and Kushchesvky. 2)On Briullov's paintings in the Academy, *Potugin.* 3) Excerpts from *The Moscow News* on North American current opinions about Kamchatka[190]

In our country we might be split apart, we might curse each other's convictions, but there is much sincerity in the desire for goodness and for a warm belief in society among our younger generation. You scold everyone, "things are all falling apart," but this very pity and despondency are testimony to your fervent desire for the building of the common cause. Do you agree // to the definition of the *common cause?* Where to! This will start a fight, but that's all right.

Isn't the time approaching for mutual understanding (not mutual flattery). Tell your witticisms, laugh, joke, but if someone is sincerely going toward a noble goal, give him credit for going toward a noble goal.

Everyone welcomed me except... (Bordello), pleased everyone. And after all, is that bad? No, it's good. All of us are searching for the common good, we are always fighting with each other, but we are all good people. Slavoph/ils/ and Westernizer/s/. The Petrine period ended with the abolition of the peasants, and, so it seemed, there would be reconciliation, but no, the war keeps going anyway. Nonsense. Potugin. On Potugin and his ravings. On Turgenev. I reread it.

February.[191]
—About Zotov. *Illustrated Gazette.*[192]
—The question of artistic quality is easily decided: write bad or better. An excellent person but he will not be able to express his idea.

—Two trials. Spasovich, poet, Vibulenus.
—In the fortress.
—*District News.*
—War, Marey, and so forth. About the Siber/ian/ university.
—About the brothel. V. Zotov.

Insult. Khristian Khristianovich.

About Bazunov.

The welfare society for the poor students at Gymnasium No. 5. *The Voice,*
No. 40, 9th February.

[There is nothing] We have a pervasive honest and radiant expectation and
desire for goodness, the *common* cause, nothing aloof, caste-like. But even when
it is encountered, everyone always holds it in disdain. The time has now come when
the commonfolk are being exposed to precisely the same depravity of thought
that existed among us in the Petrine period (it is not that I am guessing, I believe
this, and that makes it important to me). But of course, it is not in the same, you
might say, historical form as we had, but in a different form, but exposed to a depravity like ours because we have taken the beneficence of the world in the form of
depravity. And for that reason an enormous new period for the commonfolk and
for Russian life is coming.
   But still it will be seriously accepted by *a few individuals* and—the deed will
be done. //

Spasovich. *Ce n'est pas l'homme c'est une lyre.*[193] This was exclaimed with
profound trickery, i.e., as if in the form of the highest praise, but still, what could
be more ridiculous, how can he look like a lyre.
   For the commonfolk a lawy/er/ is a conscience for hire, i.e., bribed not only
by money, liberalism, praise, poetry (lyredom).

How can I then with no capital; and here the lyre thundered out; well, no talent. "Family, family" etc. Is family life worth it, isn't that really slander? This is
what the real torture is. Melensk/?/ king.

The sanctity of the family, Spasovich, but according to this line of reasoning
it is better never to bring the case to trial [sanctity] at all, because if you must always acquit the fathers. Fathers against their children—that is something else again
(Butlerov).

They punished the girl twice: with switches and in school, and as a bride and
in perpetual married life.
   You may have taken her father away from her.
   There are some cases that are difficult to turn over to public trial. Man belongs

to society. He belongs, but not entirely.

A husband and wife, they are irritated at each other, he embraced me, she is voluptuous, but she herself told me: why are you so sure of my fidelity?

What can you say in return? Where.

This is a joke. Can it be, can it be my words. You are at my feet...

Your Honor, if I am reminded of these words, then this does not belong in a public trial, this is a matter of love (kissed the feet).

But, however, if you will allow me, at that moment you confessed to her that you were suspicious.

"Your Honor, again the same etc."

But, you madmen, why then did you appear (but they are madmen. There is a vaudeville called "To the Justice of the Peace!")

And if the prosecutor brings suit against them?

A man belongs to society. He belongs, but not entirely.

There are places in my heart which the judge obviously cannot understand. I am not talking about rights. But it is simply useless, because neither the judge nor the jurors can understand them.

And so it was not necessary to spare Kroneberg /?/.

I gave birth to you. —Franz Moor's answer.[194] I consider the reasoning of this depraved man correct. —If you don't know, look it up. Schiller wrote it so long ago, after all, and the play has not been staged for so long.

Belinsky. A poet—you know, that is as if /.../.

The moral admonition consisting of: not only emotionalism, you might say, but also a deeply moral feeling, a well developed view and an ability to *control one's emotionalism.* But how to make this agreeable, for example, to the lawyer. And suddenly you have it: *c'est une lyre.*

What a great calling: to defend the innocent. But as great as it may be, it is still senseless and terribly crude. It is probably only good when the lawyer is convinced that the man is innocent, or when he knows that he is guilty but knows that the man must be spared. If he were just begging for mercy, that would also be all right.

But is this the case here: no, I am convinced; if I were not convinced, then— etc. Who would believe it?

Especially when there is a fee—I already know that this cannot be with Spasovich because he did not receive a fee.

The comic and nonserious nature of actors, why in England an actor is not considered a gentleman, a serious person. —A person *is* an actor. Vibulenus.

Actors in real life. To the English the ideal is realism, the positive, etc.

C'est une lyre—...And such lightness of soul.

And so the most humane person and a liberal, but how did he come to defend whipping...And whipping that way? *C'est une lyre.*

The child did not recognize his father. How could she recognize him? Children of that age always forget, after a long separation. Doesn't Mr. Spasovich know that? That is no reason to be angry at children.

The child adopted some bad habits, but who is to blame for that? Bad up-bringing at Coombe's, whipping at home, and her father's ignorance that there were scabs in the nose. //

Louis 17th.[195] This child should be tortured for the good of the nation. The people are not competent. This is God. *In the ideal* situation social conscience must say: let us all perish if our salvation depends only on a child's being tortured—and not accept that salvation.[196] This is impossible, but the higher justice must be *that.* The pattern of real, everyday events, of day-to-day evil is not the same as that of ideal, abstract higher justice, although this ideal justice always and everywhere is the sole *beginning of life, the spirit of life,* and the life of life. //

Who is to determine, asks Spasovich, how many blows the father can deal out, so that he will not be criticized for his harshness, for his excess (He really took to this word "excess"!). Excess, digression, uneducated people love these nice for-eign words and consider that they add force and seriousness to the style, and even beauty.

How did who determine? Why the father's own heart must decide that. Christ, embracing the children, taught how they must be regarded. Even you, Mr. Spaso-vich, must know the limit where the blows must end, if anything at all beats *sous la mamelle gauche.*

What do you want then? You want the jurors to be unable to convict Krone-berg as a torturer or, secondly, as a father. [Well so] But he could not be convicted as a father, they did not want to attack the power of a father, nor could it be at-tacked. As a torturer—that is another matter. [But you have here] So now you have proved that he did not commit any torture, it is true, you even have here Krone-berg's confession that he beat the child severely, in excess, he beat her in And all of it is stated in this confession. Mr. Kroneberg himself considered this un-fortunate. But now Kroneberg, according to the law, as you summed it up, could not be convicted for that. What more do you want, Mr. Spasovich.

No, you are a lyre, and you want more. You want not *only* the acquittal of the accused, but also the acquittal of the deed from within the man by his con-science, you want to distort the social conscience so that the victory will seem all the more brilliant, for without that victory, what sense would it make? And that's why you go off the deep end, you try to prove that it must be done that way, [that the child] the image of the child crying "Papa, papa!" seems almost funny to you. You slandered a small child in public, saying she must be whipped, you slandered her—saying a seven-year-old must not steal money. You yourself said that there were various reasons for it, the servants, Coombe, Geneva, the fact that [Krone-berg] the father was often away from home for days at a time, but at the same time you keep asserting that the child really is guilty and Kroneberg is right [word illegible]. To you, the torture seems like a good deed, *it was nothing at all, you say.* And why are you struggling so hard to distort a man's conscience? For after all, even without doing that you know that your client is not to blame, that there turns out to have been no torture (not a broken leg, was it), that he will not be punished, no, must you even eradicate all pity for the child and ridicule and falsify the genuine feelings of poor Titova? But this is too much. A "lyre" is just what it is. //

That is:

In the first place, you proved that this is not torture—this is the most important thing, and that the father must not be judged for exceeding his authority—and that is enough from you. But you feel you must obliterate [in front of the readers] from the heart of the listener that image of the girl crying out "papa, papa." It's nothing, you say, it is a trivial thing, I'm doing what has to be done. So this is what real humaneness is. No, don't obliterate that image, this is what is known as humaneness, philanthropy, love, the human heart, do not let your splendid triumph encroach upon this.

Oh, you will say: I myself said that Kroneberg is no pedagogue, that he is a bad father and you can't demand everything all at once etc.

All right, maybe you did say it, but how did you say it in the first place? Having said you had not reached any conclusion, you kept it concealed while the conclusion was straightforward, the unjustice of the power in such a father and head /?/, and secondly, you either forgot about or kept secret the fact that you had actually said that he is no pedagogue, that the girl had been neglected and that she was not to blame—that is exactly what makes the child's treatment seem so horrible to me—that is exactly it, that is exactly why. This is the injustice, this is the untruth! Whom the injustice and untruth come from does not matter, they do not even have to be from anyone, just from fate, yes that is how it is, but you know it is such a *pitiful* thing, *pitiful,* but *pity is precisely what you have to eradicate*—for a complete victory! You say you do not feel sorry for her, just look at her cheeks, this did her some good, you say—so, to whip her, and severely at that—not good.

—he belongs but not entirely.

But once it has been dragged out into the open, what can we do about it.

The sacredness of the family—

This is blasphemy. The family is too sacred to be subjected to slander. The family cannot be maintained by cruelty. The father cannot be punished (though beyond a certain limit, of course /he can/) say, up to the point of breaking someone's leg (and Spasovich will agree), but in any case, you must feel pity that the family must be based on injustice to the child (for the child is not to blame, those who make the child depraved are guilty) and you must feel pity that the child was insulted and tormented. But you must eradicate pity itself in order to enjoy a complete triumph. You lyre, you will remember Belinsky accurately.

I cannot judge the father, I cannot attack Kroneberg, although I have a perfect

125

right to feel pity, but once this case has been dragged out into the open—I must judge him. I will not concern myself with the father, his soul, his convictions, I am not competent there, but the fact is already public knowledge, it has already been dragged out into the open, and it has become a matter of conscience, I want to judge on the basis of the known facts, told by Mr. Spasovich himself. //

Why do you complicate your task: to have your client acquitted, when he was not even indictable in civil court (the leg had not been broken), with my suit, with our human, humane suit? Leave us our suit, don't spit on human love, don't contaminate a child in that one filthy part of your speech (while in another part you yourself acknowledge that the child is not to blame and must be corrected *some other way*). We regret that you *torture* the child in your speech because she has no one to stand up for her. What do you care about her cheeks? her health? We pity her, leave us our pity. After all, you task is still accomplished despite that [the father has been acquitted], the father cannot be convicted by the law of the court (what more do you want? Lyre!).

Let me say this: besides, he cannot really be convicted by the human law either: granted that he has an unjust view on bringing up a child (a poor pedagogue, as you call it), granted that he did [not entirely] not fulfill his fatherly duties and did not understand that he could only have power (in his conscience, of course, he was his own judge) when he had fulfilled his obligations; but I also know that you must not judge a family man for each and every moment in his life, for all kinds of things happen in family life. (A shaken man once told me: I love my children, and my children know that and love me, but once I threw myself on them and almost killed them, that's what would have happened if I had not been restrained). I understand that you cannot expose family life every step of the way, and it wasn't I who exposed it, it wasn't I who dragged it all out into the open for everyone to see. Besides, Kroneberg acknowledged his daughter, he wants to do everything he can for her—he made a mistake, in short, and even in my conscience I am willing to be cautious. But I will leave him—[but I], and turn my judgment to you alone! Don't attack what is basic, don't distort things, don't laugh at what is sacred, don't speak in paradoxes, b/.../.

Talent.

I remember Lamartine going to the Deputies, criticism /?/, lyre.

C'est lyre. The device was such that he seemed to praise, paying tribute to him as being a lyre, but still he himself knew that he was laughing at the man in the most caustic manner because there is nothing as stupid as equating someone with a lyre.
Of the Deputies.
She touched the lyre and began to sing.

But the lyre is still all right, just stupid, but there is also another aspect, and that is capital.

Spasovich, doing favors. Koni liked him more.

And in general

Lawyer, what grandeur and what crap.

I'll take the last speech. The Kroneberg case.—Switches, characteristic items in the speech.

Man to society—not entirely. He brought shame upon the girl.

They insulted the father. I do not know his soul. In family life a husband and wife are one: he licked my feet. Family life is impossible [if it is] in public, if it were not for the broken arm/s/ sometimes.

For that social conscience, development.

But [dist] if it is a public trial, then I can get involved in it, but the distortion of conscience, the lyre.

I will retrace the speech of the lyre.

Is that how the stenographer of *The Voice*

Excess—spent enough time on the lesson, if I may say so.

Welts from the stick, soon it will fade away, it stings, you mean this is not torture. (Through the system.)

And further, at the girl, who is frightened—

It is ridiculous to judge her for a prune, or course, one prune, or, I so say, the prune in this case was compared to banknotes. But you know it is pathetic, it must not be done for a prune.

The main thing is a long section about the child.

The family, the sacredness of the family, don't blaspheme, don't garble the facts. This is another matter. Two different matters. The family is sacred, but both pity and justice are also sacred, as the family is, and if it developed that the family had to be based on pitilessness, then it would not be worth it for the family to exist [to stand]. It is all for the good that things are not that way. The family (its ideal and relationships, the beginning of humaneness, sacred, kind feelings). Go ahead and smash ribs, but do it to someone who understands, I myself would acquit Mr. Kroneberg by the law and, perhaps, would come away from it with many favorable thoughts towards him in my heart, but leave me and my pity alone.

You say: you cannot scare her, she is "spunky" (What a word.) (A word which grates against lyricism.) How do you know and why do you need this? It is enough that there is a child in front of you, who will stand up for her?

You know, at any other trial nowadays it would have been *the environment.* But in this case the environment was too hard to pin down.

NB. Now ill repute regarding the little girl, and even the bride. And about Mr. Kroneberg (cruel). But perhaps not really cruel at all, but nervous, sick—

127

perhaps even noble, he is not an egoist, he did fight on someone else's behalf, invoking /?/ something /?/ about divinity. He is a madman, remember the Family Chronicle, he is a *bad pedagogue.*

NB. Lyre! But is it only a lyre, no and glory, how can it be without capital.

Contents of No.
Everyone welcomed me.
But after all, the whole point of the matter is in the details. They agreed to look at it as a whole.
I was interested in the *court procedure.*
War and the bordello.

The *weather* and the *bear* disturbed me (prediction).

... since the client was being threatened by too terrible a punishment for committing torture, Mr. Spasovich could not help but use all available *means.* "Now how could they not acquit him." And for that reason he was compelled to try to eradicate pity itself from human hearts, to tease the child—"spunky," you could say, to expose her secret vice (as if he were not talking about a seven-year-old and as if he does not know that physical torture reinforces that vice), to compare the prune to banknotes, to disgrace whom, then: an angel of God, hardly: to deduce and to demonstrate how spoiled she was, how she had learned to repeat the same thing over and over, and finally, to start talking about the sacredness of the family.

Let everything collapse if there is torture; Mr. Spasovich [was] is eloquent enough, but down with everything, he bowed to the switch... Such is talent and such are the obligations of a lawyer... what is all of this for... These cases do not belong in court. But what things do belong, anyway? A broken leg, bruises? Where is the limit? *The boy and the swan's feathers.* The doctor beat the boy, but pity, pity.

But just leave pity alone, do not laugh at // the whipping of the child and at her wild cries of "papa! papa!" Do not try to shame the child, do not force her as she cringes with fear to recite mechanically: *Je pas voleuse, menteuse,* face and to kiss his hand... Or was it really so unavoidable? Perhaps not? It should not have been necessary to spit on pity that way, to stifle and laugh sarcastically at the truest, purest feelings was just not called for. (Beautiful Elena). No, in this case there was a lyre and talent both. Leave pity alone. In short, something that cannot be resolved.

He felt compelled to try to prove that there had been no torture, although he himself does not know how to define it, and he is reduced to defining it as broken bones.

Or, perhaps, the lyre? O golden-stringed one! It is this goldenstringedness... etc.

Didn't you know that a four-year-old's memories fade away within a year, or surely within 1-1/2. They will say: these conclusions of Mr. Spasovich are not dangerous, the law of a child's nature is well known to all, yes, but this *is* dangerous when taken as a whole, that inspired face, the feeling of rectitude, the fire of truth—all of these things taken as a whole create a certain, decisive impression.

Why separate a father's heart from his children? Even if Mr. Kroneberg does not become separated, it is still true in general, and [ma] his heart must certainly become separated. Something of that sort will remain forever, there will be something left unsaid in their mutual glances for a long time (and that is natural, considering the nervousness on all sides).

These trials are not necessary, but, on the other hand, who is going to stand up for the child. It is such a pity, such a pity!

And you know they may even have ruined her future.
Il en reste toujours quelque chose.
Perhaps his whole heart really was washed with tears when he had to insult the child and carry on with such nonsense... or maybe not? Or is this just something being play by the lyre?—I think it is the lyre. If Spasovich had defended the other side, the lyre would have inspired him with the opposite arguments, and he would have set out to transcribe them with the same fervor.
[Talent, talent!] This is what it means to have talent! *Talant oblige.//*

Talent. You aren't exactly speaking against yourself, but you go out of your way to praise something you have never thought about before in your whole life, or you curse in another person the vices which he himself has from head to foot. They will say it is ridiculous to reason that way. But I'm not talking about that: to me this fire, this fire is excessive in such instances, that is, in every instance that could have been handled just as well without such forcing of fire—that is what really bothers me! Because you have a feeling that truth has stopped, that the man has been playing and playing so long that the lyre has taken over. For it is excessive and, in fact—a lie.

His eyes afire, his face aglow,
He weeps and all of us are sobbing.

Kill pity and there she is. She is spunky—there are her cheeks—there are her vices—there, the expert Suslova must point out the vices. But this is a child, not to blame... (It is remarkable that rosy cheeks and vices contradict each other, but there is an overall impression.) But this is not enough, like any profound psychologist, he must produce a feeling of disgust, and pity will disappear, secret vices—
Have mercy, and for that she was tortured! That is what also tormented the

father.

Agreed, but then it should not disturb Sp/asovi/ch, who knows more than anyone or anything that the 7-year-old girl is not to blame for any of this.

The conversation recorded at that time.

But still we cannot manage without capital. Now, for us to be deprived of our capital, that is absolutely impossible, [for how would we be then] [we ourselves would remain]. But apparently the mama has to go on living that way... [because by no means] and I won't give it up, because for us it would simply be impossible to be left without capital.

Now for us to do without showiness, effect, that is absolutely impossible for us. Yes, without showiness you would be doing justice, but with excessive showiness it would all be unjust.

No, but how can we manage without showiness. But still it would be impossible for us to do without showiness, because for us, without showiness, it is absolutely impossible. But still, it would be impossible for us to do without that lyre. //

Talent, yes talent is needed in everything, even in a movement.

Vain, seductive sight, unchaste sight.

The Kroneberg case.
He belongs, but not entirely.
And the judge will not understand.
Unchaste sight.
But, then, who will stand up for little ones such as these.
Where torture ends, for Mr. Spasovich it is a broken leg: but—let's listen to Mr. Spasovich, pay attention to him.
I admit that no sooner had I begun to write on Mr. Spasovich, than a new phase of the legal profession became known to me.—There were the legal eagles, there were the pincher-prodders [language], I read in many languages, etc. But then Mr. Spasovich was appointed from the court (he took off his hat). So Mr. Spasovich took up the defense, and he had to defend. Severe punishment. *All* means. But who is Mr. Spasovich like basically? *Vibulenus.*

Not a word about his biography. He is a brilliant lawyer, a talent. I admit, by his speech—Koni—he flatters the spirit of the times. But in general the question of talent—talent, nob/.../ity, Belinsky, *c'est une lyre* and how can we do without capital—everything fit together and at the same time a most holy goal: acquittal.

But let us examine the entire speech: I want to point out what kind of pitfalls await a person sometimes, what kind of distortions of feelings and concepts—especially for the sake of the holiest of goals, so that you will hear the absurdity out to the end, you will be indignant, and then suddenly you will think, "Now what could he be up to? There's more here than meets the eye! There must be a reason..." And lastly: The lyre overdid it this time with legalistics. //

...Final:
And it all got started by raising the question.
I am not a legal expert, but I still think that these questions should never have been brought up.
But still: who will defend little ones such as these? Perhaps change the law, not to Siberia but a reprimand or wardship.
But to encroach upon the family.
Impossible, impossible—but still: "papa, papa!"
Do you know what: the family, if it must stand on *"papa"* would be better off not standing at all. For this is a slander on the family.
I do not know how to solve it.
But the main thing, the main thing is why Mr. Spasovich wanted to stamp out even this "papa, papa" in our hearts, to crush our pity.
He led us along until we got used to the idea /?/
And this way immediately... //

After all, *The Voice* cannot deny that the duality of man (K. Aksakov's article in *Fraternal Aid)* is the downfall of man, but he stands up for duality, thinking that this is liberal.[197]//
About war—swords into plowshares.
Praise of war.
Paris—and the Eastern outlying areas (the Slavs). *Nota* state powers, see in the beginning.
For a Great Russian to live for himself is to live for others.
And after everything else Potugin.
The meaning of Turgenev.
V. Zotov. Slander. Obscurity in the reader's mind.
About the district press. Bordello.
High education of the peasant.
The commonfolk will pass through depravity.
For the influx of new words means the influx of new concepts.
Answer to Zotov's slander. //

Talent is essential even in a movement. Talent is the ability to say or express something well where lack of talent would say or express it poorly.
This covers the whole question of artistic quality and tendency.
They will reply, not entirely: what will you do with an artistic work, in which there is no tendency or real thought. To that I will respond that in a truly artistic work, even if it touches upon other worlds, cannot help but have true tendency and real thought. We will discuss this further. But what about Mr. Spasovich? There you go denying the true tendency and reality of thought in his defense speech, and nevertheless you are screaming that he is a talent.

That is just it, that his speech shows no talent. Overdone and from that a new law can be derived: *As soon as* an artist tries to turn away from truth, he will immediately become ungifted and at that very moment will lose all his talent.

Stenographers of *The Voice*—I think that whichever stenography is taken, one or the other, *The Voice* has sufficient means to keep a good stenographer.

Everyone welcomed me. That is good.
The ball, *Stock Exchange /News/,* is not exaltation before the commonfolk.
Everyone welcomed.
Quick, but feeble hatred so comic.
There is nothing to quarrel about, we are good people, we have an hon/est/ difference in ideas [I find].
Slavophiles and Westernizers. Petrin/e/ period.
The ball—some fine ones (see Green notebook).
Lovers of the commonfolk. Theory.
K. Aksakov. The commonfolk will overcome depravity.
For he who does not believe in the beauty of the commonfolk /not/ understands nothing about them. Not in the utter beauty of the commonfolk, but in respecting them as something beautiful. And also, light and darkness in them are together. The light, the positive side of them, is such that it will teach us and give rebirth to the entire world. The darkness is such that we, the ruined people, must inevitably come to be healed. *Chanci de nous peut profiter.*
But I would not want the commonfolk to begin with depravity. //

Spasovich. The case is finished. This case took a month.
(A lie among the lawyers, in the court.)

Bazunov—they took it for Americanism.
Although Americanism can be learned.

To pay so much—that is your decision, there is no turning back. Perhaps it would be better to give twenty per cent.

Our lovers of the commonfolk, almost all of them, regard our commonfolk as if they were a theory, and simply no one loves them as they really are. It is just the other way around, if so, it is *verboten.* I don't dare assert it.

For us it began with depravity. The feeling of chivalrous horror was pounded into us with a stick. When things had gone as far as Ermolov's saying why aren't we lords, the answer to this question followed on December 14. What is December 14? The revolt of Russian landowners who wanted to become lords, but still, everything magnanimous and youthful was embodied in them.

War. The need to overpraise ourselves before others magnanimously.

They will say—praise yourself for your science etc.

To assert one's individuality is [self-su] [requi] a requirement for self-survival. //

I am convinced that Russia will be Europe's judge. She will come to us with communism, to judge her. And Russia will decide in neither side's favor. Neither side will be satisfied with the decision.

Everything in the next century.

There will be no strong states, all forces will be destroyed by the internecine struggle of demos with the superior forces (our country will not have the superior forces). Russia must be ready. As to why Russia will be so strong, more on that later.

The Eastern outlying areas and Siberia.

Europe in the near future: internecine struggle and a quantity of progressively moving population.

The Pope—leader of communism. /.../

About Bazunov. Americanism. Our Americans: Obolensky, Ovsyannikov, Nadein.[198] Former landowner, general.
A string of settled landowners.

50 years. A well known cycle of ideas. I do not know why I should have to show that these are spirits, if I am unable to explain them myself. Our university commission,[199] at any rate, is incompetent, and if it did meet, no one knows why. Even if all its members became convinced that these are not magic tricks but particular inexplicable phenomena, they will not admit it because they would be afraid of Europe: Europe is the very place that is *paying* attention to them (definitely).

Even if going beyond my means to arrive at an explanation...

New epic poem. Two great ideas of revolt and submission, both demanding great deeds, marvelous material, indications of your own and of original material you will show us the way. *Le courage de son opinion.*

About the elections in Paris. The commonfolk were measured not by what they really are but by what /that/ they hold to be beautiful and true, what they yearn for, etc.

On Marey—about animals. Reason and belief preclude each other.

133

About spiritualism. Un mot de Sechenov.[200] Thomas and mathematical conviction. Thomas. He would have rushed to the most logical and necessary idea which is always arising from this. If I don't have the strength or means to explain this, that does not mean that it cannot be explained. *Strictly.* Even mathematics. What do you think, would mathematics have convinced the Neronov martyrs? /.../

Be a brother *ou la mort.* //

Did they go as far as fainting in our country (the lawyers), though they were telling us something about this. But it seems they probably wept. "They shed tears." All right, if he was that convinced. This is even consoling for mankind. But what if he is faking? How sad that would be then, because you know it is very possible that he is faking (for his own interests). And to think, that it is for money, how sad (but if it is not for the money, then it is respectable, of course).

And there under the cover of such an unfailing and necessary case—what depravity!

Let's have achievements, boundless, impossible, but initiatives, *our own say*—none of that.

And how Peter made our commonfolk forget how to deal with anything. *Not for youself.* If for yourself, then for everyone. And now the *zemstvo* cannot come to terms. The mediators will receive a salary. A 200-year habit of not dealing with anything.

—the bribe, so that the service turned into not getting things done but arranging deals.

My prediction.[201] Gambetta—the republic. Enemies—neighbors. But is this good? There is no doubt that communism will make some deals. The *Pope* making deals. They will turn to Russia. Russia served Europe. But truly by that time we will be independent, since we will have had two centuries to forget how to deal with anything, and we will see things differently. And here: made to forget how to deal with anything. Peter. Gambetta.

It is remarkable that this time the landholders wanted a republic, is that good? The Pope. This is all guessing. /.../

Killed: what telegrams from Paris?

He belongs, but not entirely. The individual, we can tell from a quotient how much a man relates to society, the rest we can guess, but there is something we cannot even conceive of, and this is in *every person.* For otherwise he would not be such a concrete being, and individual. //

134

True, but who will stand up for the little ones? This question, then, remains unexplained. But we cannot believe that torture begins with a broken leg. Sacredness of the family.

Lyre, capital.
But pity, at least leave us that!
Yes sir, but will they send the client into exile?
Correct.
And so, this is what the talented lawyer was reduced to. He had to finish with the sacredness of the family.

But I do not want to believe in devils: that would be too stupid and too crude.
(Little bells, a fact that seems never to have existed.)

Spasovich... Now I must either formulate in greater detail how the law defines torture, or else judge behind closed doors or else do nothing and not judge at all, provided that the leg is not broken... I don't know, I don't know, I am not a legal expert, but something must be done here. But I only wanted to say something about the lawyer's role. So here we convict them for taking a pile of money. Sometimes they take money for a good reason.

Gambetta (Communards). Because they are right. Gambetta is a puzzle.

...Catholicism, whcih has suddenly proclaimed the tremendous idea of infallibility, in other words, the idea of worldwide rule (good or bad, it's all the same), but a colossal task, the idea of ancient Rome, and this at the very time that unified Italy had turned into such a little bourgeois kingdom (Greek) along the bourgeois cliché of freedom and human rights. —As you wish, but the squashed, dying creature, weak, like a little insect—and suddenly with such ambitions (I will not give in, I will die as a ruler), this is colossal, this is worthy (I will unite with the commonfolk, they have preserved everything). —This might be.

I expressed this idea above all others in the novel *The Devils,*[202] then I met it in the *Times* in our country—but my God, what unhappiness is in store for our children, they will turn to us.
We are not that time.
Yes, it would be funny if we were not threatened with the future.
I believe in devils least of all. //

If I were on the commission, I would not under any circumstances agree to recognize the phenomenon: there I am, a professor from Saint P/etersburg/ University, and suddenly I recognize the phenomena, when not a single one of the European universities has yet recognized them, and they have only been recognized by separate individuals; that is why I think that the commission will not recognize them either; and I see, but I don't believe my eyes. That is understandable.

Thomas.
Take off the medium's coat.

Little bell under the table. None of this meant anything to me.
People are honest, I can't really get suspicious, but I have been getting suspicious for 53 years.
He made the medium angry.

Didn't Jesuitism bargain with Christ's body.
The workers are naive, they will be amazed by Christ and believe in him.
[On] Catholicism they suppose that they must carry a sword (and this is the entire difference).

To Spasovich. Sanctity of the family. We, thank God, are still Russians, and not French bourgeois who defend their family and property beyond anything you can imagine, simply because they are family and property and they comprise for them "l'ordre." No, we keep account of ourselves and even when it is "necessary" we will act sooner by conscience than by necessity. Plenty, Mr. Spasovich, plenty, come to our senses, what banknotes!... true, you are in that kind of position.

Turning from the present matter, allow me to ask you, Mr. Lawyer: do you shelter *all* instances of tyranny [of the family] under the sanctity of the family. Do you mean to say that you would not undertake the defense (prosecution) under any circumstances, afraid of the sacredness of family rights, and aren't you blaspheming here against the family. The family as such a sacred matter, [that] is, of course, impossible. I said so myself in the beginning. But it cannot be, can it, that only a broken leg... For me what you were saying about sanctity... But I was only referring to unnaturalness. //

The evil family has already destroyed itself with this, and is left with nothing sacred or worth saying.
To suggest only what God orders to the letter, no matter what.

You, I repeat, supported the father, you did well, because he is not a tyrant, because he truly loves his daughter, whom he had adopted and had not abandoned, whom he went to pick up, because here you have just a [not] bad pedagogue, an occurrence, finally, nerves... For that it must not, must not be Siberia...
—But just leave us pity.
—Yes, but if they exile him...
Now this is really falseness, and a serious, honest man swoops down like a hawk at a child, at a little girl, at our feelings.
Mr. Spasovich finished with the family.
The defense of the switches.

But these switches, if you will, are for very small children, but it would be desirable to have very small switches for these very very small children. Isn't that true? Or, maybe even switches that are not too large, not Spritzruten... "What switches these are, see, they gave a good whipping and it came out well."

But who will stand up for her? At least let someone stand up for her in print.

And so, for whipping? But here, it seems to me, the lyre has struck up. But this aspect would have been completely unnecessary for the acquittal of the accused. Perhaps to flatter the masses?

In fact, the family has been ruined, no one is being defended and all are un-happy. //

The Voice. Saturday, February 21, No. 52.[203]

In the feuilleton on Svanetien, the judgment of foreigners about Russia's future. [Of] About the people who shot themselves.

What inhumanity! And who could have defended this child.

Of course, the father, he is sitting right there, but he cannot, you see: he is being *judged* with *his child,* and he naturally cannot say a single word. That is the way the court is set up. How false! How unnatural.

Switches, whipping.

But at that point, I think. he overdid it. There is the lyre. That lyre played [rang out] quite often during the entire speech earlier, too.

The family. Here I am going to separate the matter from the Kroneberg case, here no villainy was carried out at all.

But if there had been villainy, however, such that would slip by the court. Would you have defended such a family? A better bourgeois has never existed.

The art in this is amazing, beyond all praise, if it is only regarded as art. None of his charges holds any water at all, and the lawyer himself knows that all the jurors will understand that. But our lawyer—psychologist, he is familiar with the mind and the heart of man. So what if none of his contentions holds water, so what if all the jurors understand that— // never mind! I'm not afraid! For I know that taken as a whole, as a combination, I will achieve an impression, it will work.[204]

Il en reste toujours quelque chose.

But he had to eradicate pity itself, and here is the final impression, all saved up...

But we cannot be sure that slapping across the face is the most humane thing.

I ruined my joy, filling it all up with my critique. But no one criticized this speech, the nature of the lawyers—the nature of their influence upon the jurors.

137

Like a hawk attacking a small bird, he twists it in his claws—with all the extravagance of his emotionalism. With all the force of his responsive talent.

He was put in such a position. He had to sacrifice the child, he would besmirch her, shame her: "Stealing, bad habits, the prune..."
He should have said directly: this is how the law defines torture. But don't apply it to Kroneberg...

But that would have been a terrible mistake. That wasn't enough for him, eradicate pity itself. //

But the child did not grow up in that home. These creatures force their way into our hearts when they have grown up with us. [But]

Oh, how he would have elaborated on the suffering of this little girl and embroidered on the details if he had been her defender. No, whatever you prefer, but still there is something sad about it.

Do not touch them, do not hurt little ones such as these.

In this word "spunky" there almost seems to be scorn for all her sufferings.

To touch someone's face is not "prejudice," but always a dishonor and a terrible insult. That a person's face is the image of his individuality, spirit, worth.
To put on a cheap vaudeville act, to amuse the jurors. Papas, you say. These are old, poor mannerisms (devices). This will go out of style some time or other, still new in our country.

You know, Kroneberg himself said it was painful, so why do you keep insisting that it was not painful, and that they did not consider it torture. But torture was mentioned only after that, and the main thing was to eradicate pity, to get rid of "papa, papa!" In that way the beginning was done, the case was presented in court with unnecessary // details and even gaily.

Either they will begin to act meanly or they will die sadly, clasping their hands toward God.

Agrafena—the height of art, he just touched her, and there you had: a thief, she taught the little girl, and that's what everyone would think, in order to discredit the witness. No, this is the height of cleverness. You and I, reader, would never have thought of this.
This Titova might have been exaggerating but, pity, she came to love the child. She took it for Agrafena. She thought this up. That means nothing to Mr. Spasovich. But here you have the lyre itself and not the man.

For you see, she thought this up herself. They [but they forced her] provoked her to say: *"Je suis menteuse, voleuse,* and papa didn't whip me very painfully." What was done, anyway? What is the father's power actually?

Before this: she scalded her feet /?/ with steam. This school for perversity. This is the clearest manifestation of the most extravagant emotionalism, this [looking for] is a distortion of healthy feelings and the rules of morality, it is constant, relentless to the extent that is necessary in view of government procedure, and is raised to the level of principle—oh, never was there anything more depraved, more depraving or more cynical in the Russian land. This is a school for depravity, raised to the level of something glorious [to] and held up [to] triumphant for general emulation. They know which way the wind is blowing.

I cannot make anything out of this, I am not a legal expert.

The family. Raise these things to the level of principles abroad. But in Russia not one of our sacred objects is afraid of being questioned openly, did you know that, Mr. Spasovich. Well, now you know. We Russians also are proud of our unique characteristics. Our Orthodoxy will translate the Bible on its own. We do not have sacred objects *quand-même.* Our sacred object is our faith, the sacred object is our truth /?/. We would want our sacred object to be a truly substantial, not a standardized sacred object, if not, let it not stand because it would not stand us in good stead. We will not stand pat with our sacred objects when we can no longer stand by our belief in their sanctity.

It seems that I was the first one of all of them to call the thing by its right name. I am not encroaching upon the legal profession in principle, no, but upon what it has become in our country. For we were all wagging our tongues and reciting praise. //

Let every single one of them pounce on me with the whole weight of their scorn and indignation. Never mind! I am not afraid of anything, do you know why? Because each of you, alone later, will eventually say to yourself: "You know, he is right." That is enough for me.

Samovar, she scalded her hand. Give it to him and how he will start squealing. He will even weave the banknotes into it. He would say, "He will grow up and steal banknotes." Rage, environment... emotionalism... And the sentence would have been secured. He would have secured a stipend in her name, and the public would have applauded it because she hadn't scalded the poor infant, but burned a hand.

But the nice little lyre has to play and make merry, so it rang out, and out came excess.

139

Little Petya he sat down
On a glass but did not frown,
He took his fife and played a tune
So mama would feel better soon.

How can you tell your little one to make herself saintly. Here you are big and grown, and with all your intelligence you cannot make yourself saintly, you lie and respond blindly and emotionally. (I am referring to each and every one of you, not just to Mr. Spasovich.)

Those poor, unhappy ones who try to satisfy their clients.

I ruined my copy, but you cannot let it stand as is without my protest.

No, Mr. Spasovich, don't introduce these rotten rules to us.

I do not object to Mr. Spasovich, but by not being aware of the circumstances, they may not understand, they may think that he is being serious. //

This is ideal! they will say.
But you can't really mean that all established conditions in the present state of society must be absolutely ridden with paralysis and damnation.

Before socialism it is shameful!
We do not want the golden era, but just a little more honesty!
Because there is a measure and a limit to everything.

March.   —About war and about Europe.
           —About anonymous letters.
           —About the distribution of readers by districts, conclusions.
           —*Anna Karenina*
           —*St. P/etersburg/ News,* Febr/uary/ 29.[205]
           —*Mosc/ow/ News,* No. 55, Wednesday (on forestation).
           —*New Times.* Thursday, No. 5 (Prince *Dadian and Nikolai.)*[206]
           Insult.
           Lack of education.
           —One of the local Wagners (Look up).
           —*New Times* on Bryullov (he did not like Karamzin's History), No.
6 (but in the 5th No. on the great significance of Dobrolyubov).[207]

Suvorin's feuilleton on Sunday, 7th of March. *New Times,* No. 8 (on Katkov), and in No. 7 or 6th on the great erudition of Bryullov due to his not liking Karamzin's History.

Mosc/ow/ New/s/. Saturday No. 58, 6th of March, about the arrival of Don

Carlos in England.[208]

NB. On the predominance of polit/ical/ articles in *Mosc/ow/ New/s/* above all others (look up earlier issues of this type).

Our country now has Lev Tolstoy etc.

Speaking neither pro nor contra about the essential meaning of the poem, these lines are so strange and so obscure, so uncommon somehow, that their appearance in a publication like *R/ussian/ Herald...* "This lion," is that a pun on Leo—or about his breed as lion-author, as lion-novelist, but this is more awkward, a novelist with the strength of a lion, but then what would "of kingly breed" mean.

And what cacophony, just read the line:

Our country now has Lev Tolstoy

with something half-chewed in your mouth.

English religions without Christ and God, according to Pobedonostsev.[209]

In *The Voice* (No. under the blue books) it was said that the Russ/ian/ man is rotten, but also etc. No, I did not say that.

The phenomena run after science, science runs away from the phenomena. From Aksakov's article. //

New Times, No. 9, 8th of March. Notes of *Moscow N/ews/,*—on forestation (less zeal, they say), answer: on the contrary—more zeal.

Friday, 5th of March, No. 63, *Stock Exchange News,* in the feuilleton *An Ordinary Reader of Ostrovsky.*[210]

What is better: good or evil? To him the solution is mankind. *The main thing.* /.../ Agriculture on the decline, disorder. For example, the destruction of the forests /.../ Fet: about overcultivation.[211] An indication: something is being solidly planted when agriculture is solidly established. (NB, we also cannot figure out where agriculture came from, what its connection is). Then the best people will appear. Where will they come from? The gentry perhaps, or seminarians, or will they come jumping out of an earthquake just like that.

Where the external impetus will come from—war.

About war in general.

Then Europe and, maybe, about the outlying areas.

NB. The Herzegovinians. *New Times,* according to *Moscow News,* No. 12. Suvorin's article on positive literature.[212]

Find the history.

About Saint Nil Sorsky and about *property. New Times,* 8th of March, No. 9.[213]

The Voice Tuesd/ay/, March 9, No. 69. About fishing in Ilmen (the two-bit merchants, government business, how can they without capital. About the movement of Russian military forces in Cent/ral/ Asia. English newspapers).[214]

In *New Times* about the Petersb/urg/ officials (hygiene from the magaz/ine/ *Health).*

Go to the Academy, to Ovchinnikov's st/ore/, to the orphanage, to the basements.

Sometimes war is better than peace: put in about Ilya's meeting with the blind singer Ivanishche.[215]

(The deer, Aesop's fable).

The best people: and is it possible that the law is such that there will always be Ivanishches—the environment. Where will they come from. //

Meeting with 104-year-old woman.
—(Leave it, take a peek later)
—(Spots on the sun)
—(About passports hurting productivity in Russia, the lead article in *Mosc/ow/ New/s/,* No. 59. Wednesday, March 7, NB).[216] Find Pobedonostsev's remark about passports (passport defense).

The passport is dependent upon the commune and its will, and the commune is held together all the more by the mutual financial guarantee.

To preserve the commune with free coming and going, at least until a certain time.

The Citizen from March 7 (on a translation of the Bible from Hebrew into Slavic again).

About how Russia has always been something attractive for Europe, And then *of course,* Peter's reform served to benefit the Germans much more than the Russians (see above).

New Times, No. 3 *(The Citi/zen/,* March 7)—excerpts from *Talk:* letter from a peasant about corporal punishment. NB. A falsification. Corporal punishment with switches will, in all probability, not end until all the woods of European Russia have been completely destroyed—i.e., that means it will last at least fifteen more years. For, it seems, the complete disappearance of trees will occur still and all no sooner than 15 years from now, despite the newspapers' cries that it cannot be stopped, that we will be with the bears soon.

There would be more feelings, more heart, even more reality—and not just in literature.

Reread the material.
—Old woman, 104 years old
—Reading the future in cards, the jack.
—Lizaveta Kuzminichna and the Dresden Madonna.[217]
—Nurse Alena Frolovna.
—General—stuck out his tongue.
(Lizaveta Smerdiashchaya.)[218]
—Ilyusha and Ivanishche.
—Spiritualist seance Febr/uary/ 13.[219] About Thomas the Unbelieving.
—Tongue in the mirror.
—If such ideas exist in the West, they are only socialist, communistic (a new faith, new moral bases, the old ones are thrown out, there is no need for N. M/ikhailovsky/ to be angry that they are atheists).[220] [But there is]

The Voice, No. 70, Wednesday, March 10, from America on the Central Asian question.[221]

The Voice, No. 71, March 11, Thursday, news about floggings, about Kupernik and so forth.[222]
Severe article about the commission on spiritualism. //

New Times /No./ 12, March 11. Thursday. Literary review (A muddle). About positive ideals. In the same issue: opinion on the Herzegovinian question of all the newspapers *(Moscow News).*

"What are the best people?" etc. (Words to begin the article with) or "The Harm or Benefit of War?" What a ridiculous question etc.)

The program *peut être New Times,* No. 13, Friday, March 12 (on the Eastern question—a ridiculous solution).[223] About spiritualism and about how it is deeper than Mendeleev's lecture and that its depth is due to the vacillation of contemporary people etc. And what about the people of the past? Is that how it is, what do you think? This is the search for moral comfort after the loss of religion—and that is *where the real depth is.* But to be comforted and not to vacillate is not so very easy. Where the best is and what the best is, that is the question. In that same *New Times* on positive people... Where can they be found? Where are the good people? [Where are ideals] Good people are associated with ideals. In France—in *Misérables.* In solid England—Dickens, his ideal is too modest and uncomplicated. In our times the questions have come up: Is the good really good? For example, are Christ's patience and humility good? How should the equality of people be structured—through universal love, utopia, or through the law of necessity, self-preservation, and the scientific method. But in the Gospels it is foretold that the laws of self-preservation and the scientific method will reveal nothing and will not comfort people. That people are not comforted by the progress of the mind and of necessity, but by the moral recognition [beau] of supreme

143

beauty which serves as an ideal for all, before which all men would prostrate themselves and be comforted: that, you'd say, is what truth is, in the name of which everyone would embrace each other and undertake some real action toward achieving it (beauty). How can we demand a positive ideal from our literature: from the time of Peter the commonfolk have been a Verband, but we have lost faith in ourselves. Belinsky was saved by his future dreams: of science and new foundations. I have said what is to be expected from the commonfolk, from Orthodoxy. I indicated Turgenev and so forth. But these are only attempts, [hints] hints. It is easier to draw real portraits of those who suffer from inner turmoil. Alas, all my life I kept writing about this. There exist, it is true, Karataev types— but that is only the commonfolk.[224] A family exists, portrayed by Lev Tolstoy. But this family will not last. Now what do you mean by positive achievements. You will be in no position to explain this. Potugin. *Take a look at the Potugins*— you will be forced against your will to stay with the literature of *Action*. But the reason they lack talent is because the action is not yet clearly explained and because it is still only a dream.

Collapsed and weighed down brick (*The Devils*).[225]

False idol.

We get our vacillation from our intruder, Europe, and if Europe is also vacillating, how can we help but vacillate. //

By the way, about spiritualism. Seance on the 13th of February.[226] Warding off the devils. Fakirs. Miracle, secret. Masons.

Question of the Herzegovinians. The Slavs. Byzantium. Orthodox empire.— The Slavs and their relation to us.—The war. War in general. War is in the air, in the future, our children. All the European turmoil must be resolved in the present century.

A profound silence reigned over Europe, when Frederick the Great etc.[227] The Pope—etc. France. She did not survive. She bears the idea—communism. She was deceived by Christianity, she grew weary and repudiated it as she had repudiated the conquerors. Now she wants to settle it herself and wants to be divided. But she cannot be divided—so then to get things established logically, scientifically and humanely, loving each other, working and living for each other— and being strong through each other. In short, the same church, religion, temple, but without Christ. Only they forgot that all this is utopia. They do not know whether by bread alone. Scientifically, without religion, but man will not want to give up his hardships in exchange for bread—it is impossible to propose any solution. Meanwhile, all of Europe is full of it. And our children will see it. And won't the Pope go? I said this in the novel *The Devils*. Then everything will come crashing down around Russia.[228] That is when we must be united and we will come forward with Orthodoxy.

Because spiritualism answers the great masses of the people, including frivolous believers, as well as the idle miracle-seekers and those who are simply deep believers (Pribytkova).[229]

I hardly think our scholars would ever muster up enough courage to confirm the phenomenon.

Won't our Orthodoxy mature and purify itself through its representatives and spiritual leaders in the struggle against this teaching. //

Conversing with a table, as if it were an intelligent being, is repulsive for it is crude. A man who is too ashamed to believe in a future life, suddenly bows down in the presence of a few sounds and he believes!
The phenomenon of levitating tables—must be checked. Also interesting is, if they really are spirits, why are they so weak, capricious, definitely the table, in such circumstances they exasperate the soul and the nerves.

The ancient tragedy was a form of worship, but Shakespeare was despair. What is more full of despair than Don Quixote. The beauty of Desdemona only ends up being sacrificed. The sacrifice of life in Goethe. But that is not enough: society needs real happiness and prayer—whether Shakespeare's types are positive. Shakespeare today would also introduce despair. But in Shakespeare's time faith was still strong. While now everyone really wants happiness. Everyone needs the sciences. But science has taken hold of so few people as yet. Society does not want God, because God contradicts science.—And so now people are asking literature to provide a final positive word—happiness. They demand a portrayal of people who are happy and truly content without God and in the name of science and excellence— and a portrayal of the conditions through *which all this can come about, i.e., positive portr/ayals/.*

If you will, a man must be profoundly unhappy, for then he will be happy. But if he is constantly happy, he will immediately become profoundly unhappy.
Prutk/ov/'s aphorism. (Happiness is not in being happy, but only in its attainment.)[230]

A feeling of the harmony of nature, as in Goethe.
Mathematical beliefs are the most difficult to believe. Thomas became a believer because he wished to become a believer. [Ta] I did not want to become a believer and did not believe. The taps (like a typewriter, and nothing but sus-picion, although I had no one to suspect) did not have any effect on me, the same goes for the sound under the table and the levitation and so forth (must check it). But if I had wished to become a believer, it would have been another matter. I, however, did not see any supreme mysteries: the fakir no solemnity and boyish-ness of the miracles. Short story in Paris—everyone laughs. Convicted by the justice of the peace.

Spiritualism—someone's utter mockery of people who are yearning for lost

145

truth, and someone comes and says, go ahead, knock on the table and we will give you the answer, you see, of what you are to do and where your truth is. //

"Our society is vacillating." This is easy enough to say, but no one wants to delve deeply into its disharmony. Even the old writers do not understand, nor do the critics.—One young man prepares himself and reads the Gospels, another invents a religion, preaches to the Nihilists, runs to America, [a woman] his wife, takes courses. These are all exceptions, you say? Are they really? So then where are your non-exceptions /.../ these trial lawyers? (Kupernik) They are vacillating! This very vacillation is an extraordinary sign. What do you think they will base themselves on, anyway? On science? And where has anything ever been based on science? In Europe they are still holding their ground and clinging to old outmoded precepts, while the other half of the people shout that these precepts must be gotten rid of, and it is vacillating terribly etc. (agriculture, NB).
This matter is far from resolved.

Shakespeare is the poet of despair. Where is the reconciliation. [In] It was once in belief, but belief has been lost, in what then, where is this anthill? Not with the Masons, is it? Truly, I always fancied that they had some secret, an uncanny understanding, [but some kind of] the secret of the ant. But such a secret is the equivalent of man's turning into an ant, only with intelligence. And man will not want the ant's nest. Suppose the anthill is discovered by science. There will be demands for the removal, control, and limitation of individuality. Why will I start limiting it. For bread. I do not want bread, and there will be a revolt. And it will still be a long time before man can stand up. *I do not want the kind of society where I would not be able to do evil; I want the kind that would let me do any evil I wanted to, but I myself would not want to do any evil* (excerpt from *The Raw Youth,* /from/ Atheism).[231] See Kaidanov.[232]

From love for mankind? Apropos, in England faith without God, faith in mankind. But this is the same thing.
Listen: excerpt from *Atheism* isn't that the same thing?

One man who follows this sort of thing was telling me that there are beliefs (sects) in England etc.

Excerpt about the good influence that Protestantism has and about Don Carlos' meeting.[233]

NB. A few words in the blue book.
Don Quixote: Full of pure and honest love
        True to his delightful dream—[234]

And suddenly Nikolai and Dadian.

A trip was a big event then, there were no railroads then.

Unhappiness and the single thought that he would eradicate it, this killed her long before the railroad had passed three versts, or before land-use payments.

End the *war.* With these words about evil. Because you are preaching fratricide. Maybe not. This is only the sacrifice of life. When will paradise come. Don't you see, there will be no paradise, but there will be science! There, do you see, I do not want the anthill. NB (Evil) //

Russia, of course, will not be able to solve the Herzegovinian question, as it now stands, without a declaration of war, but the time for that has not yet come.

[Hon] The English sect. They do not believe in God, but honor him as an earlier belief [in] of mankind. This actually is the deification and worship of mankind, an astonishing love, I was right. Atheism, love and sorrow.

Mosc/ow/ News, March 4, No. 56. Lead article about Chikhachev's brochure, such nonsense.[235]

Moscow News (without question the most substantial of our political newspapers) says that as long as Russia and Prussia are friendly and mind their own business, there will be no clash. But by posing the question this way it alludes only to the *as long as,* consequently it does not actually deny that unpleasant *in time.* For this is the question: when will that time be. The Eastern question has changed the center of gravity, it is not in Paris, not in *entent cordiale,* and certainly not in England. Its seed was carried by the whirlwind of circumstances to the Berlin grain field and what difference does it make if it is still buried deep in the ground: nature will take what is hers, and the grain will sprout.

The Eastern question is now in Berlin, and everything now is hiding and nestling in Berlin. The *Mosc/ow/ News* attributes even the establishment of the French Republic to Bismarck.

Just let the Republic establish itself and achieve prosperity, and right away the French will start screaming at it: now, why doesn't our strong Republic want to recoup our losses? And so again [in] the government will be forced to declare war in order to strengthen its position, that is, in order to show that it is solid and to prove how solid and strong it is. All this will take place through the inner logic of events. And communism—and in order to divert society from fear and sorrowful thoughts.

This fear that Germany has of retribution from France is meanwhile the guarantee of our peace (i.e., our peace with Germany).

They told me that Kirillov is not clear.[236] I should tell you something about

147

Dostoevsky's plan for his novel *Fathers and Children*, 1876.

Malkov. Unfinished types. Current life, Goncharov's expression.[237] Weighed down like a stone from *The Devils* etc.[238]

More sincerely.

Marshal Sebastiani.[239] The theory is superb, i.e., that under no circumstances must the Frenchman wish to be an Englishman, each one must be his own type. —To Potugin.

War and the future ideas of Europe. Communism. The fall of Bismarck. The Pope. Russia—the bulwark—all a fantasy. Is it true that we have few guns? Is it true that there are 3 to 4 million still under /?/ the Black Sea?

Novel. *Fathers and Children.*[240]
Thoughts:
—a boy is in a penal colony for juvenile criminals, he hates everyone and waits for his relatives (princes and counts) to show up. He loves the truth.

The husband killed his wife, but his nine-year-old son saw it; they hid the corpse in the cellar. The father and son embrace and tremble. The son loves his father, but the father sees that the son is shocked and is agonizing over his mother's death. Both of them meanwhile take measures to hide and be hidden. (Similar to in *Crime and Punishment.*) Finally the father makes up his mind to turn himself in for the sake of truth and for his son and for *the truth before his son.* Before turning himself in he embraces his son almost constantly (it goes on for several days) and keeps asking [himself] him: will you or will you not love the truth, honor, etc? He turns himself in so that his son may continue to love him later, if only his memory. He does not tell his son that he is going to turn himself in, but the son understands it anyway. They go there together. The father is his own accuser, with the son as a witness.
The father, now a widower after his wife's death, finds out that his son is *not his,* but by his wife's lover. Or at least he suspects it. He takes him somewhere at night, leaves him there alone somewhere on the freezing cold street, and runs away from him. Later he cannot find him.

Children who have run away themselves from their fathers.

Children, in a crowd, struggling with untruth, they win a victory, they are triumphant, etc.
NB. The dreamer type (look in old notebooks). //

The boy three days at Savior under the altar.

American duel of two schoolboys over Lev Tolstoy.

149

The boy (adolescent) shatterer of women's hearts and expert on women.

NB. For a wife it is important only that her husband remain true to her
in fact; his fantasies of other ideals and other women must not disturb her at all.
The husband's most radical infidelity in his fantasies (f/or/ ex/ample/, he falls in
love) means, for the wife, nothing in comparison to the tiniest infidelity in fact (in
the case of the completely coincidental and *unintentional* instance of inter-
course with some flighty woman who is here today gone forever tomorrow).

The bathhouse. Apollon's foot.

The entire Kroneberg case in one episode of a novel, and with Suslova[241]
testifying about the girl's vices.

Mitrofania.[242] And the lawyer cries in a frenzy—with his second-hand liberalism and strikes a common chord in other frenzied second-hand liberal hearts. Not
the wife, but Prokopia or Agaf/oni/a.

Fathers and children. Fedya's story about *Krymsk* and about his brother. In
the Frebelev school even the newest teachers raise a big storm over him; they shame
him for lying, they humiliate him in front of his friends (thus arousing in them the
evil instincts of hatred), subject him to mockery, arouse his shame and hatred—and
lead him to despair and degradation. At this point Kroneberg the father etc.

Zhemchuzhnikov and "Mother of God."[243]
Family. "For three rubles." Death with these words. What the widow, the
children, remember.

...A dreamer, he has a son to whom he seldom pays attention physically, but
(at times) he inflames him spiritually. He only imagines that he has cremated his
wife (mother-in-law, boy), but while he was still imagining it, they bring her to
him with her legs torn off (railroad). She died, *asking him for forgiveness (in Russian).* //

The reality and truth of the demand for communism and socialism and the
inevitability of the European upheaval. But then you have science—outside of
Christ and with complete faith. The things that must be discovered are the exact
scientific relations among people and the new moral order—(there is no love, there
is only egoism, i.e. the struggle for existence)—they will believe firmly in science.
The masses will rush at science first and will plunder it. The new formulation will
take centuries. Centuries of terrible discord [Despotism for the sake of one piece]
[Everything be re] But how can everything be reduced to despotism for the sake
of one piece. Too much spirit to give up for a little bread.
If there is love for one another, you will achieve your goal after all. In order
to love one another, you must struggle with yourself—says the church. Atheists

cry: betrayal of nature. The burdens of that are heavy, while this is pure enjoyment. And then the Roman church added: do not reason; obey and there will be an ant-hill. They mistook science for revolt.

It is worthwhile for the Pope to say: yes, my friends, you are brothers [ou la mort], but if the brothers do not want you, that means the world is absurd.

Communism grew out of Christianity, out of a high regard for man, but instead of *self-willed love,* the unloved take up sticks and they themselves want to take what the unloving did not give them. The Roman church is to blame for this. Mankind obeyed her, although with revulsion, but only until science came. Science rebelled, [but the Enc] and, when the time came, the Encyclopedists began to preach to the people and to the whole world that science had come and that they could get along without the church and without Christ. Then the revolution followed, it was content with very little, but then came socialism.

Science in our century refutes everything formerly held in regard. Your every sin has been brought about by your unsatisfied needs, which are completely natural and therefore must be satisfied. A radical refutation of Christianity and its morality. Christ was not acquainted with science, they say. The constant demand for a new morality (for man will not be alive with bread alone). —Property, family, they assure us, was sustained only by the old morality. The law of necessity or the law of love? But the law of science will not yield, bread is not worth it. But accept the law of love and come to Christ, then. Perhaps this is what Christ's second coming will be. But in the meantime, what will keep mankind going?

We became distracted and began to fantasize, but you should know that all this will happen, or at least begin to happen, in our lifetime. How Bismarcks fall. It will all happen when we are least expecting it. Russia, Orthodoxy. Just look at what Orthodoxy is. The Herzegovinians, the solution in the newspapers, etc.

To await humility, i.e., to conquer evil with the beauty of my love and my strict example of abstinence and self-control.

Raspail in the Chamber.[244] About love toward one's fellow man.
All of your accursed questions are correct. Humility is not strength at all!
All of your vices are due only to circumstances and your environment. And so get rid of this environment and create a new one in the name of science.

True, science is only just the beginning. There is no God because he is nowhere to be found (Mr. Shkliarevsk. arm).
Notice NB., this is really the study of the destruction of the will and the reduction of human individuality. Here then is the sacrifice of people to science.

Science is a great thing, but it does not satisfy the whole person. A man is more vast that his science. This is in the Gospels. //

151

New Times, No. 15. *Ecclesiastical and Civ/ic/ Herald* on spiritualism.
St. P/etersburg/ News on clerical vestments.

The Voice. Sunday, March 14, No. 74. *The monstrousness of the reports.*[249]
—Politics.
—Liter/ary/ criticism.
—and various indictments.

Mosc/ow/ News, No. 65 (March 13), lead article on the Herzegovinians.

Stock Exchange /News/, No. 72, Sunday. On Kupernik.[246]

Great dissention within spiritualism. There is no doubt that we will soon be reading accusations from both sides in the newspapers.

The long arm in Paris. Those who wish to believe will be convinced, those who do not will laugh.

In the morning the 15th the program. Examine the war.

Instead of the beauty of people of various types, the beauty of *rules,* and a bad person suddenly becoming good, turning his life around when inspired by normal, natural feelings. As something Christian—it is good.
    But if literature is the reverse (Action), when, it is obvious, there will be nothing, no matter how hard you try.
    "I want to suffer!"

In *The Voice,* March 15, No. 75. Hymn of praise to the soundness and maturity of the French Republic. But they forgot that the Republic will always be regarded with suspicion. And that the president (whom the army honors so much, *The Voice* notes with satisfaction) has not one single political thought in his head except for *j'y suis et j'y reste.* And it is fated always to be that way in France, that every government first of all must worry about assuming and maintaining its power and therefore only ½ of its strength can be devoted to France, and all the rest to itself. An example here is Napoleon IIIrd. //

The Voice, No. 75. Look at the places indicated with a *line.* We are most sympathetic of all to a republic because we are sympathetic toward freedom. Who could most easily be free, why we could. We have no controversy over power... Power in our country could bestow all privileges... And if there is anything that has been impeding [this] that, it is without doubt our Europeanism.

In our country the true freedom lover must be the most monarchic. That is our political strength, and we must rely upon it in order to use it for action.

To Gamma: Without having ideals, that is, without having good intentions, how can we become honest—now, I have a chance but you do not leave it to chance. I hope you will not be angry about my objection.

To Gamma. I read about Kupernik first.[247] Read *The Voice* (about a bunch of facts), read about the positive ones. Everything about ancient literature (worship). About the latest ones, about the literature of despair, about the universal human truth of Lev Tolstoy. Notes. On Don Quixote. On Shakespeare, *Dickens. Misérables* (the only ideal), in Dickens it is not ideal, in ours—*Adolescence,* in Turgenev—*Nest of Gentlefolk.* Novels of *Action,* unfortunately, did not succeed.

Beauty in the ideal cannot be achieved because of the extraordinary strength and depth of the need. In isolated instances. Remain truthful. Christ gave us the ideal. Only the literature of beauty will save us. Where are our best people. I read the anecdote about Rosen. Read about fakirs and Prince Velsky. Read about spirits. The truth of relations where the criterion is: there was faith. Then various human feelings—all of them came out of faith. Then untruth—as truth.

[The old woman]

I read an issue of *The Voice.*

Much on the Herzegovinians. *About the war.*

The Republic. The commune. Everything is full of it. The law of necessity and Christ's law. The Protestant church, an excerpt— and worship by the atheists. The best people. Accursed questions. And that is why there can be no literature. And why only the authors who still believe in everlasting order [are writing] are able to write. Those who are vacillating—yes, but this vacillation is not temporary, not uniquely Russian.

The old woman.

So, that is the plan: what and how I have read, one after the other. 16/th, tomorrow morning, *about the best people* and about *the war*—look around.

I read about spiritualism, about clerical vestments, read about Don Carlos' arrival.

In Shakespeare's time, there was still Christ, at that time it was still being resolved, but now it cannot be resolved and it has turned into literature. Disturbed by despair, questions.

In Shakespeare's time there was still Christ. At that time it was being resolved. Now it cannot be resolved and has come up again. Hamlet. Don Quixote. Accursed questions (see above). They do not know what is truth and what is not. Worship in England. In our country those who write are the ones who believe (excerpt on Protestants). The best people, the gentry, were—the best people will emerge from somewhere, will say something, come with something. Action, the Pisarevs wanted to resolve it immediately, but they did not succeed, and too little talent besides. In the West, the extremely talented writers, George Sand, did not succeed either.

Officer Druzhinin.[248] This is really an idea that Ivanishche encountered. //

In France the desire to live and communism with services of worship.

To get along with only the economic necessities, so to speak, besides the task of finding a solution for the anthill, you will need sacrifices, but will the human individuality ever agree to this? It is impossible without worship, I mean worship in the broadest sense. *Atheism and the worship of mankind.*
You will not succeed with the profit motive, there will have to be worship.

Kupern/ik/ shot for effect, so, to impress the coachman, for effect.

And so you see, the affair will end up as just trivialism, though it is an amusing affair.

All forms of morality come from religion, for religion is only a formulation of morality.

The blind singer Ivanische makes a judgment about Christ, about the absurdity of his starting to cry as he raised Lazarus from the dead.

The old woman.[249] If this fact were to be narrated artistically, i.e., if a great artist were to become inspired by it, an extremely fine picture could emerge, with meaning, with ability, and even with "the accursed questions," but under the charm of the picture you would not be afraid of the accursed question.

Besides the accursed questions we have our own questions which are also accursed. For exam/ple/. Where are our best people going to come from now? The gentry, or the commonfolk, perhaps (Fadeev), but many people do not believe in the ideals of the commonfolk and do not know them, they even say that, best of all, the ideas are completely unnecessary.
(semi-science, Russia, semi-science).
Blind singer Ivanishche is the mediocrity, semi-education, blind musician Ivanishche is a scholar, an author—he writes about whatever he feels like (About Christ, he started to cry, as an example of solutions.)

Where did he ever find out that "the Germans must be beaten."
About war, no, this war will not be easy for me.
But then the judgement about the war.
The next time about war, about Europe.
The role of the gentry, Fadeev, the ideal.

Ivanishche is now the one who solves things, while formerly the strong, the best people decided. They will say, let the best people be the ones to solve things now as well. And so it is, and there is always one final word after them, but there is much that Ivanishche does not understand, and so there is much uneasiness.

Sachs, who has the opportunity to know (because of both her intelligence and her humaneness) what this step will mean for her.[250]//

1) Gamma.
2) I read [in *Talk* the letter about birches].[251]
   On Don Carlos, Marshal Sebastian.
3) About [Prince Dadian, Mitrofania], about priests' vestments.
4) About fakirs.
   About blind singer Ivanishche (semi-education).
5) About Kupernik—3
6) About Queen Victoria's title, seriously testifying to the seriousness of the apprehensions (but the title motivated by that).
About spiritualism (all)—9+4.

I read about a bunch of facts—5.
7) I read about positive literature—10.
(commune)
About the Herzegovinians
and about European affairs.
Heard about the old woman.
11) About the robbery of the Austrian envoy.
Kaidanov.
12) The war.
13) The old woman, bunch [mi] of Aesop, of Kupernik, bunch of facts.— About spiritualism. —Blind singer Ivanishche. —About the war—and finish with Europe a little bit.
Did Ivanishche say this or did Ilya.
Moscow the 3rd Rome
Peterson—5.[252]
6th—communism and Europe.
        the war
About
        the Herzegovinians.
The belief of atheist Protestants.
I read, say, about the title, about the priests' vestments.
Blind singer Ivanishche and spiritualism.
Pumping out air. The scientific solution is in opposition to the moral one: do not steal.

It seems to me that the literature of our period has ended. The conjectural literature of the utopianists (of Action) will say nothing and will find no talents.

Once again upon the strength of the commonfolk, when the commonfolk are standing as solidly as we are now (but when will this be), they will reveal their own Pushkin.

Today I [met] had a rather curious meeting.

The war. We have many conventional concepts, about war as well.

Ivanishche always loves and tends to come up with a final solution immediately.

The literature of *Action,* you might say, is the aristocratic didactic literature— [ravings] although it is about the commonfolk—it is only the ravings of gentlemen and gentlewomen about universal equality etc.

Will a person submit his entire self to reason and to the benefits of science. He will want to do evil and to leave the atheist church of his own free will.
Atheism from *The Raw Youth.*

Union of all forces against Catholicism. 1) the war.
2) Review, MacMahonism, Gambetta—neighbors.
3) The Pope. Union of all forces against Catholicism.
4) Will go to communism. Communism. //

Origin/s/. Communism. From the decline of the conquerors. Demos—the breaking up of property. The Roman church. —Communism, will reason give moral laws, will man want to live without prayer. The church of atheists. Does science know man's nature. Will he want to make a sacrifice in return for bread. That means it is all still theory. More correct that all the utopianists. But they still have the law of love. Atheism from *The Raw Youth.* Louis Blanc and the Raspails—and the angry Communards. Why we have Mikhailovsky. This is a law. The Catholic Church can go to the ultimate extravagance. But nevertheless, concepts of morality are needed, where to get them: property, the accursed questions almost all have an anti-Christian solution. Hope placed in science.

The law of rational compliance and the law of self-will: i.e. let me do evil.

In the next no. how the positive inquiries were reflected in our country. The war.

NB. But the influence of science in our century, still wet behind the ears.

The law of rational necessity is first and foremost the destruction of the individuality (but, you say, it will be worse for me if I upset the order. I work not for love of my brother but because it is advantageous for me).
But Christianity, in contrast, proclaims much more freedom of the individual. It is not restrained by any mathematical laws. Believe, if you wish, with your heart.

And according to Christianity, and it can also be deduced from the very words of Christ, that love is the benefit, at least as far as any benefit is received, but I do everything not for the sake of some benefit, but for the sake of love. I do not wish *evil* etc.

The churches of the atheists—the Louis Blancs, Communards, rights, retribution.

Bismarck will not be able to resist, he will come crashing against Russia. Orthodoxy. —There you have real Orthodoxy. Peterson. The war. The old woman.

Rational necessity—it is all the same bread (out of stone).

Mos/cow/ News, No. 68 Tuesd/ay/, March 16. Lead article about passports. Article by Englishman Skyler on Russian literature for *1875.*[253]

The center of gravity for the Eastern question is Berlin, what about that fact that Austria is apparently stuck being the host for this movement. She must be compensated, then, in return for the German lands. //

Spiritualism. The arm in Paris. The tale would have been amusing in view of a most important psychological feature in the human soul. [We] We could bring a dead person back to life—and no one would believe it, "a trick!" This tendency is widespread and not only with miracles, but also any new, brilliant idea heretofore unheard of—this is what *Ivanishche* is carrying on about. How then do new beliefs or new thoughts become widely accepted? They will answer me very simply: there is always a woman by the name of Fama and a member of the Areopagus who do not share Ivanishche's opinion—and who come and form a group and speak out when the wind is going to change.

Maybe, I know a strange story teller, a dreamer, he would tell the tale.

But we are looking to the commonfolk for this, while the capital is by and large not the commonfolk.

Moscow News, No. 69, Wednesday, March 17. About the Herzegovinian question, about the opinion of *Russian World* on military academies and on the Petersburg newspapers.

Will Europe want to divide Turkey. Probably not.Theref., the Herzegovinians will have to resign themselves. I am not saying this is good (on the contrary, it is terribly bad for the Herzegovinians). I am only saying that this will happen. At any rate, the center of gravity on this question is Berlin, [and not anywhe] and really that of all questions, it seems.

There you have it, it is the Ivanishches who are in control, it seems, and not the Ilyas of Muromets.[254]

The bourgeois, Bismarck, and simply no one understands each other, and on that basis people are preaching peace, longlasting peace in Europe, and there are no grounds, they say, for it to be disrupted.

NB. The church of the atheists after spiritualism. But conclude spiritualism with the words that in mysticism, the need is for power. And, my friends, this must be taken into consideration—and then about the English church, the need is for prayer.

What is this all about, that there are still thieves left.
It is better to have thieves left, only that they should not steal. //

To the mother of God.
To the meek supplicant on the people's behalf. "To the ready defender and helper." Don Carlos—what a figure. He is quite some individual.

The war. Opinion of *Mosc/ow/ New/s/* and *Russ/ian/ World.*
Military and civilian.
War is better.

Mathematical proofs are hard to believe in.

Sacrifice, pray, and worship.

In our society there is little poetry, little spiritual food. Apropos, I would like to say a few words about our poets and open a new department in the *Diary...*
No. 21. *New Times,* March 20. Again in favor of destroying the forests. Teasing *The Voice* for article by Eug. Markov.[255] Surely the destruction of the forests is not such a liberal cause.

Science is theory. Does science know human nature? Do measures which rule out the possibility of doing evil really eradicate evil and evildoers? And won't voices be heard that will say, I want to have the opportunity to do evil, but... etc.

Constantinople is Orthodox, but whatever is Orthodox is Russian.

There Rome triumphed, there Julian the Apostate triumphed.

Accursed questions. All this, of course, will be much more delicately expressed (by the Pope), but the essence will remain the same.

The final contents of the March issue.
21) Communism. The Pope, Bismarck, *evil.* Russia—will she be prepared.
22) Don Carlos. Entrance. Sir Lawrence. The English public. Protestantism, an excerpt. The atheistic church. *Prayer.* Atheism from *The Raw Youth.*

23) Boborykin on Potugin.[256] Crafty device.

I read (briefly). Austria/n/ envoy 24, 25, 26. —The war. //

I read an overindulgent article about Privy Councilor's tenor of thought in upper Russia.

After Versilov's atheism, come love and sorrow.[257]

No, God is too hard to eradicate. Prayer and sacrifice. Devotion. Science, it seems, knows nothing about this. No, if anything does get established, then perhaps it will not be like the ideas of the modern Communards, and the priests of science. May God grant us that.

Catholics—they will go to the commonfolk.
They ought to annoy Bismarck.

Count of Chambord, a little bit odd, but not absurdly odd like a caricature; just respectable odd as in Don Quixote.

To Don Carlos. At that time the authorities were sending people to try to find out indirectly what he would say, would he get some sort of program started, if he were allowed into Madrid. But he haughtily evaded every attempt at negotiations, even refusing to recognize those sent to him as a warring side and actually calling them revolutionaries. Tersely, without spelling it out, but still clearly, he let it be known that "the King himself knows what he must do now" and [only] said nothing more. They left him immediately, of course, and in haste summoned King Alfonso. Then he began to shoot his generals, and in all fairness it must be said that they were loyal to him to the end.
The Englishman heard him out [cooly] gravely and, not at all moved, immediately answered // (religious questions in England were always and consistently a most important matter, to the great amazement of all civilized Russians.
(He was able to seize upon his fatal flaw, his culmination on earth, for which he was guilty unto death.) This Dobell, it seems, does not have a healthy understanding of Orthodoxy, and judges it as people judge Russia, for example. But what spiritual poverty this is when he recognizes the deformity of Protestantism but still wants to uphold it for its *good influence,* essentially for opening the doors wide and for its terrible lack of completeness. All this can be explained as the views and feelings of a truly Western person who places utilitarianism before all else, perhaps something like those government people, atheists of all countries and nationalities, who pronounce such wise dictums as: there is no God, and faith is nonsense, of course, but religion is necessary for the unwashed commonfolk because without it they could not be controlled. Leaving all questions about religion aside—what insincerity, though, lies at the base of that society [in which] and what despair for the proper development of people when there can be such [question] sentences from

159

atheistic govern/ment/ people and such *frank* articles about the utilitarianism of Protestantism (Dobell), which is stupid and wild, but which must be *upheld* because what would happen to man and society without it. This is one of the forms... [It is improper for a wise man to haggle with a youth]

As a matter of fact, is a society where there are judgments such as these really healthy. And are convictions like Sydney Dobell's about Protestantism sincere or profoundly insincere. How sincere is he in this case, but all this seems to verge on some sort of despair.

[And, however, in that society the most] (I deliberately choose the most solid of character, England.) there are profoundly—[naive] and sincere things. That is what I was told by a competent person in the know about one particular sect in England.

What despair, what a funeral march for mankind, what an unhealthy sensation, but the need, the need for prayer, for devotion: for tears, sacrifice, obedience. And evidently this has fully matured in Europe now. No, Europe's condition is frightful, and what a world in the future.

Atheism.

I repeat, the whole question of idle people is that this is all far off in the distance, and meanwhile, live, eat, drink, and be merry and do not think about your soul, the Catholic reasons that way, and so does the revolutionary.

The merchant.

No, he who has great concern for mankind and his future also has power, whoever he may be, and power to take it from others, but the people in Europe have no desire to know this.

Communism [England], the Pope, Don Carlos. England, which gave him asylum after the blood and carnage, and which Don Carlos logically relied upon after he had rejected all negotiations with his opponents, all this will stay with it for the rest of its days.[258]

Chambord. The Inquisition. A Fronde /of malcontent/ friends.

He shot the generals. —The Madrid government. In his manifesto to the Mother of God, he left, promised to return.

His entrance was completely in character.

Sebastian.

All of this is the same even now.

The war. Of course, this is all liberal, but it is hardly that, is it, isn't it more tranquil than liberal?

Of course, crafty meekness may be liberal, i.e., chiefly on the field of battle. Why, you say [tru] am I going to destroy my neighbor, and isn't it better to beat our swords into plowshares, and he [gi] surrenders very progressively if he runs off the battlefield, but going as far as appropriating the other side's property, perhaps is not so liberal (perhaps it is not even so liberal. However, it is difficult [and to say here] to settle it.

The thought is progressive and liberal, ...but on the battlefield it would be just

160

too crafty. And it might suggest to the officer the idea that he had been lured... Suddenly it dawns on the officer after such a "liberal" thought, in your style, and in return...

And so the Eastern question, i.e., the question of the unification of Orthodoxy (and nothing more) is one thing that we ought not to surrender to anyone. //

Contents of the April issue.[259]
—Churila.
—Kazan collection.
—Ivanishche.
—Spiritualism.
—Dreamer.
—Herzegovinians (!) and East/ern/ question.
Look at a *plain sheet* of paper.

Where are the best people. Yury Samarin, who could not sleep at night because of Vasilchikov's article.[260] *New Times,* No. 24, Tuesday, March 23, instead of that, the two-bit merchants full of meek craftiness /.../, Fadeev's gentry with no honor or conscience, sucking at Russia.

The war.
Note that we ourselves will undoubtedly begin finally to scorn them for their poverty, despite the fact that we ourselves are to blame for their poverty, through our cruelty and villainy, which will, no doubt, multiply in times of peace.
Gratification of desires arouses indulgence, indulgence arouses cruelty.

The war /.../
You will say that there are many great ideas, other than war, for the teaching and testing of mankind. True, but when will they arrive and won't they be over-shadowed in peace-time life by the spread of capitalism, dishonesty, villainy. Inasmuch as these things now by their own nature seem inevitable. The life of high society, their ancient isolation, and it seems, they know even less about Russia than foreigners and Lord Redstock know about her.
Lord Redstock is here in our country, incidentally. He turned. Where are the poor? (They are raging). A drop in the ocean, a drop of poison. They destroy the holy idol given by the church and look for their own. A Christ for your pocket. Sects of shakers, Milenniums /?/. Similar to spiritualists. But with Redstock they do not spin or prophesy. The crudeness of the society's development. And if so, then a new group will be the same way. Is it true that he wants to go to Moscow. What will come of him: he will found some sort of sect like the Khlysts.[261] Don't laugh and don't scoff: the Khlysts are deep, deeper than certain divine laws I could mention offered by idle minds. We hope that our clergy this time will not support the supplication of a heretic. Perhaps the force of his charm is entirely due to his being a lord and his preaching a "slam-bang faith"—as magnates of the Western

lands called our faith when they tormented the commonfolk for their faith in the last century and the century before that—but a lordly, "clean" faith. It is remarkable that all of our press seemingly ignores Lord Redstock, to bring up such facts seems to the press to be either petty or for some reason non-liberal.

Yury Samarin. Who was left then? There is nothing to preserve. Many are astonished: they are looking for the poor in order to help them, they want to give away their possessions. That is how it must be, that is how it always is at the beginning of every humane force.

Chernyshev. Young people with extremely strange traits are appearing. They come to your house and ask you to hear them out, they send you articles. I could cite several examples. It is strange that many of them seem to have fallen right out of the sky from who knows where. It would seem that the general liberal trend should have made everything generally the same. Instead they are beginning to discuss something completely different. [Unex].
Is this not the coming of an unexpected generation, which rejects its fathers who laughed at spiritual development and yet had none of their own. At any rate, this is all completely different.
And if so, then here they all are, those who worry about the future, about the whole, about all the people, and they will seize power and gain fascination. Remember what I said above about socialists.

Nothing can disturb these isolated people, nothing can draw them closer. They, in fact, stand side by side, and each does not want to know and does not see anything in the world other than himself. It is sad, although won't the optimism of the young people who threw themselves into the commonfolk yield the opposite fruits? I am *only* presenting a fact.
However, all of these may only be isolated instances, but why not take that into consideration. *We will have some more to say* about this perhaps. //

Utilitarianism of opinions. Yes, if you please, utilitarianism also. We were in a great hurry and did very little practical living, and we are ashamed of many of the most natural things because they do not fit into the theory /.../

The Voice, Thursday, No. 85, March 25. An account of the commission appointed to deal with spiritualism.[262]
An account of the commission on med/iums/: it is necessary to abstain from the immoderate use of literary embellishments.

Young people are appearing, a vigorous attack, an idea which has been dragged out onto the streets.

Alongside the horror stories about those who go to the commonfolk, you have, without doubt, the complete reverse and opposite situation—insincerity, dullness and jeering.

Of their petty fathers—heathens or profiteers, moneygrabbers and tyrants, braggarts, a right to disgrace.

Oh, I always [hoped] had a feeling that their fathers had become repulsive to them.

Apropos, I deliberately read a terribly large amount of strange things all month. I read about the society of virtue, I read about Kupernik /?/ and racked my brains for a long time trying to solve this psychological case and it seems that I solved it, but it is not much worth talking about, I read about the Herzegovin/ian/ question. Tashkent /?/. I read how the Austr/ian envoy/, I did some reading, finally, in *Russian World.*

I read the account about spiritualism.

All of them are people with one and the same folly.

I can attest to the statement in *New Times* that there are still many such people and in our times the number may even have increased. But the main thing is not that they exist, but how they judge things, and with Yury Samarin we lost a solid and profound thinker, and that is where the waste is.

They laughed at the faith of their commonfolk, while considering themselves on the side of the commonfolk.

The irony so much
Moreover, [she] she will tell him and she knows that he will say: I love you, why beat around the bush about it, so he must pay for this, after all, a woman will not give herself without being cruel.

There is a terrible ferment in all of our youth, starting with the adolescents, and in the widest range of senses. Where will this lead. The family nests [where] are being destroyed by the fathers themselves, and nothing else could emerge.

And since youth is pure, bright, and noble, young people cannot [except if from high society] start life so directly with cynicism and depravity, but instead they start with sacrifice, a vigorous attack, noble efforts, and they are not to blame for the fact that in these efforts the sense, the connection, the end, and the beginning are not at all apparent...

...Were there many *Belinskys* who suffered in their *souls?*

163

I read many newspapers.

This jeering with its cynicism and ridicule could not help but provoke a vigorous attack. It seems to me that it had to be that way.

Memento
—Write to Yushkov in *Kazan.*
—Send answer to Simbirsk Library.
—Sent to everyone?
—My brother Kolya?
—Go see Polonsky.
—Check with Soloviev[263] about the slander of *The Illustr/ated/ Gazette* (Zotov?)
—Write to the Honored Professor.
—By Smolny Monastery on Degtiarny Lane (near some boulevard) Yanikov's house, Fedor Ivan/ovi/ch Krasovsky, Prussian subject. Speak with V. V. Grigoriev 1) about the provincial press and 2) about our Asian outlying areas (will the idea about the Chinese turn out to be a fair one?)
—The welfare society for the poor students at Gymnasium No. 5.
—Where is Mitrofania?
—In an orphanage.
—Do not forget Mombelli.[264]

March 1) Mombelli
    Write: to Alchevskaya[265]
    —To Peretolchin
    —to the Honored Professor
    —a c/opy/ to Vas. Vas. Grigoriev.
    —to Otto.[266]
    —to Peterson.
It is strange not to say anything, for example, about the Herzegovinians [the scornful and arrogant tone of the account is not good].

The idea is the most noble and liberal, but I do not know whether it is a good idea for the battlefield in the heat of the action, for after such an idea all that remains is to turn around and run off the field ultra-progressively.

But it is not good if our officers proclaim their ideas on the battlefield as well as off, and by no means whatsoever can this be seen as liberal. Yes, and Europe will never forgive us for our Europeanism, she does not want us at all. //

In the April No. The infallibility of the Pope and Russ/ian/ force/d/ commune/s/. Yu. Samarin. The *higher* unity of people, which would make us distinct from Europe.

The Slavic Committee and its goal. Herzegovin/a/.

The war.

The petitioners are young people, passing them around to each other wherever they were allowed to, knaves, blackmailers, Pavlusha, cadet academies, etc.

—Churila.

—Kazan collection.

—Ivanishche.

—Spiritualism.

—The dreamer.

—Orphan/age/ or something sensational.

Avseenko. Future architecture for houses, no logs, etc. Destruction of individuality, transition to the herd instinct. /.../

—What is property?

—Strange maiden.

—The underground.

To Avseenko[267]

2. So you heave a sigh of relief that the commonfolk endured serfdom with such profound patience, they did not break away and did not curse the tsar.

1. You only wanted to attack me (a clique).

You attacked me last year, distorted the story of the woman who was hanged. There was no intelligence in literature before Pisemsky.[268]

I would not have answered at all, but I cannot forgive the distortion of my words about the commonfolk.

Mainly because in the *Russian Messenger*.

...And then he pompously starts lecturing me: why must we place our hopes /in/ the commonfolk?

But you did not get that from me.

About dipping their own empty vessels into the commonfolk.[269]

Who has an empty vessel on his head. //

Further Avseenko says: The fact of the matter is that up to now the commonfolk have not given us the ideal of the active individual.

—What? And that is after *your words* (see [no] note p. 370). So you see only kulaks and parasites?

If it were not for the empty vessel, I would tell you that you are completely shameless.

165

I do not want to lower myself to uttering one single abusive word, but it was shameful for the *Russian Messenger* to write, in connection with me, about emptied-out vessels *(Crim/e/ and Punishm/ent/* etc.).

I would suggest that what was said about me could have been expressed differently.

Russian activity is passive. But before Peter's reforms the outlying areas were more secure, colonization was stronger.
The confusion of our concepts of good and evil (of civilized people) is beyond all belief.

Didn't the *Russian Messenger* have to fight. And in '63 what about the decision about Poland? Or the Nihilettes.[270]

There are some absolute saints, are these particular instances (nurse Alena Frolovna), or a general characteristic of all the commonfolk?

You have never met the commonfolk.

You all talk about faith, while not considering it to be faith in anything. *Yes,* this is all of you.

Drunkenness, dissipation, intemperance, but along with these there are other facts, not as exceptions, but *as the general rule*—that is what the main point is. View (of the commonfolk) on crime, etc.

The commonfolk. They are depraved, but their view has not grown dim, and when it comes to deciding: what is best? their depraved acts or the common-folk's truth (i.e., their evolved concepts of good and evil), the commonfolk will not give up their truth. Oh, there are concepts which have been elaborately and erroneously worked out, but before any clash (major) with reality. NB. As, for example, the mess of *1612* ended with the Nizhny Novgorod solution. I mention this only as a sort of analogy.

"The commonfolk saved the government?" Surely this was not passive? No, action was needed here, because they were connected with it. And the mainspring only bounced right back.

At that time our political questions were perhaps better understood than they are now (the Herzegovinians, the Eastern question). Peter had nothing new to say in Russian politics. Quite the opposite, after Peter there was a bad interval for Russian politics. Then Catherine, and then all the way to the outlying areas of Russia. //

You are not worthy of speaking about the commonfolk—you do not understand the first thing about them. —You have not lived with them, but I have.

Your conception of culture does not go beyond gloves and carriages.

OUTLYING AREAS OF RUSSIA.[271]The higher meaning of this book concurs with the historic understanding that the commonfolk have about their own significance. The 3rd Rome is Moscow, and there will be no 4th.

I do not bear any grudge because of the novel *(The Raw Youth)*, it is possible, of course, that they did not read or know my novel in the *Russian Messenger*

What do we bring from Europe? What was it that the commonfolk were supposed to worship? No, it is not moral precepts at all which should be worshipped, but first and foremost—educational development, a broadening of their horizons, multiplied and reinforced by reaching an understanding of their own idea in juxtaposition with the Western European world, the historical understanding of the ancient world, the need for order.

It is quite obvious that of all our Westernizers it is not you, the Mr. Avseenkos, who have mastered all of this, and *we are bringing more than just educational development to them.* But the European lifestyle and its modern order are absolutely impossible for us to *copy,* as Potugin demands (the bourgeois and the decay of Europe). And we must not give up our moral precepts. But you will bring to the commonfolk an exposure to both ancient ideals and the latest ideals through educational development, through broadening of their horizons, and new paths will be found which will lead to our new future lifestyle and order. What are these new tasks. Service to mankind. We are bringing educational development [and in] in the widest sense of this word and that is all that we have brought. And that is not really so little. This is an impetus towards Russia's worldwide significance.

But the moral things of Europe must not be copied; vengefulness, retribution, cruelty, chivalrous honor—all of this is very bad. Their faith is worse than ours. And their humaneness, which you value so highly, is undoubtedly on a lower level than ours (the view of the commonfolk on the criminal, forgiving and forgetting offenses, the broad understanding of historical necessity—this is better in our country than in the West). The revolt of the Parisians in '93—that is not humaneness. Humane precepts are given in our faith, and these precepts of our own are better. If there is foulness, there is also saintliness right along with it. What must astound you and fill you with wonder is that the commonfolk endured all this. Because if the commonfolk are depraved, it is because they were chattel, without independent activity, they were a taxable unit.

You assent that as soon as the commonfolk show any action, they are kulaks. That is a shameless thing to say. That is not true. The nurse, crossing the Volga in *A Family Chronicle*[272] and a hundred million other facts, the action of self-denial, of nobility. A multitude of multitudes. What did you ever see in your Petersburg *besides gloves.*

The perception of the universal ancient culture of the Latins and Greeks, but nothing more.

If Victor Hugo has an understanding of secular necessity. //

They will ask: where do you see this significance of Russia? Of course, in Orthodoxy, because Orthodoxy actually commands it and leads to it: "about your affairs be like a brother and be a servant to all." Just as France was an ultra-Christian and Catholic state, Russia has always been Orthodox. Educational development has already been useful to us because no matter how much we are torn away from the commonfolk, in political ideas, for example, they still understand our service role towards Europe, that is, towards mankind. The whole question is: will we ever fully understand the *paths leading toward that.* In the March diary— I [said] expressed the fear that we will bring blood and iron.[273]

Orthodoxy—let it be Stundism![274] What we must do is to declare ourselves connected with Orthodoxy through the government. That is all that we have.

Ancient Russia was politically active, an outlying area, but *in her seclusion she prepared herself not to be righteous,* to isolate herself from mankind, but through Peter's reforms we ourselves became conscious of our own universal significance. They will say, well after all, this is because of civilization, and not because of the commonfolk? They have developed much more, and this is not at all /from/ contact with the Europ. The strength was in the native characteristics of the Russ.

And I answer that if there were no such people as the Russians, no reform could have enabled us to develop—[but] we simply would have become Englishmen, Germans. And now that we have developed, you don't mean to say that the reform happened by chance. No, it was from sources within the commonfolk. But though by now we have developed, from the beginning of the present century it was felt that too little force was being applied, that is, one cultural layer was active, while now the ranks have been broken and the commonfolk will definitely enter as an active agent. Wait a generation and you see how much the commonfolk will contribute to our action.

They understood that treasure. This was Orthod/oxy/, the pure truth outside of the truth of enlighten/ment/.

Depravity is consciously dishonest deeds, filth in the family.

Indisputedly, the stupidest of writers.

Lavretsky is a Russian figure. Pierre is also good, where the features are Russian—Prince Bolkonsky also.[275]

The chivalrous concepts of honor—but they are not always Christian, the concepts about law—but [pr.] much too much punishment, the narrow-ness of view.

—The concept of government? Ours is higher. Efficiency? In our country people knew how to get deeds done. But people in our country lost the ability, beginning from the time of Peter, but only for the duration of the cultural period when the upper layer was learning and the commonfolk were locked in ignorance. There was efficiency in our ancient world—but meagre means, low population density, separation from the world of other peoples (formerly for reason of prejudices). Russia's isolation from which she broke loose—but the outlying areas were able to guard and guide the government unity, trade, colonization. But with the reforms the activity of the commonfolk ceased through the imposed guardianship and for 200 years was replaced by governmental activity. There was much lamentable in that. //

(The Eastern question)

Our designation is to be the friend of all the peoples. *To serve them, and that way we are all the more Russian. To join all the souls of all the peoples to ourselves.*

But the reforms did not lead to imitating and copying. Great Peter was sure that we would surpass that. Educational development was needed, which consisted of knowing the worlds of other peoples, communicating with them, serving them, knowing the ancient world, the political idea was set indefinitely. Nothing new was conceived for it was there already, it did not have to be conceived again, it had only been set aside temporarily. We are bearing Orthodoxy to Europe—Orthodoxy will meet the socialists at some time. But that is not what I wish to talk about now. This is all still debatable and needs explanation—but what is not debatable is our significance for being the friend of all the national groups, the friend of people, the friend of the human mind. Why persecute the Stundists?

We will bring to the commonfolk the necessity of education *sine qua non.*

Our commonfolk are not passive. They were not as patient as [cattle] cattle. They did not even give in during the schism affair. But schismatics were servants of the tsar. The commonfolk did not want to tear the government apart with a rebellion against the landowners. What happened as a result of his doing that, not deciding it at a gathering. Feelings were peaceful among the commonfolk.

But what in the way of culture have we actually brought to the commonfolk, in your opinion: gloves, carriages.

Besides educational development, we brought science, which was developed there earlier, by the entire European *community,* and which tempted Peter so much. (In return, our country has governmental unity.) The Germans without the land, and we without the land. Why, surely we did not do this passively? No, you will say, we did this European style. If it had been European style, we would not have surrendered without a fight, we did it Russian style, recognizing ourselves as Russians. This is why I say: we returned the land as Russians. This is where the hope lies. And not in carriages and gloves.

Nature gave us awesome powers here at home and weakness when we attack.

I am not going to tell you anything about Orthodoxy [although this is all], even in comparison with the Catholicism developed by Jesuism, and with the croaking of Protestantism, but the government, but the liberation of the commonfolk with the land.

Society is built by moral precepts. You cannot bring the commonfolk anything better in the way of moral precepts (for they have Orthodoxy, and you have nothing. They are not familiar with privilege. Only science? —But science alone cannot build a society (socialism).

Humaneness. But did we really need to get humaneness from Europe? It was needed by those, like all of you, who employed the doormen and read Rousseau, it was needed by all who have become alienated, but the commonfolk did not need it. They knew how to forgive. You should read Andrey Kritsky, and that will do. //

There is dirt, but the commonfolk do not try to make their evil seem good, while we do take our evil as something good. Perhaps there are some bad things, which the commonfolk as a whole group stand for. But these are only prejudices.

The highest moral idea developed [in the We] during the entire life of the West, is advancing socialism and its ideals, and it is not possible to dispute this. But Christian truth, preserved within Orthodoxy, is higher than socialism. And at that very point we will encounter Europe, that is, the question will be resolved whether Christ will save the world or the totally opposite precept, i.e., the destruction of the will, stones into loaves.

You know, Belinsky wrote all of this—the same Belinsky that you, Avseenko, were belittling so much recently. But with Belinsky even his delusions were the truth, while with you even the truth comes out as delusion.

—Because you do not understand anything.
—But if I do not understand, why are you speaking with me so much.
—Well, I am not exactly speaking with you. Although I am addressing you, I am not speaking with you.

—They misrepresented the plot.
—Is this being fair to the author?
    —That is why I cannot even confront you and answer you.
—And in judging about intelligence, you do not think of Pushkin.
—He is writing now (with humor and concisely).
—But the reply to the *Russian M/essenger/* and then the bewilderment among the public.
—Belinsky on Tatiana.[276]
—Krestovsky being raved about.[277]
—Serfs about hatred toward the master.

—Where in Europe is this a good thing. (Picture.) Victor Hugo *Misérables.*
—The vileness of spiritualism.

Insincerity at social gatherings. (Strakhov at my place for an evening), in Prince Odoevsky, Lev Tolstoy's *Anna Karenina* etc.[278]

The commonfolk will bow before truth (even though they are depraved) and will not start a debate, while the culture will start a debate, claiming that their culture is rotten.

Culture among the commonfolk is a mystery, and at any rate, they will not resemble the cultured Mr. Avseenko, [such a] and one like him is enough the cultivated Mr. Avseenko.

The novelist of gloves, carriages, and servants.

But he will steal from me.
But how can they understand that? Obviously he will steal
(excerpt of a contradiction)
There is nothing they can bring to us. Tatiana.
You agree with Belinsky, whom you do not even know.
But you should know that Belinsky is correct, even when he is in the wrong—you have to [intell] be intelligent.
But all you have is that arrogance which always betrays the d/ullness?/ of your abilities. //

About the Kazan collection[279] *New Times,* April 8, No. 38. //
—Tacitus.
—*On the Mind and Cognition,*[280] 1st part.
—Lewes.[281]
—The Age of Alexander 1st, by Bogdanovich, by Pypin.[282]
—Literature (by Polevoy).
—by Vladim/ir/ Soloviev.[283]
—by Lassalle.[284]
—After Peter. By the historian Soloviev.[285]
—St. Augustine's Confessions.[286]
—(of Thomas à Kempis).[287]
—Zola.
—*Logic.*[288]
—Khomiakov.[289] //
Don't forget books needed: book *Common Law* by E. Yakushkin.[290]
Histoire de l'Origine des Découvertes et des Institutions Humaines. K. Ramèl—Plon.

La Chire familière et galante. Charpanter
Carlyle.
Carlyle: History of Frederick II and the revolution.[291]

—Henri Martin.[292]
—Augustin Thierry.[293]
—Prescott.[294]
—Schlözer—in Chernyshevsky's translation.[295]
—*Russia and Europe* by N. Danilevsky.[296]
—Pypin's.
—Bogdanovich's.

—Villemain, Sainte-Beuve, Taine's critical studies, Julian Schmidt, if translated.[297] //

3rd No. March.—

Literature
Provincial press and and something in the middle of nowhere.

—Write to Sonya and Elena Pavlovna.
—Go to see the Shtakenshneiders.
—To Polonsky.
—To Emilia Fedorovna.
—To Pobedonostsev.
—To Sazonovich.
—Go to the Justice's chamber.
To Pobed/onostsev/.
—Look at the children's books.
—*Govern/ment/ Herald.*
—Berezin...
—To Putsykovich.
—To Pobedonostsev.
—To the Central Administration for Press Affairs.

On the night of the 18th-19th of July, I had a dream, Anya,[298] second husband, my plot with her. Nightmare. //

To the committee for arranging the evening of music and dance at the St. P/etersburg/ meeting of artists for the benefit of needy students of the Medical and Surgical Academy the 2nd of December, 1876.

Gentlemen
Honored [by the invit] by the kind invitation of the students to the evening of music and dance, I, to my [extreme] great regret, was unable to attend, because of a sudden illness.
I regret [that] all the more because the heartfelt [to me] invitation from the students [in] and their remembering me I regard as [a great] an extraordinary honor.

With profound love and respect for Russian students
F. D/ostoevsky/ //

172

Novogorodskaya Street, house No. 9, apt. No. 28. Chernosov (near Nevsky Prospect towards the Monastery, at Konnaya, formerly Ivanov's house).

On the corner of Kirpichny Lane and the Moika, house no. 7, apt. 13, the Golovins.

Yulia Denisovna Zasetskaya, Nevsky Propsect, opposite Nikolaevskaya, house No. 100.

Elena Andreevna Shtakenshneider, on the corner of Ozerny Lane and Znamenskaya, house No.

Konst/antin/ Nik/olaevich/ Bestuzhev-Riumin, Znamenskaya, house No. 38. //

Mother on [new] by-pass No. 141, near Durdin's factory (cotton milling factory). Akulina Arefievna Eliseev—50.

Mrs. Bergman—Bolshaya Kon/naya/, house No. 6/16, 10 apt.

Anna Pavlovna Filosova. —Near Potseluev Bridge, on the Moika, house No. 94.

On the corner of Fonarny Lane and the Fontanka, house of Voronin, Mrs. Karpovich.

Kapitolina Valerianovna Nazarieva, Nikolaevskaya, No. 29, apt. 25.
Olga Afanasievna Antonova, Mokhovaya, No. 26, apt. 24.

Nazarieva, Nikolaevskaya, No. of house 29, apart. 25.

Innokenty Konstantinovich Onchukov. Corner of Nevsky and Nadezhdinskaya St., hse. of Yakovlev, No. 1/96, apt. no. 45.

Petr Nikolaevich Polevoy. Nadezhdinskaya, No. of house 7, apt. 12.

Avgusta Pavlovna Sazonovich. On corner of Fontakna and Nov Lane (between Obukhovsky and Semenovsky Bridges), house 77, apart. 32.

NB. Shpalernaya, No. 18, apt. No. 9. Vladimir Soloviev.

Vladimir Soloviev. —On corner of Gorokhovaya and the Moika, at Krasny Bridge, in Sobolev's hotel.

Sofia Aleksandrovna.
Aleksandr Nikolaevich Aksakov, Nevsky Prospect, near Malaya Morskaya, house No. 6. Gadiach.

V. I. Lamansky. 3rd Company Izmailovsky Regiment, house No. 11, apartment 4.

Khalevitskaya and Rozova. Nevsky Prospect, house No. 80, apt. No. 20.

Liubov Khristoforovna Khokhrikova, manager of the Schlesselburg Highway telegraph station.

Vs. Serg. *Soloviev.* Old Peterhof, near the rairoad station, opposite Nikolaevsky almshouse, dacha No. 7 Avenarius's.

Terty Ivanovich Filippov, Kirochnaya, house No. 17 (mailbox on the corner of Nadezhdinskaya).

Student Dolganova, Kavalergardskaya Street, house No. 6, apartment no. 9. Peska's (NB, she is asking for work, little brother and sister on her hands).

Elisey Grigorievich Levchenko—corner of Panteleimonovskaya and Liteinaya, house of Muruza, apt. No. 11.

Nevsky Pr., hse. No. 59, apt. 4. Lurie Sofia Efimovna.

Aleksey Eliseev. Marfa Alekseeva. Podolskaya Street, in Semonovsky Regiment, house of Ya. Kovalev. //

Addresses.

Nurse Prokhorovna. In 6th Company Izmailovsky Regiment, house No. 22, apart. No. 7.

Vs. Soloviev. Ofitserskaya, house No. 57, apart. 8 (on corner of Liteiny Prospect next to house with cheap apartments).

Kovalevsky (Vladimir Onufrievich) (Krukovskys NB.). On corner of 4th Row and Maly Prospect, house of Likhonin.

Polonsky. On corner of Ivanovskaya and Kabinetskaya (Vladimirskaya) house of Guro.

A. N. *Pleshcheev.* On Troitsky Lane, at five corners, house No. 27, apart. 30.

Rudin. On Grebetskaya (Yamskaya), house of Tyliakov (where the bank is), apt. No. 47.

Konstantin Ivanovich Ivanov. On Povarskaya (or on Povarsky Lane), near

Vladimirskaya, house No. 13.

Emilia Fedorovna. Petersburg Side, Sezzhenskaya Street, house of Danilov (nearer to the park, next to Borodulin's candle factory). //

Viktor Petrovich *Kliushnikov.* Nevsky Prospect, at Holy Sign, house of Kokhendorf (journal *Horizon).*

N. N. Strakhov. At Torgovoy Bridge, house of Sterligov, entrance from the Kanava, main entrance, No. apt. 19, 5th floor.

Nikolay Petrovich Vagner, on Vasiliev Island, between 12th and 13th Rows, on Bolshoy Prospect, house of Botman.

The *Shtakenshneiders.* Furshtadskaya, house No. 12, on corner of Tserkovny Lane.

Anatoly Fedorovich *Koni,* in Ministry of Justice Building on Malaya Sadovaya.

Vyborg Side, Simbirskaya Street, house of Chernaya (Chernovaya), stone building, 3rd floor, the 3rd house, not past the clinic. *Emilia Fedorovna.*

Aleksandr Fedorovich Otto. Stremianny, No. 10.

Censor Ratynsky. Nadezhdenskaya, 38.

N. A. Mombelli. Corner of Voznesensky Prospect and blind alley, house of Pal, No. 2, apt. No. 28 (2nd entrance from the alley).

House of Katner, No. 1 from Malaya Morskaya, near Isaac's. Lebedev, censor.

The dreamer.

The Grand Inquisitor and Paul.

The Grand Inquisitor with Christ.[299]

Devil was captured in Barcelona.

Privy Council, Prince D. Obol/ensky/, three stars on his suit jacket, meeting with the teacher, the affair at the police station, the crazy man running.

Idea of education for our society.
—But we ourselves have not matured enough for the idea.

—We praise ourselves for being Europeans.
—/.../
—Let us develop Orthodoxy and the freedom of the peoples.
The Greeks—Archipelago.

Debts 11th of November	75
To Pechatkin	−266 r.
To Alonkin	−425
Furniture	−140
To Vargunin	−156
	987

—How about Nad/ei/n? How many for Moscow and so forth.[300]

—Distribution to friends.

—About the merchants in the Passage.

—No. in

—Our foreign correspondence.

—On dispatch to provincial newspap/ers/.

Even the stupidity itself of some of the Alphonsine explanations increased their likelihood. //

To be an honest man is the most profitable of all.

/.../ the press will appear, but not literature.

Spirit. A non-existent fact (with a kerchief) is more significant than anything you could say, all of you together.

NOTEBOOK VI

1. Most of this notebook is taken up by notes for *A Raw Youth.* These notes were published in Russian in 1947, and translated into English in the University of Chicago Press series of Dostoevsky's notebooks for individual novels, edited by Edward Wasiolek. Thus this material is not reproduced in the present translation.

The material which remains in Notebook VI is mostly connected with Dostoevsky's editorship of *The Citizen,* a conservative weekly "newspaper-magazine" founded in 1872, and edited by Dostoevsky from the beginning of 1873 to February 1874. Dostoevsky wrote weekly political surveys, feuilletons, etc. His *Diary of a Writer* was a regular feature, and he accepted regular help from the arch-conservative K.P. Pobedonostsev (later Procurator of the Holy Synod) and his old friend Strakhov.

2. The earliest date in this notebook, apparently the time Dostoevsky learned he would be the new editor of *The Citizen.*

3. This and further notes are related to a polemic about Slavophiles and Westernizers, Christianity and socialism, among *The Citizen, The Messenger of Europe,* and *Notes of the Fatherland.*

4. An allusion to Alexander Herzen. The editors of the Russian edition of these notebooks provide volume and page references (to the 1926-30 edition of Dostoevsky's works) whenever Dostoevsky's notebook comments were later used in the actual *Diary of a Writer*—as in this case. Russian readers will want to use these references for further study and comparison of Dostoevsky's ideas. The English reader can only use Boris Brasol's incomplete translation of the *Diary of a Writer* (New York: Braziller, 1954) for comparison of his private formulations to his public ones.

5. A response to negative criticism (in 1873) of Dostoevsky's *The Devils* by populist critic N.K. Mikhailovsky and others who called his favorite heroes madmen.

6. Kirillov is one of the major characters in *The Devils.*

7. *The Devils* was partially based on the revolutionary cells set up by S.G. Nechaev. (See *The Citizen,* No. 50, 1873, for further development of this topic.)

8. Nikolai K. Mikhailovsky (1842-1904), a sociologist, literary critic, all-authoritative expounder of populist and socialist ideas. His best known critical essay is a survey of Dostoevsky called *A Cruel Talent* (1882).

Here as in Volume One of *The Unpublished Dostoevsky* the words *narod* (people, commonfolk), *narodnyi* ("of the people," national), and *natsional'nyi* (national) present problems for the English translator.

9. Moscow address of V. Pribytkova, a minor writer.

10. Famous case where a provincial governor's hunting party ruined peasant fields and animals. The party was stopped by peasant force, and he started a campaign of vengence on them. A young prosecutor began a case against the governor, but he was acquitted and given a dinner of honor.

11. A.N. Pypin. See Note 25, Notebook IV.

12. The 200th birthday celebration of Peter the Great.

13. A Caucasian religious sect—whose virtually illiterate interpreters of holy writing won a following, which, along with the Protestant Stundist success, made Dostoevsky wonder about the state of Russian clergy.

14. Letters praising women's philanthropy by the Archpriest Avvakum (17th century) had just been published.

15. There was a Petersburg Art Exhibit in early 1873, and Dostoevsky wrote against

tendentiousness in art. See *Diary of a Writer*, No. 13 (1873).

16. A critique by V. P. Burenin (Jan. 1873) of N. Nekrasov's long poem *Russian Women* (in *Notes of the Fatherland*), about the wives of the Decembrists. See *The Diary of a Writer*, No. 13 (1873) for Dostoevsky's detailed comments on this.

17. Bismarck and Emperor Wilhelm visited Petersburg, March 1873.

18. An 1873 court case in which an actress daughter refused to help her impoverished mother and brother; the court rejected the mother's petition.

19. This and other statements from the entries here are developed in the *Diary of a Writer*.

20. Dostoevsky's anti-Catholicism is well known—as in *The Idiot, The Brothers Karamazov.*

21. No. 10 contains "a certain person's half-letter," (see *Diary of a Writer*, ed. Brasol, p. 67), a rejoinder to critics of *The Devils.* The comments in this entry of the notebooks are used in the half-letter.

22. V. G. Avseenko, a liberal critic.

23. Nikolai I. Kostomarov, the historian. See Note 10, Notebook II.

24. See Turgenev's "Bezhin Meadow" *(A Hunter's Notes).* Also *Diary of a Writer*, No. 10 (1873).

25. A note to explain what *The Citizen* would be with Dostoevsky as editor.

26. Dostoevsky apparently had special responsibility for the sections he says are under his editorship.

27. Dostoevsky's *Diary of a Writer* started with No. 1 (1873) of *The Citizen.* Where he says "I" or "mine" below he is often referring to this. The "Current Life" section was written by Dostoevsky and others.

28. Pamfil Danilovich Yurkevich (1827-74), Dean of History—Philology Faculty, Univ. of Moscow, engaged in polemics against Chernyshevsky in the 1860s.

29. M. P. Pogodin was a regular contributor to *The Citizen*, writing on Slavophilism in *No. 9.*

30. Vasily Ivanovich Kelsiev (1835-1872), after a complicated intellectual life, had become a fervent Slavophile, an expert on schismatics *(raskolniki),* possibly part model for Shatov in *The Devils. The Citizen* published a necrology and, later, unpublished works by Kelsiev.

31. *The Citizen* published several stories and novels by its founder-publisher, V. P. Meshchersky.

32. Comedies by A. F. Pisemsky ("Intrigues") and D. Kishensky in 1873.

33. Several women writers appeared—or were scheduled to appear—in Dostoevsky's paper: N. P. Shalikova, Kokhanovskaya, S. M. Loboda, and V. I. Pribytkova.

34. Terty Ivanovich Filippov, a member of the editorial staff of the paper from its inception. His writing for it was mostly on church subjects.

35. Strakhov had already contributed to the paper before Dostoevsky took over.

36. Possibly Vsevolod Soloviev; more likely Dostoevsky intended to make Nikolai Ivanovich Soloviev (1831-74) editorial secretary—he had been Dostoevsky's collaborator on *The Epoch.*

37. One I. Bogdanov had submitted a sketch "At the Station."

38. In No. 4 (1873) Dostoevsky wrote a review of an article in *Talk* on "Our Monasteries."

39. Several issues of the paper contained letters from women.

40. A brochure by Rostislav Fadeev, "Russian Society in the Present and Future (What Shall We Be?)."

41. Pseudonym of Alexei Sergeevich Suvorin (1833-1911), one of the most influential

Russian journalists and publishers in the last part of the 19th century.

42. *The Story of the Travelings in Russia, Moldavia, Turkey and The Holy Lands of the Monk Parfeny of the Afonsk Holy Hills Monastery.* One of Dostoevsky's favorite books, taken abroad in 1867 and used for various scenes in *The Devils, A Raw Youth* and *The Brothers Karamazov.*

43. *Selected Saints Lives* (1861-62) 11 issues of which Dostoevsky owned and a new edition of which was announced in 1873.

44. *The Citizen* was involved in a polemic over N. A. Polevoi's *Russian Folk Tales.*

45. Dostoevsky's Siberian notebook, published in 1936. *Zven'ia,* VI.

46. Henry Stanley. Simultaneously with the announcement of *The Devils* in the *St. Petersburg News* there was an announcement of Stanley's book on how he found Livingstone—an illustrated translation of which was to be published in 1873.

47. Pope Pius IX published one in 1864; possibly Dostoevsky is referring to new 1870 proclamations on Papal infallibility.

48. Ivan Fedorovich Gorbunov (1831-95), an actor, raconteur and writer with whom Dostoevsky often performed at public readings.

49. Apparently someone reminding the newly-appointed Dostoevsky that her submission was already in the editorial office.

50. An excerpt from Evgeny Salias's novel on *The Pugachev Revolt,* published in No. 12 (1873).

51. *The Citizen,* No. 12 (1873) contained a letter-report by a Russian tourist who visited the Vienna Exhibition of 1873.

52. Dostoevsky rewrote and published a humorous sketch by I. S. Gensler in No. 10 (1873).

53. K. P. Pobedonostsev's "From London" appeared anonymously in No. 27 (1873). A current news item was the visit of the Shah of Persia to London, with attendant anti-Russian sentiment. All of Pobedonostsev's many contributions to *The Citizen* were printed anonymously, usually with the signature "ZZ."

54. N. Konstantinov, "Panslavism and the Greeks." the *Russian Messenger* (1873).

55. *The Diary of a Writer.*

56. S. Maksimov, author of a book ("Grain-sack..."), was told by Dostoevsky's opponents to go write for conservatives like Dostoevsky.

57. *A Guide to Calesthenics* by K. A. Shmidt (1873).

58. An essay in No. 13-14 by R. Popov, "Home Industries and Artel Organization of the People's Work."

59. Reference to announcement in *The Voice* of public readings and cheap editions of the authors mentioned further—and a letter about high mortality in orphanages.

60. Dostoevsky returned to I. Bogdanov a study called "Carpenters."

61. Last line of a poem by L. Papkova, published (and rewritten) by D. in No. 24.

62. An essay by Putsykovich in No. 25.

63. Dostoevsky printed instead a report on reforms concerning private lawyers.

64. Continuation of T. I. Filippov's article on "The Petersburg Society of Lovers of Spiritual Enlightenment" (started in No. 22).

65. "Report on the Vienna Exhibition," No. 20-23.

66. Nothing by Kelsiev was in No. 24.

67. D. D. Kishensky's "No Good Comes if You Drink the Dregs."

68. Poems by Nemirovich-Danchenko, S. Konstantinov, and L. Papkova were printed—

and laughed at by Dostoevsky's opponents. Dostoevsky often rewrote the especially bad poems himself.

69. "The Khiva Campaign."

70. Kishensky's play was (the author said) written for the commonfolk theater, and he was worried lest the censorship imagine it as a call for the commonfolk to attack merchants. He assured Dostoevsky this was not true at all, that he firmly believed the Russian people could have no connection with the Western International.

71. Dostoevsky's own pieces "A Fix in the Village Izmailov," "Wall to Wall," and "The Story of Father Nil" appeared in this section.

72. No. 25 came out June 18, 1873, with Dostoevsky's own analysis of Kishensky's play and the sketch on Khiva, probably prepared by Dostoevsky.

73. Three poems by Nemirovich-Danchenko—later of Moscow Art Theater fame.

74. A lead article on Prussian military training—and a *Times* report on the visit of former Spanish Queen Isabella to the Vatican—and the remark that the Vatican would now look to democracies for help, not monarchs.

75. *The Citizen,* No. 30, contained an article on Bobrovsky's book on Russian cadet academy education.

76. *The Citizen* argued the bravery of Russian soldiers was best testified to by this hostile Hungarian's comments.

77. Report on the Shah's visit to Liverpool and Manchester; after England he traveled to Russia—all of this reported in Dostoevsky's paper.

78. A Polish miller who sold his wife to a 65-year-old man. The court could find no appropriate law in the Codex, but sentenced them to almost five months in prison.

79. Refers to a polemic over Professor Katkov's views on the structure of Russian universities.

80. A court case against a monk, Father Nil.

81. In the summer of 1873 Meshchersky left Dostoevsky to handle all the financial affairs of the paper, including paying contributors—which led to much unpleasantness for him. The normal essay and fiction rate was 5 kopeks per line, except for Strakhov who got 7.

82. Nemirovich-Danchenko was then paid for all his previous contributions; he had complained bitterly—and relations between Dostoevsky and him remained bad.

83. For editing the issue.

84. I. Yu. Nekrasov.

85. Strakhov reviewed a Russian translation of Charles Darwin's *The Origin of the Species* in No. 29.

86. For his article on Bobrovsky's book (see Note 75 above) Dostoevsky and he soon had a serious falling out ideologically

87. See Note 21, Notebook IV.

88. Lev Tolstoi.

89. A line from popular verses Dostoevsky could first have heard at a factory after his exile: "A marvelous country across Altay/ Threw an elbow into China."

90. Dostoevsky's neologism: *darvaldaia.*

91. See Note 40.

92. Golyadkin in *The Double.*

93. Apparently the polemic on education of the commonfolk and different needs for different locales.

94. Nikolai S. Mordvinov (1754-1845), an important government official.

95. M. M. Speransky (1772-1839), statesman, advisor to the Tsar.

96. Puns on Tolstoy's name: *zatolsteet, zatolstel.*

97. A polemic with Fadeev's brochure which said technical education was essential to Russia now.

98. A new text of Lermontov's play *Masquerade* was published in *Russian Past (Russkaia starina),* along with notes telling a great many new facts about the circumstances of the duel in which he died in 1841.

99. Pushkin had his reservations, but wrote a great deal about Peter—including his *History of Peter the Great.*

100. Dostoevsky persistently misinterpreted Pushkin all through his career, particularly his story "The Stationmaster" (one of the *Belkin Tales,* 1830), which Dostoevsky mistakenly saw as a philanthropic tale.

101. Dostoevsky is making a case for his side here, and with Gogol it is more plausible than with Pushkin; see especially Gogol's *Selected Passages from a Correspondence with Friends* (1847), which, however, Dostoevsky had ridiculed in *The Village of Stepanchikovo.*

102. One of the main figures in the Decembrist Uprising (1825).

103. See Note 40.

104. An article by E. Markov in *The Voice* (Sept. 1875) on the young generation of the seventies and their movement "to the people."

105. (Dresden Madonna. A copy of Holbein the Younger's madonna (1525-26) was in Dresden.

106. A long "poem" about Christ. In 1877 Dostoevsky returned to this idea; in the Bible which belonged to him these words are marked: "He was there in the wilderness for forty days, being tempted by the devils." (Mark I, 12).

107. Dostoevsky considered S. M. Soloviev's book on Peter (publication noted in *The Citizen,* No. 1, 1873) an idealization. Dostoevsky's negative attitude to Peter is repeatedly expressed in the notebooks.

108. A lead article on the success of people who moved from the Ukraine to Siberia; report on the failure of other resettlement efforts and need for special institutions to manage resettlement.

109. Published in 1869 by Popov, an old friend of Pobedonostsev.

110. Dostoevsky's wife's younger brother, a successful landowner-farmer.

111. V. P. Pechatkin, a bookseller who handled editions of Dostoevsky's novels.

112. G. F. Kozhanchikov, owner of a large bookstore and distributorship. He sold, on consignment, *The Devils* and *Notes from the House of the Dead,* getting a 30% discount from Dostoevsky.

NOTEBOOK VII

1. The statement in the first paragraph of Note 1, Notebook VI applies to Notebook VII as well.

2. On February 26, 1873 Dostoevsky wrote M. P. Pogodin: "Perhaps you've heard that I'm an epileptic! On the average I have one attack per month, and that's the way it's been for many years, since Siberia, the difference being that for the last two years to get back to normal after a fit it takes me *five* days, not three as it used to for almost twenty years. And now a strange thing—it's been almost five months since my last attack."

In January 1873 Dostoevsky discussed his sickness with Vsevolod Soloviev, who reported:

He told me he had an attack not long ago.

"My nerves have been upset since childhood," he said. "Two years before Siberia, during my various literary unpleasantnesses and squabbles, a kind of strange and un- bearably tormenting nervous sickness started. I cannot describe those disgusting sensations; but I remember them graphically; it often seemed to me that I was dying, here it was— real death came, and then went away. I was also afraid of lethargic sleep. And a strange thing—as soon as I was arrested, suddenly all traces of my disgusting sickness disappeared; never again, neither on the way, nor in prison in Siberia, did I even experience it again; I suddenly became robust, strong, fresh, calm... But during imprisonment my first attack of epilepsy occurred, and since then it has never left me. Everything that happened to me before that first attack, the smallest events of my life, every face I had seen, every- thing I read and heard I remember in the finest detail. Everything that started after the first attack I very often forget, sometimes I totally forget people whom I knew well; I forget their faces. I've forgotten everything I wrote after imprisonment; when I was finishing *The Devils* I had to read everything from the beginning, because I had even forgotten the names of the characters..."

Dostoevsky's younger brother reported that when he was young Dostoevsky would leave notes saying he might fall into lethargic sleep today, so don't bury me for such-and- such number of days. —A similar fear was one of the main ones expressed by Gogol in his "Testament."

3. In the beginning of April 1874 Dostoevsky was feeling overworked by *The Citizen* and started calculations to make the *Diary of a Writer* an independent publication—which he did a year and a half later.

4. *A Raw Youth.*

5. See Dostoevsky's letter to his wife, July 1/13, 1874. In his letters to her he describes many talks with children—and she helped him collect similar material.

6. One of the most hotly-debated subjects of the seventies was education for the common- folk, and considerable attention was given to it by *The Citizen.*

7. This is the first outline for *The Brothers Karamazov.*

NOTEBOOK VIII
(1874-1875)

1. The statement in the first paragraph of Note 1, Notebook VI applies to Notebook VIII as well.

2. In St. *Petersburg News,* No. 117 (1873) article on J. Beavington Arkinson's *An Art Tour to Northern Capitals of Europe* (London, 1873).

3. A report on the capricious birching of a young peasant girl by order of a low court.

4. A murder which was reported in *The Kievan.*

5. *The Citizen;* No. 23 (June 10, 1874) contained an article on Prussian government measures against the church. The author, probably with Dostoevsky's approval, notes that Bismarck's measures go against the tradition of state-church relations.

6. Dostoevsky wanted to visit a prison colony of juvenile criminals. The matter con- tinued to interest him, and with his friend A. F. Koni, he did make a visit in December 1875.

7. Subscribers to Dostoevsky's paper who also ordered *The Idiot* directly paid no postage.

8. In 1873 Dostoevsky—with his wife's capable help—became his own publisher. The first announcement, for *The Devils,* of such sale was in 1873. The Dostoevskys continued to print and privately market his books until the end of his life—by which time he managed to

get out of debt.

9. Apparently an advance from Nekrasov of 2000 for promising to publish his new novel in *Notes of the Fatherland.*

NOTEBOOK IX

1. Dostoevsky began this notebook in September, and used it regularly from November 1875 through April 1876, primarily for his *Diary of a Writer* (January-March 1876).

2. Belyaev's (1810-73) book was published in 1859 in Moscow.

3. The lead article in *The Voice* was on the attitudes of the Russian and foreign press to revolutionary propaganda, with references to Marx, Bebel, Liebknecht and Lassalle.

4. The paper reported a speech by Disraeli and wondered whether only English interests (not Russian, Turkish, etc.) lay in Egypt and the Mideast.

5. One of two unsigned letter-articles by a so-called former Russian teacher who said revolutionary propaganda was rampant in Russian schools, blaming in part Katkov and Leontiev's *Russian News* for confusing the real issues of education.

6. Mikhail G. Chernyaev (1828-99), a general, conqueror in Central Asia, publisher of the conservative newspaper *The Russian World.* In 1876 made commander of the Serbian Army—which soon capitulated to Turkey. Dostoevsky knew him personally and wrote about him several times in the *Diary of a Writer.*

7. Khlestakov—the empty-headed, prattling hero of Gogol's *The Inspector General.*

8. Andrei G. Filonov (1831-1908), pedagogue, defender of old-time classical education who called on students to betray each other to the supervisors.

9. Vsevolod V. Krestovsky (1840-95), fiction writer, former contributor to *Time,* author of anti-nihilist novels.

10. Count E. A. Salias de Turnemir (1842-1902), a historical novelist. See Note 50, Notebook VI.

11. Vasily G. Avseenko (1842-1913), in addition to being a critic, wrote fiction on high society, published in Katkov's the *Russian Messenger.* Dostoevsky often polemicizes with him in the *Diary of a Writer.*

12. Rostislav Fadeev (1824-83) a conservative, monarchist, general and social observor. See Notebook VI, Note 40.

13. The papers reported on the "Ovsyannikov case" in November and December 1875. S. T. Ovsyannikov, a millionaire flour merchant, was accused of burning down a Petersburg mill belonging to another millionaire—but rented by Ovsyannikov, who stood to gain a great deal from the arson. He was deprived of rights and sent to Siberia. Mass bribery of officials, although uncovered at the trial, was not fully investigated. The trial of such a notable individual was a major social and journalistic event.

14. Rostislav Fadeev's proposed confirming nobility on rich merchants (in his book *Russian Society in the Past and Present,* 1874).

15. F. M. Reshetnikov (1841-71), an important "plebian novelist," author of *The People of Podlipnoe,* of whose last days the poet Nekrasov had told Dostoevsky in 1875 during conferences on the publication of *A Raw Youth.*

16. Allusion to verses by Dennis Davydov: "Just look: our Mirabeau/ Lashes old Gavrila/ Across his whiskers and face/ For a rumpled jabot."

17. Yukhotsky—hero of a high-society novel by Avseenko, entitled *The Milky Way,* curdled by Dostoevsky in the April 1876 issue of *Diary of a Writer.*

18. Refers to articles on poet A. K. Tolstoi and his death, including a letter from Turgenev on the subject.

19. *The Voice* reported on these November 9, and Dostoevsky visited a colony for juvenile criminals in December (see *Diary of a Writer,* January 1876).

20. The issue contained reports on George Sand's *Flamarande* and *Les deux freres,* and A. Wynter's *The Borderlands of Insanity and Other Allied Papers* (London, 1875), one of the main points of which is the thinness of the barrier separating sanity from insanity.

21. The names (of some high officials) derive from the Russian verb "to suck."

22. Turgenev. In *The Devils,* portrayed as Karmazinov, Turgenev is made to say the water-pipes of Karlsruhe are dearer to him than anything in Russia.

23. Cited in No. 287 (Nov. 1875) of *The Moscow News,* quoting memoirs about Lamartine.

24. The Simbirsk monument to the great historian and writer was unveiled in 1875.

25. Two papers ironically reported that a Moscow intellectual turned medium (apparently M. Katkov) had been in contact with Gogol's ghost, who was dictating to him Part II of *Dead Souls* as it was in the burned manuscript.

26. "There will be trouble and distress for every human being who is an evil-doer, for the Jew first and for the Greek also."

27. The subscription price was lowered five rubles.

28. The fortieth anniversary of Turgenev's literary career was noted in 1876. Dostoevsky did not send the telegram apparently.

29. In Russian, "vykormok" (a baby fed by someone else, not its own mother).

30. The conservative paper, compared Russian radical thought to Dostoevsky's hero—a creature ashamed of its own mother (i.e., Russia) and chasing after Frenchmen.

31. The report that the Austrian government had cut off food to 65,000 refugee Herzogovinians was denied.

32. The report that 10 clergymen who had officially refused to teach theology in schools; the censor wouldn't allow Dostoevsky to publish comments on smoking priests.

33. The Odessa Committee of the Council of Trade reported that partly because of competition from the United States, Russia would no longer be a primary factor in the international grain market.

Lemoin wrote that if the English insisted on having Suez, what would keep Russia out of Constantinople, etc.

34. A major part of Mikhail Lermontov's novel, *A Hero of Our Time* (1840).

35. Report on England and Suez.

The question of compulsory education was reported to be under serious discussion in government circles.

36. Poretsky quoted examples of bad style.

37. In Russian, "stoloverchenie"—reference to the "table-turning" of spiritualism.

38. The brochure entitled *Pro Nihilo* was an attack on Bismarck.

39. See Note 13 above.

40. *The Voice* (November 29, 1875) reported a 23-year-old man had wounded himself seriously, and a note was found in his pocket saying: "I have already killed more than one person and ruined many; I am a robber and cannot go on living in this world. Afanasiev."

41. The paper reported that Russia supported the uprising and demanded freedom for all Christian provinces of the Ottoman Empire.

42. The Belgian paper had reported a major change in European territorial holdings was

in the works, and that Russian diplomats were playing a large role in this. The paper was violently criticized for this by many other papers in Europe.

43. An agency of the Russian government gave ten thousand rubles to the victims in the uprisings in Bosnia and Herzegovina. Dostoevsky believed therefore that the government was more energetic in its help than the Slavic Committee.

44. The vacuum in the vaults was partly to thwart thieves.

A midwife named Kukolevskaya had come to Petersburg from the deep provinces to do socially useful work. A doctor, whose mistress she became, stole her money and threw her out into the street.

45. G. R. LaRoche, "Music Sketches." *The Voice,* (Nov. 26, 1875), on A. Fominitsyn's opera *Sardanapalus.*

46. A. S. Suvorin. Dostoevsky states Suvorin's point of view.

47. An official named Limberg got drunk and started bothering a woman teacher named Morozova and her friend on the street—and was beaten up by a college math student named Kovalsky. A policeman testified, however, that he "found Limberg lying on the ground, and Morozova was sitting on top of him and beating him, along with Kovalsky." The judge sentenced her to four days arrest for "indecent posture and disturbing the peace." Limberg and Kovalsky got five days, the former fined twenty rubles, the latter ten.

48. The first of a series of entries for a planned essay-attack on Turgenev, whose Westernizing liberalism was anathema to Dostoevsky. Their long history of enmity is well known; Turgenev considered Dostoevsky unbalanced, and Dostoevsky pilloried Turgenev in the form of Karmazinov in *The Devils.* Dostoevsky was especially critical of Turgenev's novel *Smoke,* where in Chapter XIV the hero Potugin makes fun of the Russian folk epics, particularly one about Churilo (Churila) Plenkovich.

49. Turgenev and his life-long love Pauline Viardot translated a number of works of Russian literature, including Gogol's "Tale of terror" "Viy" (from *Mirgorod,* 1835).

50. An allusion to Potugin's words about being a "samorodok" in Chapter XIV of *Smoke.*

51. Allusion to a description of 18th-century clothes in Casanova's memoirs, an excerpt of which was published in the premier issue of Dostoevsky's magazine *Time* in 1861.

52. Alludes to Potugin in Chapter XIV, talking to a young man, a nihilist, about monogamy and the descent of man.

53. "The Impolite Koronat" was a story by M. E. Saltykov-Shchedrin in *Notes of the Fatherland* (No. 11, 1875) as one of the *Wellintentioned Speeches.* An excerpt from *A Raw Youth* was published in the same issue. The attitudes of Dostoevsky and Saltykov-Shchedrin to the problem of education were—as usual—exactly opposite.

54. " 'The peasants are coming and they are carrying axes,' lines probably invented by some earlier liberal landowner"—Dostoevsky put this in the mouth of Stepan Verkhovensky in *The Devils.* The words "the landowners suffocated us for a long time" are the beginning of a revolutionary poem.

55. L. Stechkina, a new woman writer, publicly protested serious editorial cuts made in her story "The First Storm" published in the *Russian Messenger* in 1875.

56. Directed at Turgenev.

57. See Notebook I, Note 11.

58. A story by A. Nezlobin called "The Circle—From the Notes of a Social-Democrat," a negative portrayal of revolutionary youth.

59. A brief necrology of M. P. Pogodin.

60. Chapter XVIII.

61. Litvinov in *Smoke,* Chapter XXIV, talking to Irina.

62. "My dear sir" ("Milostivyi gosudar' moi") is used several times in Turgenev's story "The Dog."

63. Gubarev—a negative character in *Smoke.* Another negative character says women can save themselves only by using sewing machine and artels.

64. The "Unknown Person" ("Neznakomets") was A. S. Suvorin's pseudonym. In the feuilleton noted he attacks Ovsyannikov's defense attorneys.

65. Actually, Dostoevsky meant Stanza VI of the Dedication of Byron's *Don Juan.* See following entries.

66. The judge in the Morozova case. See Note 47 above.

67. In Chapter XIV of *Smoke* Potugin says Russia would have nothing to lose if everything they invented disappeared from the earth. He had visited the Crystal Palace of the London Exhibition—with its display of all man's most sophisticated inventions. Dostoevsky's attack on the Crystal Palace, as a symbol, is well known (see *Notes from the Underground*).

68. Lt. Pirogov is a bland and cowardly character from Gogol's "Nevsky Prospect" (1835).

69. *Smoke,* Chapter XXV, Irina is given a seat. A. S. Menshikov, former Commander-in-Chief, was sent as ambassador to Turkey by Nikolai I in 1853.

70. Dostoevsky's daughter Lyubov (1869-1926).

71. A large article-ad on Volf's bookstore appeared in this issue. And the defense at the Ovsyannikov trial protested negative press coverage.

72. Maria Tebrikova (1835-1917) was a writer and leader of the women's rights movement of the 70s.

73. For Dostoevsky pride was a great sin—and he judged Pushkin and Pushkin's heroes on a scale of pride. See Dostoevsky's "Pushkin Speech" in *Diary of a Writer* (August 1880).

74. An essay in *The Russian Messenger* (No. 11, 1875) quotes Plato saying, "Tyranny comes only from democracy, not from other forms of government, for extreme freedom is reborn as the strongest and most unrelieved slavery." Dostoevsky liked the thought.

75. The polemic comments directed at N. K. Mikhailovsky probably result from personal encounters in 1875 when *A Raw Youth* was appearing in *Notes of the Fatherland.*

76. Eliseev's suggestions were in a piece on reasons for the departure of seminarians to regular universities.

77. August von Kotzebue (1761-1819), popular German dramatist.

78. Suvorin is not quoted exactly, but the gist of his view is given by Dostoevsky.

79. Refers to the large fee taken by Spasovich for defending insurance company interests in the Ovsyannikov trial.

80. Probably A. A. Saburov, a high government official.

81. One of the main leaders of the 1825 Decembrist uprising, for which he was hanged.

82. To the Russian envoy. See Note 69.

83. See Chapter I of *Smoke.*

84. It contained a report on the meeting of a Russian church group discussing closer relations between the Catholic and Orthodox Churches.

85. The conflict between French republican parties was a matter of great interest to Dostoevsky. The voting results were reported by telegram.

86. A student ran an ad here asking for work as a doorman.

87. The lead article reported Gentry rights were broadened—and government service made even less a requirement.

D. I. Mendeleev reported his colleagues' work showed spiritualism to be totally without basis.

88. Suvorin said this apropos of Pogodin's death.

89. Rurik, Sineus and Truvor—all ancient founders and rulers of Russia.

90. Suvorin ridiculed Klokachev (see Notes 47 and 66). Morozova's husband wrote the judge demanding he apologize to his wife; the judge gave the letter to the police and claimed he was being threatened with a duel. The Mayor ignored the judge's complaint.

91. Dostoevsky quotes from a translation of Aristotle *(Politics,* III, 5, 4) appearing in *The Russian Messenger* (No. 11, 1875).

92. Suvorin said Volf could be among the leading publishers for children.

93. See Note 48 above.

94. A paraphrase ("seminarian" replacing "bourgeois") of two lines from Pushkin's "Genealogy of My Hero."

95. In an essay on novels by Trollope and Sheller-Mikhailov, Soloviev used ideas from Dostoevsky's *A Raw Youth*—and praised Dostoevsky very, very highly as artist and social observer.

96. An article which said the case was good for shedding light on many hidden and un-hidden problems of Russian society—and the Russian court system. It criticized the role of the press—which wrote too lightly and prejudicially about the trial and its principals in progress.

97. The *Voronezh Telegraph* reported three monks had been accused of murdering a girl named Vereshchagin.

98. During a robbery a young relative of the rich victim killed a woman cook—and was in turn killed with the same crowbar by his comrades, who were afraid he would betray them. They were not found.

99. Skabichevsky published an article in No. 10 (1875) of *Notes of the Fatherland,* part of which reexamined Turgenev's famous piece analyzing the two types.

100. Dostoevsky described the children's party at the Club of Artists in *Diary of a Writer.* (Jan. 1876).

101. An ironic and imprecise quote of a character in Gogol's play about a play "Departure from the Theater."

102. Title of a successful comedy (1875) by N. Potekhin.

103. That is "Scratch a Russian and you'll find a Tatar."

104. Suvorin was extremely scornful of the spirits called up by mediums—and the whole spiritualism fad.

105. Suvorin quotes Ya. P. Polonsky's verses on the new devils to this effect. Compare this whole entry to Dostoevsky's January 1876 *Diary of a Writer* (Chapter III) on spiritualism.

106. David Friedrich Strauss (1808-74), German theologian and philosopher who tried to prove Bible history mythical.

107. Orlov—a prisoner described by Dostoevsky in *Notes from the House of the Dead* (Part I, Chapter 4).

108. Dostoevsky discussed courts and trials in special detail with his friend A. F. Koni. M. E. Kovalevsky was a court reformer, founder of a juvenile detention farm.

109. Marie Edme Patrice Maurice de MacMahon (1808-93), Marshal of France and second president of the third republic.

110. Potekhin, a defense attorney in the Ovsyannikov case, protested the way he was being treated in the press, especially by Suvorin.

111. Sylvio—romantic hero of Pushkin's story "The Shot" (1830). *A Hero of Our Time*—Lermontov's novel, whose hero Pechorin can be placed in the same category with Sylvio.

112. Eduard Kotlubai (1822-79), a Polish historian.

113. No. 358 reported on shady money collections from peasants, and on a priest who shot himself—after his superiors had ignored clear warnings.

114. Gaius Gracchus (153-121), sponsored changes from aristocratic to democratic rule.

115. In the second edition of P. N. Polevoi's *History of Russian Literature* (1874).

116. The Society was celebrating its tenth year—with much publicity and support of the Tsar. See *Diary of a Writer* (Jan. 1876, Chapter III).

117. The state courier who lashed a horse—when Dostoevsky was a child in 1837—is immortalized in Raskolnikov's horse-beating dream, and described in *Diary of a Writer,* trans. Brasol, p. 184 ff.

118. Hero of the philanthropic story (of that title) about peasant life, by D. Grigorovich.

119. *The Last Day of a Condemned Man.*

120. Tacitus, *Annales,* I, 22-23. Vibulenus causes mutiny by histrionic lies about his brother being killed.

121. Dostoevsky had three editions of Tacitus in his library, one in Russian, one in French, and this one: Taciti Opera, ex recens. G. Ch. Crolini, editio secunda, curante F. Ch. Exter. Biponti, 1792. 4 volumes.

122. He has in mind Kalika Ivanishche, a character from an epic folk song *(bylina)* about Ilya Muromets.

123. *The Voice* blasted Olga Shcherbinskaya's *Reading for Children* (1875).

124. Dostoevsky was rather hostile to Lermontov—who was quite ugly.

125. See Note 68 above.

126. Start of a Sevastopol song, partly written by Leo Tolstoy, first published by Herzen in 1857.

127. F. Rückert's poem *Des fremden Kindes heiliger Christ,* which Dostoevsky used for his story "A Little Boy at Christ's Christmas Tree."

128. A Russian State Councillor donated one silver kopeck for a monument to Lermontov in Piatigorsk—and entered his name in the donation book.

Thersites—an ugly, foul-mouthed mythological fellow who rails at Agamemnon in Book II of the *Iliad.*

129. There was a troop train wreck near Odessa in which 120 men were injured (3 killed). The papers were calling for setting of responsibility.

130. Viktor F. Golubev, director of the Orlov-Vitebsk Railroad had ordered a car cleared for his own use—and the Russian Minister of People's Education was thrown off—after which Golubev publicly humiliated himself before the Minister. This was described by Suvorin in a feuilleton(1873)—which Golubev labeled slander. But Suvorin won in court.

131. In a Samara district court several peasants were tried for disinterring and driving a stake through the body of a woman who was reputedly a witch—they thought she was causing misfortunes in their village. They were released.

132. A. A. Grigoriev's poem "Art and Truth. Elegy—Ode—Satire" juxtaposed Shakespeare and Ostrovsky's "truths." Apparently Dostoevsky had a very negative opinion of Ostrovsky's *Wolves and Sheep* (1875).

133. A. F. Gusev (1842), professor in the Kazan Theological Academy, author of turgid religious essays.

134. I. N. Berezin, *Russian Encyclopedic Dictionary* (St. P., 1875). Dostoevsky's critique of the entry on himself went into the *Diary of a Writer.* See Brasol, pp. 196-97.

135. "On Educating the Commonfolk," *Notes of the Fatherland,* No. 9 (1874).

136. The reasons why Dostoevsky published *A Raw Youth* in the normally antipathetic *Notes of the Fatherland.* This was arranged by Nekrasov, probably knowing Dostoevsky would be favorably inclined after breaking with *The Citizen.*

137. In 1875 in Leipzig E. L. Kasparovich published the first collection of secret documents and official material connected with the Petrashevsky Circle, entitled *The Society for Propaganda in 1847.*

138. See Dostoevsky's story "The Peasant Marey" (1876).

139. Hang Belinsky's portrait, that is. An allusion to Nekrasov's lines about portraits of Gogol and Belinsky in *Who Can Live Well in Russia.*

140. According to Russians, suicide forced by drawing lots.

141. Lines from a poem by D. Averkiev in 1875.

142. In Semeonov three men and a peasant woman killed two old ladies to rob them; they performed a religious burial service so they wouldn't be haunted by their ghosts. Pavlusha—see Note 98.

The Vyatka suit involved some peasants' case against Kalinin who had illegally grabbed their land—but troops were used to put down the peasant disturbance which followed.

143. Topics covered: French National Assembly struggles, Disraeli and Gladstone in England, unification of Italy and protests of the Pope, upcoming presidential elections in the United States and the centennial of independence, the Europeanization of Japan.

144. Near the Aral Sea Russian troops under Skokelev massacred two thousand locals while losing one man. Presumably this pleased Dostoevsky.

145. K. P. Kaufman (1818-82) commanding general in Turkestan.

146. A train wreck on the Odessa Railroad killed almost 200 of 400 new recruits, causing public outcry for something to be done about the railroad companies.

147. K. N. Leontiev (1831-91) was still to write his most influential political works.

N. Ya. Danilevsky (1822-85), creator of "scientific Slavophilism," published *Russia and Europe* in 1869, developing a theory of mutually watertight civilizations—Slavdom being not necessarily better than, but certainly different than the West.

148. A report that two children had been asphyxiated on a train.

149. Dostoevsky calls "vuiki" women who say "vui..." (i.e., French *oui*) badly.

150. Peter Grigoriev, Alexandrinsky Theater actor, author of many vaudevilles.

151. A very negative review of Shcherbinskaya's book, especially the story "Kitty Cat," and an attack on Volf.

152. A report on scandals and fistfights on a holiday in Moscow.

153. Chichikov—hero of Gogol's *Dead Souls.* Skvoznik-Dmukhanovsky—the Mayor in *The Inspector General.*

154. In the entry—reaction to reports that the Minister of Transport was angry about a train-wreck, a railway official had dragged a woman off a train, the theft of 184,254 rubles from the Church official by a peasant.

155. Paraphrase of the Kabala on a bookman, in Russian *nav'iuchennyi knigami chelovek.*

156. Published in 1848.

157. The poet Tyutchev told Dostoevsky that *Crime and Punishment* was superior to Hugo's *Les Miserables.* See Dostoevsky's letter to Alchevskaya, April 9, 1876.

158. Dostoevsky is wrong. Pushkin's only printed comment on Hugo was to call him "uneven" and "crude."

159. Pen-name of liberal historian G. K. Granovsky.

160. A survey of big trials, including Ovsyannikov, a 28,000-ruble bank robbery and a

400,000-ruble stock fraud.

161. Granovsky attacked the autocratic conduct of the railroads.

162. A reaction to reports of fires started with kerosene lamps—mixed with associations of the Paris Commune fires.

163. Articles dealt with education, and a professor of theology's attack on "spiritualism."

164. G. S. Veselitsky-Bozhidarovich head of a Paris society to help Herzegovinian refugees. Dostoevsky met him in Petersburg—apparently this prompted the "Slavic" entries which follow.

165. See Note 117.

166. See Note 138.

167. Vasily V. Grigoriev (1816-81), scholar of Eastern studies, monarchist, 1874-80 editor of *The Government Messenger* and head of the censorship bureau. Dostoevsky frequently met and talked to him, liked him, and was apparently influenced by him.

168. Two children were left orphans after A. Perova was murdered by her lover—who committed suicide. See *Diary of a Writer* for January 1875.

169. Both P. N. Svistunov and M. A. Nazimov were Decembrists.

170. Kroneberg was tried for flogging his seven-year-old daughter—and, thanks to a vigorous defense by Spasovich, acquitted. Dostoevsky was furious. Fetyukovich's behavior in *The Brothers Karamazov* is modeled on Spasovich's. On the case in detail and Dostoevsky's opinion of lawyers and the adversary system see *Diary of a Writer*, February 1876 (Brasol, pp. 210 ff.).

171. An involved quarrel. *Russian World* defended Dostoevsky from an attack, aided by misquotations of third parties, in the *Gazette.*

172. Chapter XIV of *Smoke.*

173. K. P. Pobedonostsev, Dostoevsky's arch-conservative friend, head of the Holy Synod.

174. This paper repeatedly published feuilletons, comments and poetry making fun of the *Diary of a Writer.*

175. A long story by Turgenev.

176. See Note 75 above.

177. *Historical Studies and Essays* (St. P. 1876). Pobedonostsev said Peter treated serfdom merely as an existing fact—he was neither for nor against it especially.

178. This idea was fully developed by Dostoevsky in his Pushkin Speech (1880), and in the 1876 *Diary of a Writer.*

179. In his book he noted the internal passport system was set up in 1724.

180. V. D. Spasovich (1829-1906) a brilliant lawyer and especially later, in the eighties, a literary critic.

181. Alexander F. Bazunov, a bookseller who published several of Dostoevsky's books, and took subscriptions for the *Diary of a Writer.* In January 1876 he went bankrupt and left the country with some of Dostoevsky's money.

182. "A thought when uttered is a lie"—taken from Tyutchev's poem "Silentium."

183. Refers to Dostoevsky's stay in the Peter-Paul Fortress and his fellow members of the Petrashevsky Circle.

184. *The Petersburg Gazette* printed the Avdeev necrology virtually word for word.

In an epigram on Gamma (Gradovsky), D. D. Minaev made fun of Gradovsky's efforts to write poetry.

185. Reviewing the January issue of *Diary of a Writer,* the *Petersburg Gazette* said that "Dostoevsky's mind has sick traits."

186. Refers to discussion of founding a university in the Siberian city of Irkutsk. In the other item a brave captain officially accused his colonel of various misdeeds, and the court (unconcerned with those complaints) convicted the captain of insubordination and sentenced him to sixteen months in prison.

187. A quote from Pushkin's romantic lyric "The Poet."

188. Unidentifiable.

189. Tsar Nikolai I.

190. Item No. 1 here refers to a libel case involving Petersburg papers; No. 2—in *Smoke* Potugin calls K. P. Bryullov a nonentity; No. 3—the Vladivostok newspaper reported America insisted it could continue its illegal liquor trade with Siberians, and proposed Russia sell Kamchatka.

191. Beginning of entries for the February 1876 *Diary of a Writer.*

192. Zotov blasted the first issue of *Diary of a Writer* here, saying Dostoevsky's style was ponderous and ugly. Also: "He hasn't the slightest wit. Many of his ideas are so strange that they could stem only from an imagination inclined to be sick."

193. A number of these next entries deal with the Kroneberg case and Spasovich's speech in defense. (See Notes 170 and 180 above.)

194. In Schiller's *Die Raüber.*

195. Louis XVII, who died in prison at age 10.

196. Compare the "Rebellion" chapter of *The Brothers Karamazov.*

197. In *The Voice* Gradovsky accused Dostoevsky of having contradictory ideas about the commonfolk—as good and bad, given to glorious ideals and miserable habits. Dostoevsky replies in the March issue of *Diary of a Writer.*

198. D. A. Obolensky, a member of the State Council: on Ovsyannikov see Note 13. Nadein—a bookseller who took over from bankrupt Bazunov.

199. St. Petersburg University commission to study the claims of spiritualism.

200. I. M. Sechenov, a fierce materialist, made Professor at St. Petersburg University in 1876.

201. In the March issue of *Diary of a Writer,* "Dreams about Europe" and "Dead Power and Future Powers." Gambetta was leader of the bourgeoisie republicans in France.

202. Through Shatov, Part II, Chapter 1. And also in *The Idiot,* Part IV, Chapter 7. On Dostoevsky and Catholicism see also Brasol, p. 264, particularly the note.

203. In the piece alluded to a Frenchman says the future of aging Europe belongs solely to Russia.

204. Dostoevsky illustrates this contention brilliantly with the lawyers in *The Brothers Karamazov.*

205. The prolific writer Boborykin lamented the failure of Russians to honor her writers—especially Dostoevsky.

206. Nikolai I deprived Prince Dadian of his ranks for using soldiers as peasants.

207. In the course of lauding painter Bryullov, the paper notes he didn't like N. Karamzin's *History of the Russian State.*

In an earlier issue Suvorin claimed Dobrolyubov was more important than Boswell.

208. Don Carlos—pretender to the Spanish throne. Dostoevsky writes of his bloodletting role in *Diary of a Writer,* March 1876. (Brasol, p. 259 ff.)

209. The observer mentioned by Dostoevsky in *Diary of a Writer,* this note tells us, was Pobedonostsev.

210. The "ordinary reader" was critic A. M. Skabichevsky, attacking Ostrovsky's play

The Rich Fiancees (1876).

211. In an article in the *Russian Messenger* (No. 1, 1876), poet A. A. Fet argued against socialism, said if the whole world were covered with aluminum phalansteries, Russian peasants wouldn't live in them. And renting land to peasants was dangerous because they would overuse it in three or four years.

212. Actually a pseudonymously published article in *New Times* by S. A. Vengerov on contemporary literature. He reproaches overly-vicious negative criticism seeing this (and society in general) as the reason for a lack of new positive heroes.

213. Suvorin reported on a new book dealing with the property holdings of churches and monasteries, which showed that the monastery named after fifteen-century mystic Nil Sorsky (who preached that monasteries should not own property) was very wealthy.

214. One report on well-to-do merchants poaching brazenly in areas where even the peasants didn't dare fish, and an English report expressing fear of Russian actions in Central Asia getting close to India.

215. See Note 122.

216. Internal passports were (and are) required for all Russians, and many barriers prevented getting passports good for traveling abroad.

217. Lizaveta—a Dresden friend. The madonna—apparently the Dresden copy of Holbein.

218. Mother of Smerdyakov in *The Brothers Karamazov.*

219. On February 14 (not 13th) Dostoevsky was present at a spiritist seance at A. N. Aksakov's—along with Leskov, Boborykin and others. See *Diary of a Writer,* Brasol, pp. 310 ff.

220. Mikhailovsky criticizing *The Devils, Notes of the Fatherland,* No. 2 (1873), 322-23.

221. An anonymous brochure called "Russia and England in Central Asia. A Problem," calling for the two countries to sensibly agree, was published in New York.

222. An election official, drunk, staged a mock-trial in his office, using peasants from the street as "prosecutor," etc.—and then birched, execution-style, a colleague. Kupernik was accused of shooting at passing coachmen. See *Diary of a Writer,* March 1876.

223. The paper unrealistically called on the Turks to satisfy part of the Christians' demands— after the Turks had obviously crushed the Herzegovinian uprising.

Mendeleev's St. Petersburg University commission had examined the spiritualistic claims and was to make a public speech.

224. Platon Karataev—Leo Tolstoy's ideal man (peasant) in *War and Peace.*

225. See Chapter 1.

226. See Note 219.

227. "A profound silence... Europe," quoted from I. K. Kaidanov's textbook of history (St. P., 1841).

228. Part II, Chapters 1 and 6.

229. Varvara Pribytkova, author of the story "The Sickness of Our Time."

230. Kozma Prutkov—fictitious author of purposely ridiculous "aphorisms."

231. Part III, Chapter 7 of the novel. Also Brasol, pp. 259 ff.

232. See Note 227.

233. See Note 208.

234. Quote from Pushkin's poem "A Poor Knight," quoted in *The Idiot* (Part II, Chapter VII) and *The Devils* (Part II, Chapter VI).

235. Chikhachev's brochure "The Chances for War and Peace" (Paris) said England and Russia had no basic hostilities in spite of the Eastern problems, nor did Germany and Russia. The paper disagreed.

236. Important character in *The Devils.*

237. "Tekushchaia zhizn'," a phrase perhaps used by Ivan Goncharov in talking to Dostoevsky, but its first documented use is in the 1873 *Diary of a Writer.*

238. See Part I, Chapter 1.

239. Comte Horace Francois Sebastiani (1772-1851), Napoleonic general. The anecdote is used in *Diary of a Writer,* March, 1876. See Brasol, p. 263.

240. Dostoevsky got the idea for a novel on the theme of conflict between fathers and children in the early 1870s. Parts of *A Raw Youth* and *The Brothers Karamazov* deal with the theme.

241. Dostoevsky probably has in mind Appolinaria Suslova's younger sister (the first woman doctor in Russia), Nadezhda Suslova. See Fyodor Dostoevsky, *The Gambler, with the Diary of Polina Suslova* (Chicago, 1972) and Beatrice Stillman, "Sofya Kovalevskaya: Growing Up in the Sixties," *Russian Literature Triquarterly,* No. 9 (Spring 1974), 277-302.

242. Mother Superior Mitrofania (Baroness P. G. Rosen) was tried (1874-75) for forging notes for huge sums and falsifying a will.

243. Probably refers to poet Alexei Zhemchuzhnikov (one of the inventors of Kozma Prutkov).

244. Francois Vincent Raspaid (1794-1878), scientist and politician, involved in revolutionary activity in 1830 and 1848.

245. The reports in that issue included Gradovsky's accounts of spiritualist activity, various facts about murders, robberies and suicides—including a 13-year-old boy—and about a masquerade at which someone's finger was bitten off.

246. See Note 222.

247. See Note 222. Here Dostoevsky goes over topics to appear in the March 1876 *Diary of a Writer.*

248. Alexander Druzhinin (1824-64), liberal "esthetic" critic, best known for his story "Polinka Sachs" (1847), in which a woman boldly divorces her husband for a lover—who fails her—and she confesses she still loved her husband.

249. The old woman, a centenarian, is described in *Diary of a Writer* (March, 1876), see Brasol, p. 240 ff.

250. See Note 248.

251. A peasant wrote in saying the best way to popularize education among peasants was to outlaw physical punishment (birching) for anyone who finished a commonfolk school.

252. Nikolai P. Peterson, a pedagogue of Slavophile leanings. Dostoevsky quotes him in *Diary of a Writer.* See Brasol, p. 247-48.

253. A special commission was working on passport reforms.

In the English periodical *Athenaeum* Skyler published "Continental Literature in 1875," discussing Leo Tolstoi, Dostoevsky, A. K. Tolstoi and others, praising highly *Anna Karenina* and *A Raw Youth.*

254. Ilya Muromets—hero of Russian folk epics.

255. *New Times* made fun of conservationists like Markov. Dostoevsky defended the cause in his June issue (1876).

256. Boborykin wrote articles on spiritualism (see Note 219), but must have brought up Potugin's name when talking to Dostoevsky.

257. A major character in *A Raw Youth.*

258. See Note 208.

259. Only spiritualism and the Herzegovinians made it into the April issue (1876).

260. Samarin (died 1876) was a Slavophile, so concerned for Russia's fate (a necrologist said) he couldn't sleep all night after reading the article about deforestation. See Brasol, pp. 272-73.

261. A flagellant religious sect. See Brasol, 268-69.

262. The commission (see Note 223) met with various mediums—who soon refused to cooperate, fearing the truth would be too obvious.

263. Vsevolod Soloviev.

264. Nikolai Mombelli (1823-1902), along with Dostoevsky, one of the members of the secret action group within the Petrashevsky Circle. Dostoevsky often met him in the seventies.

265. Christina Alchevskaya (1843-1918) wrote Dostoevsky three letters on *Diary of a Writer,* especially in connection with education of the commonfolk.

266. Alexander Otto was sent by Turgenev to Dostoevsky to collect (an apparently non-existent) debt of 50 thalers.

267. See Note 11 above. Avseenko attacked Dostoevsky's idea on the commonfolk (February, *Diary of a Writer),* and Dostoevsky replies in the April issue. See Brasol, 273-93.

268. The hanged woman (Olya) is in *A Raw Youth,* which Avseenko attacked in two different magazines.

In an essay on Alexei Pisemsky's plays, *(Russian Messenger,* No. 10, 1874), Avseenko condemned the theater of Gogol and others for "descending" to the world of bribe-takers, lacking ideals, etc.

269. Avseenko said, "all the confusion enmeshing those shouting about dipping their own empty vessels into the commonfolk has resulted from an incorrect posing of the question, mixing up two different things," and that the ideals for the peasant still had to be found in Europe.

270. In 1863 the *Russian Messenger* had been violently against Polish—and Russian—rebels and revolutionaries.

271. Title of a book by Slavophile Yury Samarin (1868-71).

272. An important "fictional memoir" (1856) by Sergei Aksakov.

273. See Brasol, p. 259.

274. Dostoevsky discusses Stundism in one of the sections of the January 1877 issue of *Diary of a Writer.* Brasol, p. 566 ff.

275. Lavretsky—Slavophile hero of Turgenev's *Nest of Gentlefolk.* Pierre Bezukhov and Prince Andrei Bolkonsky—main heroes of *War and Peace.*

276. In V. Belinsky's eighth and ninth essays on Pushkin. Dostoevsky's ideas were different. Compare V. G. Belinsky, *Selected Philosophical Works* (Moscow, 1956), pp. 211-95 to Dostoevsky's "Pushkin Speech."

277. Apparently writer Vsevolod Krestovsky, author of *The Petersburg Dens* (1863).

278. In Romantic writer Vladimir Odoevsky's descriptions of high society in "Princess Mimi" (translated in *Russian Literature Triquarterly,* No. 9, 1974).

279. In this issue S. A. Vengerov criticizes *The First Step* (Kazan, 1876), a provincial literary miscellany.

280. Hippolyte Taine's *De l'Intelligence* (1870) in Strakhov's translation (1872) was in Dostoevsky's library.

281. George Henry Lewes (1817-78). His *Physiology of Common Life* (1859), in Russian, was in Dostoevsky's library.

282. M. I. Bogdanovich, *A History of the Reign of Alexander I and Russia in His Time* (1869-71). A. N. Pypin, *The Social Movement in Russia during the Reign of Alexander I* (1871).

283. Probably the gift Dostoevsky had received from Soloviev (to be one of Russia's greatest philosophers), his dissertation *The Crisis of Western Philosophy. Against Positivism* (1874).

284. Ferdinand Lasalle, *Collected Works,* 1870 (Vol. I), in Russian, was in Dostoevsky's library.

285. S. M. Soloviev, *The History of Russia.*

286. St. Augustine had not been translated into Russian. A new Latin edition, edited by K. von Raumer, appeared in 1876.

287. Pobedonostsev's translation of *The Imitation of Christ* (1869) was in Dostoevsky's library.

288. In Dostoevsky's library was M. Vladislavlev, *Logic* (St. P., 1872).

289. Dostoevsky's had Volume One of Khomyakov's *Complete Works* (Moscow, 1861).

290. The book, (Yaroslavl, 1875), was in Dostoevsky's library.

291. Thomas Carlyle's *History of Frederick the Great* (1858-65) and *French Revolution* (1837).

292. Author of *La Russie et l'Europe* (1866).

293. His *Conquête de L'Angleterre par les Normands* and parts of *Lettres sur l'histoire* had been translated into Russian by 1876.

294. William H. Prescott (1796-1859). In Dostoevsky's library was a 2-volume Russian translation of his *History of the Reign of Ferdinand and Isabella the Catholic.*

295. Chernyshevsky was co-translator of August Ludwig von Schlözer's *Vorstellung der Universalhistorie* (St. P., 1861-69), 18 volumes.

296. Danilevsky's essays appeared in book form in 1871.

297. Henri Villemain (1790-1870), critic and historian of literature. Charles Saint-Beuve (1804-1869), well-known critic (and popularizer of Russian literature). Taine—Dostoevsky refers to his *Essais de critique et d'histoire* (Paris, 1858). Heinrich Julian Schmidt (1818-86)— his histories of French and English nineteenth-century literature had been translated into Russian by 1876.

298. Dostoevsky's wife.

299. See Ivan's poem in *The Brothers Karamazov*—still years in the future for Dostoevsky.

300. M. N. Nadein. How many copies of the *Diary of a Writer* should be given to his store for distribution.